# Izabela the Valiant

# Izabela
# the Valiant

The Story of an Indomitable Polish Princess

ADAM ZAMOYSKI

WILLIAM
COLLINS

William Collins
An imprint of HarperCollins*Publishers*
1 London Bridge Street
London SE1 9GF

WilliamCollinsBooks.com

HarperCollins*Publishers*
Macken House
39/40 Mayor Street Upper
Dublin 1
D01 C9W8, Ireland

First published in Great Britain in 2024 by William Collins

1

# Contents

# List of Illustrations

**The Polish-Lithuanian Commonwealth**

SWEDEN

*Baltic Sea*

Riga

RUSSIAN EMPIRE

LITHUANIA

*to Russia*

*Dvina*

Smolensk

Königsberg

PRUSSIA

Gdańsk

*to Prussia*

Wilno

*Szklów*

PRUSSIA

Berlin

Grodno

*Niemen*

*Dnieper*

SAXONY

Dresden

Poznań

*Vistula*

Warsaw

*Wołczyn*

*Siedlce*

*Terespol*

*Nieborów*

*Puławy*

Lublin

P O L A N D

Breslau
(Wrocław)

Kraków

Zamość

*Sieniawa*

*to Austria*

Lwów

*Brzeżany (Berezhanyi)*

Kiev

*Granów
(Granov)*

H A B S B U R G   E M P I R E

*Danube*

Vienna

Podolia

*Międzybóż
(Medzhybiz)*

*Kamieniec
(Kamyanetz
Podíl'skii)*

○ Estates

First partition, 1772

0          200 miles

0          200 km

OTTOMAN EMPIRE

The Polish-Lithuanian Commonwealth

SWEDEN

*Baltic Sea*

Riga

*Dvina*

Smolensk

RUSSIAN EMPIRE

Königsberg

Gdańsk

*to Prussia*

PRUSSIA

Wilno

*Szklów*

Grodno

*Niemen*

*to Russia*

Berlin

Poznań

*to Prussia*

SAXONY

*Vistula*

Warsaw

*Wołczyn*

Dresden

*Nieborów*

*Siedlce*

*Terespol*

*Puławy*

Lublin

Breslau (Wrocław)

Kraków

Zamość

*Sieniawa*

Lwów

*Dnieper*

Kiev

HABSBURG EMPIRE

*Danube*

Vienna

*Brzeżany (Berezhanyi)*

PODOLIA

*Granów (Granov)*

*Kamieniec (Kamyanetz Podil'skii)*

*Międzybóż (Medzhybiz)*

○ Estates

Second Partition, 1793

0          200 miles

0          200 km

OTTOMAN EMPIRE

**The Grand Duchy of Warsaw, 1807–14**

SWEDEN

*Baltic Sea*

Riga

Danzig (Gdańsk)

Königsberg

Wilno

*Szkłów*

Smolensk

*Dvina*

PRUSSIA

Grodno

RUSSIAN

*Niemen*

*Dnieper*

Berlin

Poznań

*Vistula*

Warsaw

*Międzyrzecz*

*Wołczyn*

EMPIRE

SAXONY

Dresden

*Nieborów*

*Siedlce*

*Terespol*

*Gruszczyn*

*Puławy*

Lublin

Breslau (Wrocław)

Zamość

Kiev

A U T R I A N   E M P I R E

Kraków

*Wysock*

*Sieniawa*

Lemberg (Lwów)

*Brzeżany (Berezhanyi)*

*Granów (Granov)*

*Danube*

Vienna

*Kamieniec (Kamyanetz Podil'skii)*

PODOLIA

*Międzybóż (Medzhybiz)*

O   Estates

——  Frontiers, 1814

▨  Added, 1809

0        200 miles

0        200 km

OTTOMAN EMPIRE

The Kingdom of
Poland, 1815–31

SWEDEN

*Baltic
Sea*

Riga

*Dvina*

Smolensk

Königsberg

Wilno

*Szkłów*

RUSSIAN

Danzig
(Gdańsk)

P R U S S I A

Grodno

*Niemen*

E M P I R E

Berlin

Poznań

*Vistula*

Warsaw

*Międzyrzecz*

*Wołczyn*

*Dnieper*

SAXONY

*Nieborów*

*Siedlce*

*Terespol*

Dresden

Breslau
(Wrocław)

P O L A N D

*Gruszczyn*

*Puławy*

Lublin

Kiev

Zamość

Kraków

Kamieniec
(Kamyanetz
Podil'skii)

*Sieniawa*

*Wysock*

Lemberg
(Lwów)

*Brzeżany (Berezhanyi)*

*Granów
(Granov)*

A U S T R I A N   E M P I R E

*Danube*

Vienna

P o d o l i a

*Międzybóż
(Medzhybiz)*

O T T O M A N   E M P I R E

O   Estates

——   Frontiers, 1830

0 ............ 200 miles

0 ............ 200 km

## Czartoryski Forebears

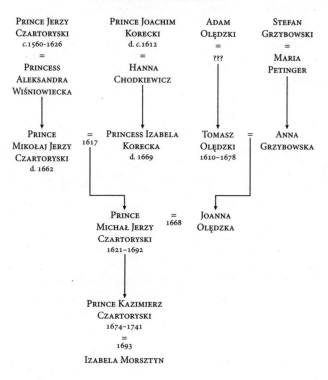

PRINCE JERZY CZARTORYSKI
c.1560-1626
=
PRINCESS ALEKSANDRA WIŚNIOWIECKA

PRINCE JOACHIM KORECKI
d. c.1612
=
HANNA CHODKIEWICZ

ADAM OLĘDZKI
=
???

STEFAN GRZYBOWSKI
=
MARIA PETINGER

PRINCE MIKOŁAJ JERZY CZARTORYSKI
d. 1662
= 1617
PRINCESS IZABELA KORECKA
d. 1669

TOMASZ OLĘDZKI
1610–1678
=
ANNA GRZYBOWSKA

PRINCE MICHAŁ JERZY CZARTORYSKI
1621–1692
= 1668
JOANNA OLĘDZKA

PRINCE KAZIMIERZ CZARTORYSKI
1674–1741
=
1693
IZABELA MORSZTYN

## Morsztyn Forebears

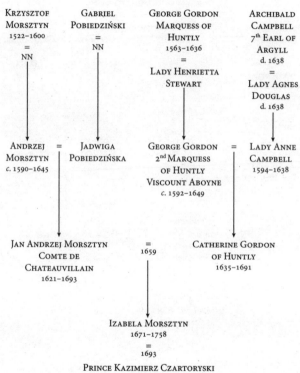

KRZYSZTOF
MORSZTYN
1522–1600
=
NN

GABRIEL
POBIEDZIŃSKI
=
NN

GEORGE GORDON
MARQUESS OF
HUNTLY
1563–1636
=
LADY HENRIETTA
STEWART

ARCHIBALD
CAMPBELL
7th EARL OF
ARGYLL
d. 1638
=
LADY AGNES
DOUGLAS
d. 1638

ANDRZEJ   =   JADWIGA
MORSZTYN      POBIEDZIŃSKA
c. 1590–1645

GEORGE GORDON   =   LADY ANNE
2nd MARQUESS         CAMPBELL
OF HUNTLY            1594–1638
VISCOUNT ABOYNE
c. 1592–1649

JAN ANDRZEJ MORSZTYN        =        CATHERINE GORDON
COMTE DE                    1659     OF HUNTLY
CHATEAUVILLAIN                       1635–1691
1621–1693

IZABELA MORSZTYN
1671–1758
=
1693
PRINCE KAZIMIERZ CZARTORYSKI
1674–1741

# THE FAMILIA

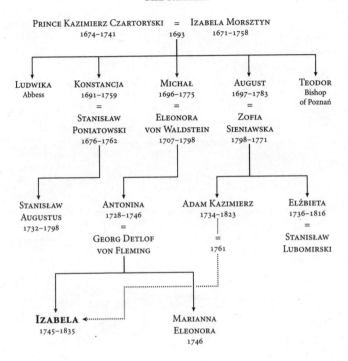

# IZABELA'S FATHER

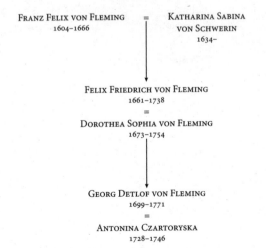

# Izabela's Children

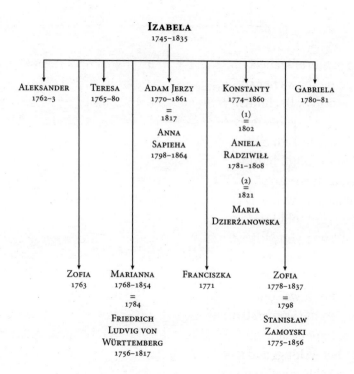

**Izabela**
1745–1835

**Aleksander**
1762–3

**Teresa**
1765–80

**Adam Jerzy**
1770–1861
=
1817
**Anna Sapieha**
1798–1864

**Konstanty**
1774–1860
(1)
=
1802
**Aniela Radziwiłł**
1781–1808
(2)
=
1821
**Maria Dzierżanowska**

**Gabriela**
1780–81

**Zofia**
1763

**Marianna**
1768–1854
=
1784
**Friedrich Ludvig von Württemberg**
1756–1817

**Franciszka**
1771

**Zofia**
1778–1837
=
1798
**Stanisław Zamoyski**
1775–1856

# Preface

Two prints of Izabela hung on the walls of the London flat I grew up in. One shows her sitting at a harpsichord in a fetching toque with an expression both childish and saucy. Another, based on a watercolour by the Prince Regent's favoured artist Richard Cosway, has her standing by a balustrade with a little dog at her feet, and the tilt of her head and expression I found hard to resist. I cannot remember when I was told she was my great-great-great-great-grandmother, but I grew up loving those images, as well as that of her husband, whose portrait in the drawing room I am told I used to salute as a child.

When I first visited Poland in my late teens, I went to see the Czartoryski Museum in Kraków, where Izabela's spirit hovered over an amiable jumble of works of art and family mementos zealously guarded by her devotees. But it was only much later that I began to appreciate that there was more to the woman than the accepted biography would allow. Gradually, it became clear to me that her collections, her building and gardening projects, her writings and her cultural patronage were not just expressions of a remarkable creative mind; she was, I came to appreciate, the original performance artist, living out her life through them.

With time, I also became aware of an aspect of her which had not been discussed in the family, namely that most of her offspring were not sired by her husband. I discovered that I was descended from two of her children, at least three of her lovers, and not from him – nobody is. Her rich emotional life was inconvenient to subsequent generations, and in most Polish studies it is either overlooked or dismissed as part and parcel of

1

rococo mores. But it was much more than that; it was an expression of her character just as important as any other. And it is that remarkable character which lies at the heart of this story of a vulnerable but resilient girl caught up in extraordinary events.

The vast fortunes and grand connections should not obscure the fact that what happened to this woman, her family and her world happened to millions of human beings affected by power politics, tyranny and war. Not only was her world physically ravaged by armed conflict; its traditional structures and hierarchies were crushed by autocracy and replaced by alien administrative organs serving centralising regimes. Izabela's story is also in many respects the story of this part of Europe.

The family archive held at the Czartoryski Library in Kraków is a treasure house of information. But it confronts the researcher with huge problems. Not only is there so much that one has to pare down and leave aside passages by all members of the family which one longs to quote, but many of the letters have no date, others only a day of the week or a date without the month. The year is often added later in a different hand, and in many cases demonstrably wrong. They are mostly bound up in a sequence which is often incorrect. As letters were frequently opened by the secret services of the three partitioning states, much is left unsaid, yet tantalising phrases to the effect that the details will be filled in when the correspondents meet suggest importance. They are also full of nicknames and code words, many of them impenetrable.

Much of what has been written about Izabela and her family is based on faulty memory or accounts tailored to fit the patriotic narrative and cover up inconvenient facts. The most detailed work on Izabela's husband, by Professor Tadeusz Frączyk, was unfinished when he died, and was not revised before publication, so that too is unreliable. While I have tried to establish the facts as accurately as possible, I am aware that much remains hidden, and hope that more will come to light with time. And there is so much more to Izabela than I could possibly fit into a book of this length.

I have restricted the number of actors in Izabela's life to the bare minimum to spare the reader an avalanche of Polish names. I have used the place names current at the time, adding present-day names in brackets where appropriate. The question of the value of the sums of money quoted is a thorny one. In the period which concerns this book, values were given sometimes in *czerwony* (gold) *złoty* and sometimes in *złoty polski*, and it is often not clear in which. This poses a major problem, as in the first two-thirds of the period covered by this book there were eighteen *złoty polski* to one *czerwony złoty*. The *czerwony złoty* was, at 3.5 grams of gold, equivalent to the Dutch ducat in use throughout most of Europe, which, allowing for minor variations, can be taken as roughly equivalent to the British pound. Later, there were only nine *złoty polski* to the ducat.

The translations from Polish, Russian and French are mine, those from the German archives are by Vincenz Hoppe, and that of Elise von der Recke's journal and other German sources by Angelica von Hase.

My thanks for their patient assistance go to Dr Janusz Pezda and Dr Paweł Wierzbicki of the Biblioteka Książąt Czartoryskich in Kraków; to Dr Jacek Krochmal of the Archiwum Główne Akt Dawnych in Warsaw; to Ewa Rutkowski of the Bibliothèque Polonaise in Paris; and to Anna Oleszak and Albert Walendowski of the Wojewódzka Biblioteka Publiczna im. Hieronima Łopacińskiego in Lublin. I am greatly indebted to Dr Grażyna Bartnik-Szymańska for sharing her painstakingly acquired knowledge of the registers of the Parish of the Holy Cross in Warsaw; to Konrad Niemira for his useful tips on Paris and Spa; to Michał Przygoda for his iconographic expertise and insights; to Professor Alina Aleksandrowicz for her erudite guidance; and Professor Elżbieta Wichrowska for her advice on many areas and particularly with regard to Helena Radziwiłł. I should like to thank Vinzenz Hoppe for his professional research in German libraries and archives, and Stanley Finger for his explanation of Benjamin Franklin's armonica. Above all, I must thank Clare Alexander, Arabella Pike and my wife Emma for encouraging me to tell the story of this extraordinary woman.

Adam Zamoyski

1

## An Arranged Marriage

I zabela's wedding was hardly a 16-year-old's dream; she was little more
than an accessory in an important deal. It was nevertheless a splendid affair. The church, a jewel of late baroque architecture, its octagonal
interior a wedding cake of exquisite stucco decoration, was filled with
the grandest in the land. Though some wore French court dress, most
of the men were resplendent in traditional Polish costume of silk, velvet
and sable buttoned with jewels, their gem-encrusted oriental sabres at
the hip. The finery of their ladies was wreathed in quantities of diamonds, rubies and pearls. The bridal couple had been blessed on the
previous day by one bishop, and their union was sanctified by another,
the '*Illustrissimus Excellentissimus et Reverendissimus*' Bishop Antoni
Wołłowicz, as the parish register, the *Liber copulatorum*, put it, and it
was accompanied by gun salutes provided by the private army of the
bride's father.[1]

While her dress may also have been sumptuous, the bride was draped
in a muslin veil to hide the ungainly wig concealing the baldness and a
face covered with scabs left by the bout of smallpox she had barely survived. Her groom was a prince, handsome and charming, but not to her.
He had known her since childhood, never fancied her, and had recently
fallen in love with another. He had done everything to resist the match
before yielding to parental pressure, and regarded it as his 'misfortune'.
So did his sister. As the bishop began to give the matrimonial blessing,
she left her pew, and, rushing up to her brother in tears, embraced him
'as though she were bidding him an eternal farewell', in the words of one

of those present, who added that 'the scene was too extravagant not to give rise to the wildest conjectures'. When the ceremony was over, her prince walked away, leaving Izabela at the church door.[2]

They were brought together again at the wedding breakfast, in the nearby country residence of Wołczyn belonging to her grandfather, Prince Michał Czartoryski. The single-storey house, built entirely of timber, presented a long façade behind which sprawled no less than thirty-six rooms. It was approached across two forecourts flanked by stone wings with accommodation for guests and a *cour d'honneur* adorned by statues along its sides.

The two hundred or so guests were seated at tables spread around the 'great room', the 'parade room' and the 'gallery' of the house. The walls were of larch, the floors of rosewood, ebony and other woods set in elaborate patterns. The walls were hung with tapestries as well as mainly Italian paintings and portraits of kings and ancestors, frequent references to whom were made in the speeches delivered during the banquet.[3]

These speeches took the form of versified panegyrics in the tumescent prose of the Polish baroque literary tradition, richly interspersed with superlatives in Latin. No fewer than three Jesuit and one Piarist Colleges had each confected a paean for the occasion, along with contributions from individual rhymesters, all competing in a tournament of hyperbole. The groom, Prince Adam Kazimierz Czartoryski, was assured that he was 'of such noble ancestry that history could furnish none better'. 'In your very person you are so endowed that if today crowns and sceptres were only awarded to virtue and service none would pass you by,' gushed one eminent man of letters. He praised the prince for his 'generous wisdom and ripe good sense' for choosing a bride who would 'multiply his princely house and its fame, bringing felicity to himself and his illustrious forebears'. She was described as a lady rich in her own and her ancestors' virtues who had been piously brought up to shine as an example of every excellence. From this 'beautifully and carefully matched couple' the Motherland could in all certainty expect great things.[4]

The banquet was followed by a fireworks display around a mythological scene in which the young couple emerged from a Roman 'temple of sacred friendship' erected for the occasion in the formal French garden, cut through the middle by a canal dominated by a statue of Neptune atop a grotto with a gushing cascade.[5]

The festivities would no doubt have been even more elaborate had the wedding not been rushed. As the bride and groom were first cousins once removed, he being a generation and eleven years her senior, a dispensation had been sought from Rome. In the interim Izabela had visited a peasant cottage bringing food for a child stricken with smallpox and caught the disease herself. Given the possibility of her succumbing to it (it had carried off her mother and baby sister when Izabela was just 1 year old), no time was wasted once the document arrived.

It was a purely dynastic union. An only child, Izabela was the conduit for the transfer of a dowry of 800,000 złoty (around £45,000 in the money of the day), and the couple would inherit the entirety of her father's fortune on his death. The wedding had also provided a pretext for the hosts to entice their political opponents into negotiations, and over the next five days of banquets, dances and theatricals the assembled grandees discussed possible common action at the next parliamentary session. One of the most prominent of these, Prince Michał Radziwiłł, had sent over two huge carts piled high with game of every sort for the wedding feast and invited the whole party to his palatial residence at Biała, where the junketing continued in splendour with more balls, ballets and theatrical performances. Whether the newlyweds went too is not known. They were not needed there; they, or rather Izabela, had fulfilled their purpose.[6]

After a few days at her father's estate of Szereszów, they went to another family country house at Oleszyce where he appears to have left Izabela for a time with only her French governess, Mademoiselle Petit, for company. They adored each other, and Izabela would probably have been happy to spend the rest of her life there. A modest country house had replaced the castle that had once stood on steep earthworks, and these provided them with their principal diversion; they would roll each other up in a sheet and then, by pulling hard on it, propel the other down the slope at stomach-churning speed. But her marriage had propelled Izabela into a vortex that would swirl her around Europe and turn her into anything but a simple country girl.[7]

She may have been ill-prepared, but she did not lack spirit. 'I have never been beautiful, but I have sometimes been pretty', Izabela wrote twenty years later in a retrospective 'portrait' of the kind much in vogue at the time. 'I have beautiful eyes, and as all the movements of my soul can be seen in them, that makes my physiognomy attractive . . .' She listed her features as a pale complexion, a fine forehead, a nose that was 'neither good nor bad', 'a large mouth, white teeth, an agreeable smile and in all a pretty face'. 'I am tall rather than small, I have a svelte waist, breasts too small, ugly hands, a charming foot and in general graceful movements,' she continues. 'My figure is like my mind; the greatest merit of one and the other is that I have always been able to make the most of them.' 'A careless upbringing' had left her with what she called the 'enthusiasm' with which nature had endowed her, and she described herself as of a gay disposition, easy-going, loving and trusting. And if her enthusiasm and small breasts left him cold, her husband was too kind a man to resist such qualities for long. Although the ravages of smallpox had begun to wear off, she was physically not to his taste, as she well knew. Yet that did not stop him fulfilling his duty, as Izabela would give birth to his son within a year, on 9 October 1762.[8]

'To attempt to describe the soul, the heart, the mind and other attributes of Adam Czartoryski is both difficult and vain,' she would later write, explaining that no words could evoke 'that rare mixture of virtues and the most noble intentions', or his sensitivity, kindness, tender manner and educated mind. Her words are echoed by almost everyone who met him. Intelligent, learned, witty, amusing, charming, with exquisite manners, gay, benevolent, honest, are adjectives which recur in people's accounts of him. They also describe him as the quintessential *grand seigneur*. When he gave him an audience in Rome, Pope Benedict XIV said he had never met a more worthy young man. Adam did not drink or gamble, and if he did have weaknesses, they were a touch of vanity and an excessive fondness for the company of women.[9]

Both Adam and Izabela had a good sense of humour, which must have helped. 'I married my husband without love,' Izabela would later admit, 'and only felt for him a tender friendship which he deserves more with every day that passes.' This was just as well, as she had been married to a man of whom much was expected.[10]

# A Royal Dynasty

The Czartoryski were descended from the Grand Dukes of Lithuania, one of whom had ascended the Polish throne in 1386 and founded the Jagiellon dynasty, which in its heyday reigned over more territory in Central and Eastern Europe than the Habsburgs. The last of the Jagiellons died in 1572, by which time his Czartoryski cousins had declined into penury and insignificance. They only began to emerge from this in 1693, when the slightly hunchbacked Prince Kazimierz Czartoryski, a shy, stuttering 18-year-old, made an advantageous marriage.

His bride was the daughter of the poet and former Treasurer of Poland Jan Andrzej Morsztyn and the Scotswoman Catherine Gordon. Her father, George Gordon Marquess of Huntly, had been beheaded in Edinburgh in 1649 for his loyalty to Charles I, and Catherine was brought up in France by her mother, Anne Campbell, daughter of Archibald Earl of Argyll. Catherine became lady-in-waiting to Louise-Marie duchesse de Nevers, last of the Gonzagas of Mantua, who had come to Warsaw in 1645 as consort to the King of Poland. It was there that Catherine met and married Morsztyn, and in 1671 gave birth to a daughter, named Izabela.

Morsztyn had headed a faction which hoped to put a Bourbon on the Polish throne, and when they failed he moved to France, where he was given the position of secretary to Louis XIV and the title of comte de Chateauvillain. His daughter, Izabela, was then 12, and she spent her youth between Paris and Versailles. When she returned to Warsaw as the wife of Kazimierz Czartoryski, her salon attracted the leading intellectual lights of the day and exuded a French culture and a modern spirit of enquiry not-ably absent from the houses of most Polish magnates of the day. A woman of character and ambition, she was determined their five children should attain the highest positions, and brought them up accordingly. One became a bishop, one an abbess, while the other three, Konstancja, Michał and August, were to affect the course of history.

Michał, born in 1696, was intelligent and cultivated, with a dominant personality and strong political instincts. His caustic wit and tendency to say what he thought did not always go down well with his peers, but he was highly regarded. He married Eleonora von Waldstein-Wartenberg, a Bohemian countess who numbered among her ancestors the renowned General Wallenstein. She brought him a considerable dowry and bore him three daughters.

The second son, August, born in 1697, was also clever and well-educated, and while he suffered from an excess of vanity his fine looks and noble figure, along with what one contemporary described as 'a kind of magic' in his manner, earned him much popularity.[1] 'He has an exquisite taste for the arts as well as all-embracing and profound know-ledge,' wrote the French writer Bernardin de Saint-Pierre, adding that 'the qualities of his heart are even greater'.[2] Greater still was his luck.

Although he started out as a soldier, fighting the Turks as a Knight of Malta and winning his spurs in the Austrian army under Prince Eugene of Savoy, his greatest triumph was to win the hand of Zofia Sieniawska. As the last scion of the powerful Sieniawski family she inherited its prestige along with its vast estates. By marrying Count Stanislaus Ernst von Dönhoff, the last of the Polish branch of that family, who conveni-ently died four years later, she became the greatest heiress in Europe. Her fortune was so immense that on his death several courts, including those of Vienna and Versailles, took an interest in her marriage plans.

August Czartoryski was the least endowed of Zofia's suitors, who included the Bourbon comte de Charolais, an Infante of the Portuguese house of Braganza, princes of Holstein and Brunswick, and half a dozen Polish magnates. One of these sought to ridicule Czartoryski by bribing his tailor to disclose what he would be wearing on the day all the suitors were to pay court to her and dressing up his numerous servants exactly like him. But August's charm won him Zofia's heart and her hand, and a fabulous fortune with them. She owned more than twenty estates, thirty towns and some 700 villages, as well as salt, iron and tin mines, along with several leases on valuable crown land.[3]

Although he was now the wealthiest man in Poland, and possibly in Europe, August did not take his new-found riches for granted. When the managers of Zofia's estates and her tenants came to pay their dues, August would check the accounts with care, and, once he had finished, tell the marshal of his court to carry the money to his wife. The marshal would lead a procession of servants bearing the barrels of coin to Zofia's apartment and, bowing, announce that 'his highness the prince sends your highness the yearly income from the estates in her dowry'. To which she would reply: 'please thank the prince and carry this gold back to him.'[4]

According to Polish law, a woman's dowry remained her property, and should be returned in the event of divorce. The customary prenup-tial agreement also assessed the groom's total wealth, half of which would become hers on his death. These arrangements were dictated not so much by regard for women as the determination of the bride's family to safeguard its property in the event of there being no issue from the marriage. So although the husband generally administered his wife's property as if it were his own, from a financial point of view the mar-riage was more of a partnership than elsewhere in Europe.

Michał's and August's sister, Konstancja, a strong character of uncom-promising views known as 'the hail cloud' for her disapproving stare, contributed to the family's fortunes in a no less practical way.[5] In 1720 she married Stanisław Poniatowski, a man who had risen from the minor nobility and obscure, possibly Jewish, parentage to become an outstand-ing general under Charles XII of Sweden and to forge such a reputation for himself that after that king's death he was approached with offers of service on behalf of George I of England and the Regent of France. 'He was a man of extraordinary merit', according to Voltaire, 'a man who at every turn in his life and in every situation, where others can show at most only valour, always moved quickly, and well, and with success.'[6]

These three siblings, supported by their forceful mother Izabela and their well-chosen spouses, were regarded in Poland as the leading family of the day, on account of their wealth, which had regilded their regal title, their intelligence and their sense of purpose. They and their associates came to be referred to simply as 'the Family', *Familia*.

Their purpose was to restore their country to its former greatness, by reforming its constitution and reviving its institutions. They had been prepared for the task by a careful education conducted under the eagle eye of their mother whose French upbringing marked them; they embraced the spirit of the age, being the first magnates in the country to abandon the traditional semi-oriental Sarmatian dress and adopt French fashion, they spoke languages and believed in education as the basis of a better society and a saner polity.

The once powerful Polish Commonwealth, made up of the Kingdom of Poland and the Grand Duchy of Lithuania, was the largest state in Europe after Russia, and in many respects the most progressive. But it had suffered badly from the ravages of war during the seventeenth century. Impoverished by unfavourable economic models and bedevilled by archaic social structures and an excessively idealistic constitution, it had lapsed into a state of anarchy.

From the late Middle Ages the king's right to rule had been subject to the approval of the parliament, the Sejm, and when the Jagiellon dynasty died out in 1572 it was the entire electorate which chose the next ruler. As no Pole liked the idea of another Pole getting above himself, they usually settled on a foreign prince from a reigning house and he was usually succeeded by his son. Even then the fact that the successor had to be elected produced discontinuity and unrest at the end of every reign. And the king's prerogatives were severely restricted by the Sejm. Yet this was itself hamstrung by a perversion of the principle that major decisions should be unanimous, and the veto of a single deputy could effectively block legislation. This was exploited by Poland's three neighbours, Austria, which hoped to control it, Russia, which was determined not to allow a well-ordered state to block her expansion into Europe, and Prussia, a second-rank power on the rise, desperate for more territory. All three were bent on preventing its regeneration and had no difficulty in finding a deputy who could be bribed or bullied into blocking any salutary measure.

In 1697 Russian troops forced through the election of the Saxon Augustus II, known as 'the Strong'. He was more interested in introducing the manufacture of porcelain to Europe at Meissen than governing Poland. He encouraged a state of indolent anarchy which suited most Polish magnates and the minor nobility, the *szlachta*, united in their dislike of paying taxes to ensure the proper functioning of a state which would only hinder them in the exercise of an unbridled way of life which they regarded as their God-given right.

The magnates, who had accumulated vast fortunes and captured the highest offices of state by making it impossible for the king to award them to anyone else, lived 'in a style almost royal', in the words of the British diplomat Nathaniel Wraxall.[7] They had their own courts, staffed not only with servants but also with poor *szlachta*. These would perform non-menial service, maintaining their status by always having a sabre at their side, even when waiting at table. Apart from the non-noble paid staff who performed the menial functions, many magnates maintained exotically attired servants for show, such as the 'laufers' whose job it was to run alongside their ladies' carriages in operatic costumes in order to open the carriage door, or the 'hajduks' in pseudo-Hungarian dress and the pages in 'Spanish' dress with a plumed helmet who attended their masters and mistresses with no particular function to perform. These courts were governed by marshals, stewards, masters of the stables, of the wardrobe, the cellar and so on. The lady of the house would have a gaggle of young noble girls to attend her wherever she went, on the understanding that she would bring them up and find them husbands in due course, providing them with a trousseau and a dowry, thereby extending the influence of the family to whom they and their spouses would be eternally indebted.

Although the salaries were low, the young nobles were adequately kitted out. 'They had to have fiery horses with rich harnesses because in the capital or during visits they made up a cavalcade around the carriage in which the lord or the lady drove out,' records one contemporary. The carriage itself would be drawn by horses of the prevailing fashion, and if that happened to be for piebalds, lack of availability would be dealt with by painting greys to look like them. Manes and tails were also often dyed crimson or green to add panache, the horses' heads were adorned with gilded helmets, while coachmen and the grooms riding at the back of the carriage wore gaudy liveries with plumed headgear.[8]

As well as the armed support of the nobles they employed or who felt beholden to them, such magnates often had a body of regular troops. The British ambassador James Harris estimated that August Czartoryski had 375 servants and attendants of one sort or another in his Warsaw residence alone, and an army of between three and four thousand troops.[9] Over and above that, such magnates could count on the unquestioning support of their creditors: in the absence of banks many people would deposit their savings with the local strongman, for which they received a percentage, and would therefore do everything to ensure he prospered. The power exerted by such individuals led to minor civil wars in support of rival candidates for the throne and to violent score-settling.

Augustus II was forced to abdicate in 1704 by reform-minded Poles who elected a compatriot, Stanisław Leszczyński, in his place. With the support of Charles XII of Sweden and of France, whose Dauphin, the future Louis XV, married his daughter, Leszczyński gained independence from Russia. But when Charles XII was defeated five years later, he had to flee and Augustus II was reinstated by Tsar Peter the Great who forced the Sejm to limit the Polish army to 18,000 men in return for a guarantee to defend the Commonwealth's territorial integrity, and its obsolescent constitution, thereby ruling out any reform.

On the death of Augustus II in 1733 the Familia considered putting August Czartoryski up for election, but when Stanisław Leszczyński came forward once again they backed him. He was duly elected, and Voltaire composed an ode in celebration. But within days Russian troops were on the march; they assembled a thousand *szlachta* with instructions to elect Augustus' son. Stanisław's supporters were scattered around the country, and August Czartoryski fell back on Gdańsk with him to await the promised French military support. But although France and her allies declared for him in what became known as the War of the Polish Succession, Louis XV was more interested in seizing Habsburg territory closer to home than helping his father-in-law in Poland. He gave Stanisław the former Habsburg province of Lorraine to rule, while his supporters in Poland had to make their peace with the new king, Augustus III, who can only be described as an overweight oaf.

The Familia concentrated on enhancing their influence in the country, partly through strategic marriages. August's daughter Elżbieta married

Prince Stanisław Lubomirski, a man of sense and substance who shared their aims. One of Michał's three daughters, Aleksandra, married Prince Michał Sapieha, prominent in a clan which wielded power in Lithuania. Another, Antonina, was wedded to a comparative newcomer to Poland.

Count Georg Detlof von Fleming was from a family that may have originated in the Netherlands but had ensconced itself in northern Germany. He himself had made a career in Saxony in the service of Augustus II and built up a fortune in Poland by buying tracts of land and farming them efficiently. He was physically attractive, but coarse in his manners, devoid of grace, choleric and prone to violence. 'Fleming was more German than Polish,' noted one contemporary, 'a boring man, quite eccentric.' He nevertheless identified Poland as a land of promise, converted to Catholicism and built a church to validate what was an entirely pragmatic move. Although he resented Michał Czartoryski's bantering superiority, he also identified the Familia as the major force in the country and willingly dedicated himself and his fortune to their royal ambitions by marrying his daughter Antonina, with whom he had a daughter he hoped might one day be a queen.[10]

That daughter was born on 31 March 1745 in the house of her grandmother Eleonora in Warsaw and was christened Elżbieta Dorota Balbina. Beginning with the Morsztyns' daughter, all the Czartoryski women christened Elżbieta, the Polish form of Elizabeth, used an Italianate variant of the name, Isabela.* Her mother died of smallpox the day before Izabela's first birthday, and two days later her baby sister was carried off by the same disease, aged only thirteen days. Fleming consoled himself by marrying his late wife's sister, another Konstancja, but she too died of smallpox only a couple of years later. He then found companionship in his mistress Marya Tymanowa, the only person who knew how to calm his violent rages.

His daughter was brought up by her grandmother Eleonora, 'a lady of holiness and kindness', in the words of one diarist, pious and observant in her faith, devoting much of her time to saying the rosary.[11] She presumably gave Izabela religious instruction, and as she had taught

---

* Adam Kazimierz's sister Elżbieta, who married Stanisław Lubomirski, was also called Izabela, but to spare the reader confusion I will refer to her as Elżbieta.

her own children to read and write, along with arithmetic, she probably taught her these as well. But the rest of Izabela's education was left to her French governess, Madeleine Petit. It consisted mainly of studying Charles Rollin's *Histoire Ancienne* and *Histoire Romaine*, along with other illustrated French books on the Middle Ages and the Renaissance. It was not a demanding upbringing, and she records that she was left to herself much of the time: 'alone, in the country, I enjoyed a pleasant youth', she later reflected.[12]

Eleonora spent most of the year in the country at Wołczyn but for the winter moved to her Warsaw residence, a building in the rococo style with a courtyard at the front and a garden behind known as the Blue Palace for its patinated copper roof. It was not far from the grander Czartoryski Palace on Krakowskie Przedmieście, where Izabela's great-grandmother and namesake lived and where her grandchildren and great-grandchildren often congregated. The matriarch's French upbringing and cultural preferences must have had some effect on the girl, if only at the level of manners and deportment, and, as she would later note, 'good taste'.[13]

Even closer to the Blue Palace lay the Ogiński Palace, home of Izabela's aunt Aleksandra, who would become a lifelong friend and influence. She had married a Sapieha and, on being widowed a couple of years later, would be forced by her father Michał Czartoryski to marry Michał Kazimierz Ogiński. The ceremony had taken place in secret on the eve of Izabela's own wedding at Wołczyn in order to forestall another suitor. Ogiński was a cultivated man, a distinguished soldier and accomplished musician, but the marriage was childless. Aleksandra compensated by bringing up the orphaned daughter of one of her sisters-in-law, Helena Przeździecka, who became a close childhood friend of Izabela, even though she was seven years younger.

The Familia had come to the conclusion that only with one of their own on the throne could they hope to bring about the desired reforms. August was the obvious candidate; distinguished, charming and affable, he would front the enterprise while his elder brother, Michał, would direct policy and his brother-in-law Stanisław Poniatowski acted as executor. August was a little old, but while he had been holding the port city of Gdańsk for Stanisław Leszczyński, awaiting the French fleet and troops which never came, on 1 December 1734 his wife Zofia had given birth to a son, christened Adam Kazimierz. This meant that if the need arose the Familia would be able to field a younger candidate.

Much care went into preparing young Adam for a royal destiny. By the time he was 20 he had travelled widely in Germany, Switzerland, France and Italy. Of an intellectual bent, he sought out the luminaries of every town he visited and learned the language of those he met, and others besides, mastering no less than eighteen according to some sources.[14]

Despite their mother's view of France as the fount of all that was most progressive in Europe, Michał and August had singled out England as being the least badly organized state in Europe. In 1753 their nephew, Konstancja Poniatowska's son Stanisław, was sent to London to study the workings of the constitution, the economy and social institutions. Four years later, his cousin Adam was despatched there with the same purpose. His father had arranged for him to be mentored by Lord Mansfield, Lord Chief Justice of the King's Bench, the foremost jurist of his day.

With the outbreak of the Seven Years' War in May 1756, Frederick II of Prussia overran Saxony and Augustus III had to take refuge in Warsaw, Poland being neutral. As he was ageing, the prospect of an election loomed, and Warsaw became a diplomatic nexus, even Spain sending an ambassador. England, which was open to the idea of supporting the Familia, posted Mansfield's nephew Lord Stormont there. His instructions from George III read: 'You shall carefully and diligently cultivate the friendship and acquaintance of the chief among the Polish nobility, but more particularly that of the prince Czartoryski, count Poniatowski and count Fleming whom you may assure of our particular regard and esteem, making them at the same time a suitable compliment in our name . . .'[15]

Meanwhile, Adam's sister Elżbieta Lubomirska was in Paris, using her friendship with the king's mistress Madame de Pompadour to drum up support for the Familia's plans at the French court. She was also busily promoting her brother's cause with the Duchess of Anhalt-Zerbst, pressing her to induce her daughter, the Russian Grand Duchess Catherine, to do likewise in St Petersburg.[16]

Stormont did as he was instructed but would not commit Britain to act, while France only managed to introduce an element of chaos. Her foreign minister, the duc de Choiseul, wished to interfere as little as possible, but Louis XV operated his own diplomatic network, known as *le Secret du Roi*, with two agents in Warsaw, each with different instructions.

As no other foreign power showed any sign of commitment and knowing that Russia would feel bound to intervene in any case, the Familia resolved to seek support there. On his return from England in 1759, Adam was despatched to St Petersburg. He was received with honour, to the extent of being addressed as *cher cousin* by the Empress Elizabeth. He was also honoured with the favours of Countess Praskovia Bruce, lady-in-waiting to the young Grand Duchess Catherine and a figure of influence at court.

His father had decided that it was time he married, and, given that she would inherit Fleming's fortune, which must not be allowed to drift elsewhere, the 16-year-old Izabela was the obvious choice. To his great regret, Adam was summoned back to Poland and had to cut short his affair with Countess Bruce. Regret turned to despair when he was told whom he must marry. He put up a struggle, valiantly supported by his sister who detested Izabela, but was eventually pressured into agreeing. They were duly married, on 19 November 1761.

The political situation began to change in January 1762 following the death of Russia's Empress Elizabeth. She was succeeded by her nephew, a mad German from Holstein who had been invested as Peter III, whom Adam had befriended in St Petersburg. Assuming they could count on his support, August and Michał felt that there was no point in waiting for Augustus III to die and decided to use a constitutional form of revolt known as a confederation to push through the election of their man before the incumbent king's death. In the spring of 1762 Adam was sent to Paris, presumably to apprise the French court of the Familia's plan and try to obtain its consent and possibly its support.

# 3

## Almost a Queen

It says something about their relationship that, less than two months after the wedding, in January 1762, Adam presented Izabela to the King of Poland, Augustus III, and when he set off for Paris in the early spring of 1762, he took the barely educated 17-year-old with him. To avoid unnecessary courtesies and etiquette, and out of what she called 'a rush of laziness', Izabela decided to travel in the uniform of an officer of his regiment of foot guards.[1] This turned out to be a mixed blessing.

'We were sailing down the Rhine when I heard that there was a fair on at Mainz and I insisted on disembarking there,' Izabela relates. 'I lost my husband in the crowded streets, took fright, and not knowing what to do, went into a shop.' The shopkeeper, a lecherous fat woman, grabbed Izabela and began kissing and fondling her, only stopping when she discovered the pretty young officer was a woman.[2] Izabela continued her journey dressed as one.

The next stop was the watering place of Spa. This was, according to an Englishman who visited it a few years later, 'the most delightful spot for its natural beauties, and its social habits'. It was frequented by 'from nine hundred to a thousand of all descriptions and characters,' he explained, 'a motley crew of crowned heads, princes, bishops both temporal and spiritual, barons and boutiquiers'. The small town nestling in the hills was a fief of the Bishop of Liège, and his bankers acted as croupiers. A retired French officer officiated at the duels which regularly resulted.[3]

'I did not take the waters, as I was feeling so well,' writes Izabela, but she derived 'much amusement' from observing those that did. 'There was a fat Englishman who always sat there without uttering a word. He would drink his eight glasses, then get up, approach my husband and, every day, say: "My dear Prince, I must compliment you: you have a wife who has the prettiest foot in the world." Having said that, he would sit down again and remain silent until the next day, when he would say the same thing.'[4]

Izabela may have shed her male attire, but the tomboy lived on beneath her dresses. One day she hired a buggy to go for a drive. Descending a slope, she was annoyed when another tried to pass her, and told her coachman to use his whip. The horses bolted and disaster was only averted by the boy leaping from his seat onto the shaft and managing to halt them just in time. He was badly hurt in the process and could not walk for a month. 'Such things cannot be paid for,' he said when Izabela offered him money. 'But one grows fond of people for whom one has done something like this, so as a reward I would like to serve you and never leave you.' He duly accompanied her to Poland and served her for thirty years breaking in horses and driving carriages, and the son he had there would become one of Izabela's favourite footmen.[5]

Izabela did not take to Paris, where they went next, and left few records of what she did or saw there. She did describe accompanying Adam to the salon of Madame Geoffrin, where literary luminaries would meet and often read their latest works. Afraid of making a fool of herself in such company, she played safe by saying nothing. But while she did not think much of what was being said, she became aware that her silence was taken as a sign of stupidity by some and arrogance by others.[6]

What made her feel particularly awkward was that everyone she met was talking about Jean-Jacques Rousseau's novel *La Nouvelle Héloïse*, which had been published the previous year, and which she had never even heard of, let alone read. To hide her ignorance, she asked a miniaturist to paint a couple of scenes from the book. He took the commission seriously and consulted the author, then living north of Paris at Montmorency, on which episodes to pick. Rousseau was intrigued to hear of the interest of a pretty young princess and asked a Polish acquaintance to invite her to come and see him.

'Without knowing a line of his works I nevertheless felt inside me that Rousseau must be an exceptional being, that I must see him,' Izabela wrote. 'Proud of having been noted by him, I drove to the meeting with the excitement one feels before a novelty or a new play.' Adam accompanied her, and Rousseau received them seated on his bed wearing a 'round' wig and a coat of coarse brown cloth. His 'fat' and 'ruddy' companion, Marie-Thérèse Levasseur, whom he would later marry, was also present. Izabela admitted to feeling 'overawed' as he began speaking. 'I did not open my mouth, as that was what I always did when I felt so greatly inferior to those around me,' she recorded, adding that the whole exercise turned out to be pointless, since she could barely understand a word he said. 'But I do remember his face and his room, his wig and his wife. Rousseau was not tall. I think he would have been ugly if he had not had so much wit and genius. His eyes were small but bright and sparkling.'

The visit lasted no more than half an hour. 'I do not remember the conversation, but I do remember very well that Rousseau put forward a metaphysical opinion, that he shouted like a deaf man as he supported it, that this annoyed my husband, who was with us and who got up to leave. Rousseau followed us, shouting and still arguing the case he had put forward.'[7]

Adam and Izabela travelled on to London, where he presumably called on some of his acquaintances from previous trips. It is also probable that he sounded out those in high places on possible reactions to the Familia's plans. He would certainly have taken Izabela to the theatre: during his first stay in London he had developed a passion for it, and she was quickly won over.

They were back in Poland by 1 June 1762, when Adam was invested with the Order of St Andrew by the Russian ambassador on behalf of Tsar Peter III, a mark of honour which augured well for the Familia's plans. But within weeks the situation changed radically. Fearing for her own life, Peter's wife, Catherine, persuaded her lover and his brother officers to carry out a coup and remove him to a prison, where he would shortly be murdered.

It so happened that Adam's cousin Stanisław Poniatowski had been Catherine's lover during his stay in St Petersburg a couple of years earlier. On 13 July 1762, days after seizing the throne, she sent him a letter which began: 'I am sending Count Keyserling to Poland immediately to make you king after the death of the present one, and in the event that he could not succeed on your behalf, I wish it to be Prince Adam.'[8]

Whether Izabela was excited at the idea of becoming queen will never be known. Adam was not. Although he canvassed on behalf of the Familia and was elected as a deputy to the parliament, the Sejm, which met on 4 October that year, he was not a political animal. He would probably have enjoyed the role of hereditary sovereign in some kingdom with a well-established monarchy where he would be able to spread enlightenment, but that was not what the Polish throne offered.

The Polish-Lithuanian Commonwealth was a curious political construct in which the king was essentially the executive of the elected lower chamber, the Sejm, and the nominated upper one, the Senate. He had little power other than that of patronage. Although Adam's regal lineage and personal wealth would have put him in a strong position, he would still have had to steer a cautious course around the restrictions imposed by conservative elements at home and suspicious neighbours abroad. He had a great ability to charm and inspire devotion, but he would not have enjoyed putting up with opposition, as he did not like his opinions challenged.

On 6 October Izabela gave birth to a boy, who was christened Aleksander Jerzy. The senate of the city of Gdańsk, where Adam had been born twenty-eight years before, struck a large silver medal larded with royal symbols to commemorate the event. A little under a year later, on 2 September 1763, Izabela gave birth to a daughter, christened Zofia, but the child died only two months later. And only a couple of months after that, on 27 December, Aleksander died, too. Infant deaths were so common in those days that the event would probably not have been as traumatic as it would be to mothers of later generations. But the death of these physical ties to her husband would have been made the more painful as Elżbieta Lubomirska was taking every opportunity to denigrate her in his eyes and those of their father. The two siblings felt what Adam admitted was 'an exclusive tenderness' for each other, and she could not bear to see him happy with another.[9] Her behaviour made life so miserable for Izabela that she sought solace in her cousin Stanisław Poniatowski and soon began to entertain stronger feelings for him.[10]

The end of the Seven Years' War earlier that year facilitated the Familia's plan of an armed confederation, since it left plenty of soldiers looking for employment. While travelling around the country with Izabela canvassing support among the *szlachta*, Adam recruited some of them to reinforce his father's and his uncle's armies. But Catherine, who had originally endorsed the Familia's plan for an armed confederation to seize the throne, changed her mind. Her new foreign minister Nikita Panin advised her to wait until the death of Augustus III. The effort and expense incurred by the Familia was not wasted; when Augustus did die, on 5 October 1763, they were well prepared to force the election of their candidate.

The first step was to pack the Convocation Sejm, which set the rules for the election and vetted candidates, with as many Familia supporters as possible. Despite the recent loss of her baby daughter and her 14-month-old son, Izabela joined her husband on his election trail, heading off into the south-western parts of the country escorted by a couple of thousand lancers and hussars to ward off the armed supporters of the principal candidate, the late king's son Frederick Christian. He had the backing of France, his sister being married to the Dauphin, and of Austria, since the Emperor Joseph II was his uncle. But he died unexpectedly on 21 December, only two and a half months after his father. This opened the field to others, notably the Hetman (commander-in-chief) Jan Klemens Branicki and Karol Radziwiłł.

Suspecting Keyserling of being too close to the Familia, Panin sent his nephew, Prince Nikolai Repnin, to Warsaw to assist and at the same time keep an eye on him. While Keyserling favoured August Czartoryski or his son Adam, Panin felt that Poniatowski's lesser standing would make him more beholden to Russia. He based Russian policy on close alliance with Prussia, and Frederick II of Prussia feared a Czartoryski stood a better chance of regenerating Poland. In order to pre-empt this, in April 1764 Prussia and Russia would sign a treaty, one of whose clauses bound them to prevent any constitutional change in Poland.

In March 1764 Russian troops marched into Poland to keep in check the likes of Radziwiłł, who had a formidable militia, and Branicki, who commanded the Polish army. The parliamentary elections duly gave the Familia and its supporters a majority in the Convocation Sejm, which convened on 7 May and the following day elected Adam as its marshal. Some 2,000 Czartoryski troops took up positions in and around Warsaw, with about twice as many Russians in reserve. Realizing they would be outvoted, the Familia's opponents registered their protests and left.

Marching back to protect his own estates, which were threatened by Russian troops, Karol Radziwiłł passed through Izabela's father's estate of Terespol, looting it thoroughly, capturing his sixty-strong militia and making off with his mistress. An incandescent Fleming assaulted one of the Radziwiłłs' supporters in Warsaw on hearing the news. Michał Radziwiłł, who defied a Russian force which had come too close to his residence at Biała, was defeated and, as a warning to others who might defy Russia's policy, his palace was looted, with every pane of glass being smashed and textiles ripped from the walls, while his steward was whipped by Russian soldiers.[11]

As marshal of the Convocation Sejm, which would sit from 7 May to 23 June 1764, Adam was able to put through legislation governing fundamentals, such as tariffs, weights and measures, the budget, the army, the administration, down to the paving and lighting of streets. The Familia's ideas were at last being given form, and their hopes soared, but Adam let them down. He repeatedly declared that he did not wish to be king, believing his cousin Stanisław would make a better one. The two had known each other since childhood, shared many interests and tastes, and were united by the same outlook and ambitions with respect to their country. On 7 September Stanisław Poniatowski was elected, choosing to rule under the name of Stanisław II Augustus. Izabela would not be queen.

# 4

## *Love and Betrayal*

With their cousin's coronation on 25 November 1764 a new era dawned for Poland, offering Adam and Izabela fresh opportunities. Having an intelligent, educated man on the throne changed the whole dynamic of Warsaw both politically and socially. This was noted by more than one foreign visitor. 'I confess that I found the air of a Republic refreshing, after having passed so long a time in such a despotic country', noted the British diplomat James Harris, arriving in Warsaw after a posting to Berlin.[1] Casanova, who turned up in Warsaw in 1765 on his way back from St Petersburg, also found it congenial. He dined with Adam and Izabela on his first evening in town before going on to enjoy the prima donna of the opera, which led to a duel that nearly cost him his life, and regretted having to leave.

Adam continued to sit as a deputy in the Sejm but devoted most of his time to what he felt was the best way to further reform, through satire and example. He wrote didactic articles and satirical pamphlets, commissioned translations of English and French plays and wrote five comedies, which were performed on the public stage and in amateur performances in schools and private houses.

In 1765, he took command of the Cadet Corps, originally styled the School of Chivalry, established by the king to form military and civilian cadres. He drew up the curriculum and a catechism aimed at instilling civic virtue in the cadets and recruited teachers, often from abroad, as in the case of Jeremy Bentham's friend the Essex clergyman's son John

Lind. He also assumed command of the regiment of Lithuanian Foot-guards, which he reorganized.

The 19-year-old Izabela was left free to enjoy all the pleasures Warsaw had to offer. The Royal Castle had become another family home, with Stanisław Augustus presiding over lively court festivities and entertainments; the Czartoryski Palace on Krakowskie Przedmieście rivalled it in lavish hospitality under the urbane gaze of August, and his country house at Wilanów outside Warsaw was the setting for idyllic parties.

The city also lent itself to amusement of every sort. It was small in area, consisting of a couple of dozen palaces surrounded by timber workshops and hovels, many fine churches, three hospitals and one of the greatest public libraries in Europe. The population numbered nearly 60,000. The streets struck foreign visitors by their mix of colourful Sarmatian costume with French dress, the sober German style of the middle class and the beaver hats and black gabardines of the numerous Jews. The carriages of the aristocracy, with their exotically clad attendants added a theatrical note.

Although most balls were given at the Royal Castle or aristocratic palaces, there was much entertainment in public spaces. The Saxony Gardens were the scene for promenading during the daytime and balls at night, hosted by the king or various aristocrats, which were open to all who appeared admissible to the guards at the gates. 'There could be nothing more enchanting than these balls,' wrote a German traveller. 'Some parts of the Gardens, lit up with coloured lanterns, created a magical contrast with the deep shadows of other areas. Under the great tent people danced the *polonaise*, in others it was the *anglaise* or the *contredanse*. Polite merriment reigned everywhere, and the mask allowed greater freedom, enhancing the pleasure, since it allowed all classes to approach each other for a while.' Another was shocked at the ease with which members of the lower orders were admitted to what he described as 'bacchanalian' feasts.[2]

Izabela had gained in self-confidence and was well placed to take advantage of such entertainments. She had made herself at home in the quarters assigned to her on the ground floor of the Blue Palace. Accessed through a small hallway, they consisted of a drawing room, a bedchamber and two smaller rooms, along with a dressing room. Two of them had windows over the front courtyard, the other two over the garden and the Saxony Gardens beyond. Izabela had had the apartment decorated with plenty of gold leaf; the dressing-room ceiling was entirely gilt. Her drawing room and bedchamber walls were covered in damask with green and yellow-brown floral motifs, one of the smaller rooms was lined with lemon-yellow silk, the other with painted wallpaper. Other than that, white and gold predominated, with gilt sconces on the walls and white-painted furniture with marble or yellow leather tops. The drawing room was dominated by a sofa with a heap of cushions, and occasional tables were scattered with porcelain figurines.[3]

If an inventory of her wardrobe drawn up around 1768 is anything to go by, she was well kitted out for such entertainments. Written in a mixture of mis-spelt French and Polish words, it lists two 'Robs', nine dresses, 2 'Robronts' (presumably *robe ronde*, a dress with panniers), six dressing-gowns, nine fur-lined overcoats, two 'deshabilles', four 'salops' (presumably informal indoor gowns), one 'mantyl', a whole page of furs (mainly sable), a crimson Cadet uniform along with white waistcoat and breeches, a blue one with crimson trimmings, a green tail-coat, several waistcoats and pairs of breeches, a collection of men's headgear, including two beaver hats, one with a white plume and gold braid, five more with various different trimmings, three 'English' leather caps covered in silk and velvet, and another of card covered in velvet; and a summer wardrobe consisting of eight dresses, four 'Robronts', as many 'ruboszans' (presumably *robe de chambre*), seven coats, six 'deshabilles', twenty-two hats, four skirts, two 'salops', a summer man's uniform, grey frock coat, several waistcoats, and four coats made of light wool, a page and a half of masques and fancy dress, including peasant, Turkish and other costumes, seven pages of trimmings, another six 'salops' and a page of 'half-salops', followed by pages of various linen items, trimmings and so on.[4]

This appears to have been partly stored in her dressing room, whose other contents included a tea set, a coffee service, an inkwell and writing implements, a whole page of silver accoutrements for washing, pots and bottles for creams, powders and scents, a page and a half of gold trinkets, souvenirs, costume jewellery, all of it gold with semi-precious stones. The pages are of folio size and densely written.

The position of women was stronger in Poland than elsewhere in Europe, and not only on account of their greater financial independence; for centuries they had grown used to holding the fort while their husbands were away, at elections or sessions of the Sejm, at distant trade fairs or at war, leaving them in charge of running not just the household but the court and the estates as well. And if in the provinces their behaviour might be restricted by local censure, this was not the case in Warsaw. A German traveller noted that they put a passion and energy into their dancing unknown elsewhere in Europe and dressed in unconventional ways, and it was not uncommon for a lady to receive gentlemen at home bare-breasted.[5]

'The world does not produce females more winning, polished, or calculated to charm in conversation,' wrote another British diplomat. 'They have neither the shyness and coldness of the English, nor the reserve and haughtiness of the Austrian women. Ease, joined with grace, and animated by the wish to please, render them infinitely agreeable. In beauty they may dispute the palm with any country; and their attractions are commonly heightened by all the refinements of dress and coquetry. It is not my intention to apologize for their levity; still less to excuse their libertinism; but those imperfections and faults are probably more the result of situation, than of natural depravity of licentiousness. In a court and capital such as Warsaw, under a prince such as Stanislaus, it is not easy to resist the seduction of example, added to the torrent of immorality.' He had already noted that 'The dissolution of morals among the upper orders, is not one of the least extraordinary and characteristic features of the capital and country from which I am writing.'[6] According to Bernardin de Saint-Pierre, 'the hymen does not possess any chains that they cannot break, and divorce is frequent among them.'[7]

Izabela enjoyed the balls and the amateur theatricals popular at the time and was praised for her histrionic talents. 'Born with some advantages and charms, from a very early age I received the homage of men,' she later confessed. 'This flattered my pride, and from the earliest times I was a coquette,' she added.[8] It is not known whether she resisted the seduction of example, but there is no evidence that she was sexually promiscuous or even particularly active. She was still a child at heart and seems to have enjoyed captivating by her verve and style more than anything else. The poet Adam Naruszewicz wrote an ode on her sleigh, representing it as a chariot of gold driven by Cupid, in which her heavenly beauty outshone the grace of swans and the colour of roses, and tortured the hearts of people.[9]

In July 1765 Adam gave a party at the king's summer palace Łazienki to celebrate the birth earlier that year of their daughter Teresa, and this was followed by a masked ball given by Fleming, accompanied by fireworks and gun salutes. On her name day, which was also the anniversary of their wedding, 19 November, Izabela was honoured in flowery terms at the first night of an opera dedicated to her.

Adam occupied an apartment with a similar layout on the opposite side of the hall, and his was dominated by a working library, with all the latest publications on subjects that interested him; as well as the *Grande Encyclopédie* of Diderot, to which he had subscribed, it contained books on oriental literature and mathematics. It also contained a few paintings, a collection of medals and some oriental objects, including a huge sultan's headdress.

These separate living arrangements were the norm at the time and did not signify any distance between Izabela and Adam. They had been married for over five years, had produced at least three children and another was on the way. Adam loved the company of women and flirting with them. In Prussia, where he was sent in 1766 to negotiate with Frederick II, he sired a boy, whom he would entrust to his sister Elżbieta to bring up, along with her own illegitimate son.[10] The absence of other known descendants out of wedlock, however, suggests he was not particularly wayward. His relationship with Izabela was based on companionship and mutual respect rather than love, which would not necessarily preclude sexual relations, but Adam's attitude did lead her to look elsewhere.

Her friendship with Stanisław Poniatowski had developed into love before his election but it was unrequited, as he was in love with Adam's sister Elżbieta Lubomirska and saw Izabela only as a dear friend. From the moment he ascended the throne, he was besieged by other women. As one might expect of a handsome, unmarried king, he was the object not only of sincere feelings but of calculation, as people pressed their wives, sisters and daughters on him to obtain rank and favour. He had installed a certain Madame Leulier, or Lullier, in a house where he could meet whoever he chose, but discretion was hard to achieve in the circumstances. Gossip and intrigue swirled around his person, and some of it must have concerned Izabela, as on one occasion he swore to Adam that there was nothing inappropriate between them.[11]

Adam would drop Izabela off at the Royal Castle when he had things to do, or, as the king put it, he went off to seek his own pleasure elsewhere. By the summer of 1767 Izabela and Stanisław had become lovers. She would claim that although she was flattered and gratified by his advances, since it annoyed her sister-in-law, she did not give in. But she did.[12]

Adam did not feel any jealousy towards his cousin or begrudge him the crown. 'If great genius, superior qualities, and the finest feelings in a king of Poland were sufficient to ensure the happiness of this nation, then ours would have nothing more to wish for,' he wrote to the English diplomat Robert Murray Keith.[13]

Michał and August Czartoryski had wished for more. They felt they had won the election for Stanisław and expected to implement their programme jointly with him. Tensions emerged as he brought his brothers into their daily meetings. They had insisted the Sejm grant them princely titles, which stuck in the craw of the Czartoryskis and Lubomirski, and they encouraged him in his eagerness to reform everything at once. Michał Czartoryski urged caution, believing that the fundamental measures already enacted should be allowed to solidify before further action was taken which might ruffle feathers at home and alarm the country's neighbours. The king resented the way his uncles assumed a right to direct policy and was convinced that his uncle August felt he had stolen the crown from him. Relations were not improved by Stanisław Augustus promoting people they disapproved of, such as Franciszek Ksawery Branicki. No relation of the Hetman Jan Klemens Branicki, Franciszek Ksawery was a swashbuckling lout of obscure parentage who had saved the future king much unpleasantness and possibly his life in St Petersburg when he had been caught in flagrante with the Grand Duchess Catherine by her husband.

The king had assumed his past intimacy with Catherine, which had been based on intellectual affinity and mutual respect as much as physical love, would allow him to communicate directly with her. But Catherine and her foreign minister Panin regarded Poland as a dependency and preferred to leave matters in the hands of their man on the spot. Keyserling had died shortly after the election, leaving only Repnin as the agent of Russian policy in Warsaw, and he assumed the attitude of a proconsul in a distant province of the Roman Empire.

Repnin was 'a worthy man, very feeling and humane, of great natural parts, and very agreeable', in the words of the British diplomat James Harris, who pointed out that 'the power that suddenly fell into his hands was capable of turning the head of a much greater man'. He was only 29, possessed of striking looks, a polished manner and a swagger born of success. He had earned the rank of general in the field and that of ambassador to Berlin through his marriage to Panin's favourite niece, Princess Natalia Kurakin, before getting posted to Warsaw. Harris observed that 'the tone he takes is so high towards the men of the first distinction, and of such an overbearing gallantry towards the women, that it is quite shocking'.[14] Habituated by the Russian court either to command or obey, he behaved, in the French contemporary historian Rhulière's phrase, like 'an insolent slave'.[15] He was encouraged in this by the nature of the society in which he found himself; the state of affairs over the past decades had bred moral corruption; for too long those who stood up to power had been punished, the craven rewarded. But things were changing. The Polish polity was being reformed and the country was beginning to develop commercially and even industrially.

This did not suit Frederick II of Prussia, who wanted Polish territory to round off his domains. He imposed drastic tariffs on goods flowing down the Vistula past his possessions in East Prussia and flooded Poland with debased silver coinage. He now persuaded Catherine to join him in intervening on behalf of their co-religionists in Poland, Protestant and Orthodox, insisting that all disabilities against them be lifted – something neither would ever tolerate in their own dominions.

Non-Catholics in Poland were the least discriminated against dissidents of any country in Europe, but the demands put forward by Frederick and Catherine would have given them political power which even Repnin could see would be unacceptable. But his and the king's attempts to explain this only made Catherine feel that her will was being thwarted. Egged on by Frederick, she dug her heels in.

Michał Czartoryski was for pausing further reforms and dissolving the Sejm, which would delay and possibly defuse the issue. But the king determined to press on. His uncles therefore decided to distance the Familia from the throne. Repnin tried to bully the Sejm into thwarting the king and enacting the legislation demanded by Catherine, but while it happily voted against the king's proposed reforms, it also confirmed in perpetuity the disabilities of the dissenters.

In his desperation, Repnin turned to the malcontents such as Karol Radziwiłł who had opposed the election of Poniatowski, gone into exile and had their estates sequestered. Using flattery, the promise of reinstatement and hinting that they would be allowed to dethrone Stanisław, he duped a number of them into supporting him; but when they realised they were supposed to pass legislation in favour of the dissidents, they too baulked. Repnin then tried intimidating Michał and August Czartoryski into supporting him, by sending Russian troops to occupy their estates, to no avail. Hoping to bring the Sejm to order, on the night of 13 October 1767 he sent Russian troops to arrest four senators, including two bishops who had been particularly outspoken, and drive them out of Warsaw into exile in Russia.

Izabela was involved in these events, though it is not clear exactly how. She was in love with the king and repeatedly rejected the advances of Repnin, who had fallen violently in love with her. According to one contemporary who claims to have heard it from Repnin himself, the king was so desperate to use Repnin to shield him from Catherine's rage that, 'seeing the ambassador prince Repnin burning with love for [Izabela], and her inflamed with love for himself, went to her and exposed the terrible position he was in, weeping in front of her'. According to this source, he told her that while it broke his heart to give her up, he must make the sacrifice in order to keep his throne and begged her to go to Repnin and 'requite his love and submit'. According to the same source, the king had used her to arrange a secret meeting with Repnin at the house of Madame Leulier, at which the decision to arrest the senators was taken. This seems unlikely, as does another theory: that it was Fleming who pushed his daughter into Repnin's arms out of fear of losing his estates.[16]

In her own account, recorded some four years after the event, Izabela gave a different version. She confirmed that Repnin 'was in love with me, and was poorly received'. 'The troubles which overtook my country soon gave him the opportunity to show me how dear I was to him,' she related. 'My family and my husband had strongly irritated the empress by constantly opposing her every wish. Prince Repnin received orders with the most severe instructions against them. [. . .] she commanded Prince Repnin to have them arrested and to confiscate their properties. She wrote that his life depended on his obedience. The princes would have been lost if Prince Repnin had not had the generous courage to disobey her. I felt it my duty to be the price of so much kindness; and I will add that whilst giving myself in the spirit of gratitude, I believed I was giving in to love.' This account is also unreliable, as Izabela was at that point trying to justify Repnin.[17]

The abduction of the four senators had the desired effect, and on 25 March 1768 the Sejm passed the legislation on the dissenters along with a new 'eternal treaty' with Russia. Believing he had achieved his ends, Repnin was triumphant. To show what he thought of Polish society and its customs, and to demean the Familia, he hired the theatre for the evening of Ash Wednesday and had a comedy put on. 'At this play no one was present, but the prince, his suite, and the Princess Czartoriska,' noted Harris.[18]

Repnin's triumph was short-lived. Just over a week earlier, on 29 February, a group of the same malcontents whom he had manipulated against the king met at the little town of Bar in Podolia and, fired by nostalgia for the good old days of anarchy as well as hatred of the supposed political and moral depravity of the new order, formed a confederation in defence of the faith and the motherland.

Adam must have seen this coming. Back in January 1768 he had decided to leave the country. Although there were probably diplomatic motives involved, he may also have wished to get Izabela away from Warsaw. He could not go at once, as she was heavily pregnant. On 15 March she gave birth to a daughter, christened Marianna Julianna, who was without doubt the king's and was generally assumed to be such in Warsaw society. Scurrilous quips circulating on the subject would certainly have been brought to her notice and she probably looked forward to getting away. Spring was late that year, the weather cold and stormy. In April she borrowed some money from the first banker in Warsaw, the polonized Scotsman Piotr Ferguson Tepper, and they left on 25 May. They took with them their treasurer, Jan Chrystian Blum, the renowned beauty and friend of Adam Jadwiga Ciechanowiecka, the young Familia henchman Michał Zabiełło, Dr Wolf and various servants, nine people in all. French agents in Warsaw informed their foreign minister, Choiseul, that they were considering settling in France.[19]

Their first stop was Dresden, the seat of the Elector of Saxony. This visit may have had something to do with the wish of the king and the Familia to engage the support of the Saxon court; Stanisław had for some time entertained hopes of counterbalancing the influence of Russia and Prussia by opening up channels of communication with the Catholic powers in Germany, the Habsburgs, and France.

From Dresden, Adam and Izabela made their way across Germany, heading for Spa, and she had once again taken to wearing one of her military uniforms. As their carriages rolled into Frankfurt, they found crowds lining the streets, with people up trees and on roofs to watch them pass. 'This surprised us greatly, particularly when we heard cannon-shots and loud Hurrahs!,' Izabela records. 'We kept going, not supposing for a moment that this was meant for us. Reaching the inn *The City of Rome*, we found the civic authorities and the magistrates waiting to receive us at the foot of the steps bowing low and delivering a speech which struck us as the height of extravagance. We were ceremoniously ushered into a chamber in which dinner was served, and we were begged to allow them to watch us eat. It was like a dream or some kind of joke, and I kept asking for an explanation, but only got knowing smiles in return. Then I suddenly thought I heard someone say *Your Majesty*, and gradually all became clear.' The young King of Denmark Christian VII, three years Izabela's junior, was known to be passing through Germany incognito on his way to Paris. 'He was very young, small, blond and pale, and my man's clothes and dress had led them to conclude that I was the King of Denmark. We had three carriages and a multitude of servants, another reason to suppose that I was one of the kings of this world.' When she protested at their addressing her as 'Your Majesty' they merely understood that the king wished to remain incognito. 'In the end I decided to stop protesting and accepted the crown,' she concluded. But her royal status was to be tried further.

'That evening, the host of the inn entered to announce that a young lady wished to speak to me,' Izabela continues. 'I was intrigued and told him to bid her come in. She was pretty, but she had only come to see me to put an end to the sorrows of an old and infirm mother. She told me she had an only brother who was in the service of Denmark and asked me to give him leave so he might make an advantageous marriage and thereby help his poor mother. "Mademoiselle," I said, "If I were the king your brother would have his leave, but I am not." However much I swore and protested, she would not get up but wept in floods while clutching my knees. Seeing that I would never be rid of her, I asked her to wait a moment, saying I would be back and then she could decide what was to be done. I hurried into the next room, removed my man's clothes and reappeared as a woman, with my chest bared . . .' Izabela embraced the astonished girl, asked for her brother's name and regiment, and, on meeting a Danish count in Spa few days later, asked him to convey her plea to his king, who graciously granted it.[20]

They reached Spa on 1 July and took lodgings in the Hôtel de Lorraine. Izabela bought a guidebook and had visiting cards printed, meaning to stay for some time and enjoy the social life – according to the registers, 808 people graced the resort that year.[21]

Adam left for Paris after four days, taking only one person with him. He called on Choiseul to find out whether there was any possibility of engaging France in support of a potential alliance of the king, the Familia and the Confederation of Bar, but was given to understand that the French court did not rate the king or the Familia. Disappointed by this, he distracted himself by visits to Madame Geoffrin and meetings with Grimm, Diderot and d'Alembert.

This time, Izabela did take the waters. She also frequented the theatre, bought books and took part in the social life of the place. After five weeks, she travelled with her party to Brussels, where she spent nine days sightseeing and going to the theatre, which put on a special performance for her, and she made the required donation, of 50 gold zloty, just over £50 at the time.[22] From there she travelled to Calais, where she joined her husband on 17 August, and together they sailed for England.

Two days later they were in London. They were received by their Argyll cousins and the Duchess of Portland, as well as other acquaintances Adam had made during previous trips. They then they set off on a tour which took them as far as Birmingham, staying either in country houses or inns (bills for their dinners at hostelries and inns along the way provide an interesting insight into the staples of the day – 'chicken fricassy' and lamb's sweetbreads feature overwhelmingly).[23] A special 'entertainment' was arranged in their honour at the Duke of Portland's seat, Welbeck Abbey, at the beginning of September but they did not go, as Izabela was unwell. But back in London they did attend an event which must have provided some amusement, a ball on 10 September in honour of the actual King of Denmark.[24]

On 14 September they left London for Dover. They spent the next five months in Paris, which Izabela liked for its amenities rather than its society, finding it shallow and arrogant. Her attitude shines through her description of a supper to which she had been invited by the duchesse d'Orléans at the Palais-Royal.

'A huge number of candles, rooms overloaded with candles, and a throng of women, that was what I saw on entering. I felt I was walking on thorns, not knowing what to say or where to put myself.' The duchess came to her rescue. 'We talked until it was time for supper. I myself said almost nothing out of fear of saying something wrong. We sat down at the table. I was placed beside the duchesse. Towards the end of supper a fat woman whose very red breasts overflowed the edge of her dress to a disagreeable extent suddenly began to speak, to announce that she had received a letter from her cousin Monsieur d'Adhémar. I was informed that this woman was Madame de Clermont from one of the country's grandest families. Not being able to find the letter, she began to tell us its contents. On his way back from Russia, her cousin had passed through a province called Li Li Lithuonia or Lithuania where, he wrote, people lived in holes in the ground which were covered in snow in winter and where if the children ventured out for a moment they were invariably eaten by bears. At first I was astonished by this description of the province in which I had been born and brought up. Then, looking at young Zabiełło who was like me a Lithuanian and seeing his fury at this story, I was suddenly seized by a fit of uncontrollable giggles, which astonished everyone. People were asking me what was making me laugh. I wanted to avoid answering, but pressed on all sides, I agreed and told the duchesse d'Orléans that I was laughing with joy at having escaped the bears of Lithuania, which happened to be the land of my birth.'

When supper was over the company moved to another room where they sat down to play *trente et quarante*. Izabela seated herself next to an old lady who at one stage asked her to lend her some money as she had run out. At which point Madame de Clermont shouted across the table: 'Madame, I would hold onto your money as I warn you that Mummy cheats.' To which Izabela replied, 'very loudly and with spirit': 'Madame, in my country the children who get eaten by bears would never say such a thing of their mother.'[25]

If Paris had left her cold, the sensations she had undergone in England made a profound impression on her. What struck Izabela as they travelled around the country staying at or visiting country houses was how the English landscaped their parks, in contrast to the French, whose taste for formal layout prevailed in Poland. It set her thinking about the relationship between houses and their surroundings, between culture and nature, and would have far-reaching repercussions. But it was not the only revelation she had experienced in England.

In London, Adam and Izabela had made the most of the theatres, attending all the performances by David Garrick. While Adam saw theatre primarily as a didactic medium, Izabela appreciated it as a means of emotional expression and a way of bringing to life events and human passions. And while she was striving to educate herself by reading books, it was what she had seen and heard in England that had widened her horizons and stirred her imagination.

# 5

# A Tangle of Lovers

O n their return to Warsaw, on 13 March 1769, they were greeted
with two printed panegyrics by budding poets welcoming the fact
that Adam would bestow on his homeland the benefits of the learning
and experience acquired abroad. He did, by enriching the curriculum
of the Cadet Corps and despatching two of its pupils whose talent he
had noted, Józef Orłowski and Tadeusz Kościuszko, to Paris on a bursary to study drawing and cartography. Izabela was not mentioned in
the panegyrics, though she too had come back with ideas that would
enrich Poland. She was not yet 24 but the experiences of the past couple
of years had matured her both emotionally and intellectually.

Although, as she claimed, she had become his lover partly out of a
childish urge to annoy Elżbieta Lubomirska, she had fallen in love
with Stanisław Augustus. Yet he had shown weakness and betrayed
her by pushing her into the arms of Repnin. He had also used her, on
that Ash Wednesday at the theatre, merely to demonstrate to the
whole of Warsaw that he was the master and sneered at their decen-
cies. But he was also, when not truculently parading his power, an
intelligent, cultivated and sensitive man who was deeply in love with
her, and when she returned from abroad she found him waiting for
her and they resumed their affair. But only a month after her return,
in mid-April 1769, he was recalled by Catherine. He was desolate and
begged her to leave him at his post and to at least help pay his debts,
but she was inexorable. He left in June 1769, not before having made
Izabela pregnant.[1]

What she felt at his departure is difficult to tell. She was compassionate by nature, and his misery moved her. She also felt a twinge of guilt, as he had told her his recall had been motivated by Catherine's displeasure at his having spared the Czartoryskis and partly out of jealousy of Izabela. This was untrue: in April Catherine rewarded him for his services with the Order of St Alexander Nevsky, and she recalled him because she required his military talents on the Turkish front.[2]

Seven months after his departure, on 14 January 1770, Izabela would give birth to a son, christened Adam Konstanty Feliks Paweł, though the last three names would be dropped and replaced by Jerzy, in memory of her father. He was held over the font not, as was customary, by relatives and grandees but by two paupers of the parish. Since meeting Rousseau, Izabela had read several of his works and been profoundly affected by them; the selection of beggars as godparents to her child was a statement clearly moulded by his sentimental outlook. The ceremony was followed by a grand reception at the Royal Castle presided over by the king and the whole Familia. Although the boy was without doubt Repnin's, he was firmly asserted as the future head of the princely house of Czartoryski.[3]

It is easy to assume that Adam knew Marianna and Adam Jerzy were not his offspring, but while he could not have failed to be aware of his wife's amorous relationships, one cannot entirely exclude the possibility that he occasionally performed his marital duties. And it is not unusual for those most intimately involved to be ignorant of such things. Either way, he assumed the role of a dutiful father.

George Burnett, a clergyman and surgeon who was a friend of Robert Southey and Samuel Taylor Coleridge, spent some time living with the Zamoyski and Czartoryski families and observed that while English husbands are 'curious to know, whether the population of their domestic territories is attributable exclusively to their own exertions, or whether it has been at all promoted by foreign succours', it is 'a question of less anxious interest in Poland, and a husband perhaps acts wisely in treating it with philosophic indifference'.[4] Nowhere in in his correspondence or his behaviour did Adam show any reserve in accepting Izabela's children as his own. 'I give warm thanks to God for the rare benefaction of deigning to bestow on me such children as you,' he would write to Izabela's next son many years later.[5]

Repnin's removal from the scene was certainly propitious. But his successor, Prince Mikhail Nikitich Volkonsky, did nothing to improve the political situation. Poland was in a state of civil war, with the Bar confederates rampaging around the country, pursued by Russian and less enthusiastically by Polish royal troops. The Porte had declared war on Russia in October 1768, and her ally France despatched officers and money to support the Barians. The ineptitude of Russian policy had defeated its own purpose, by undermining the authority of the king she had chosen and pushing a hitherto friendly Polish state into rebellion. The optimism of the first years of his reign had evaporated and Warsaw had lost much of its charm for Izabela.

Her rural childhood had left her with an enduring love of nature. As the novel attractions of city life waned, the yearning for bucolic pleasures grew. She accompanied Adam on the occasional visit to Wołczyn, but that was a long way off. Closer to Warsaw, only some twenty hours' drive, lay his parents' Puławy, which they also visited. But life there was hardly bucolic, as like other Polish magnates' residences it swarmed with servants, officials and courtiers.

The twin inconveniences of having to travel long distances to their country estates and of not being able to get away from hordes of attendants when they got there had long inspired some to seek rural retreats near Warsaw. A hundred years earlier a Lubomirski had built himself a refuge which would be called Łazienki after its bath-house and enlarged by its later owner Stanisław Augustus. In 1674 the Sobieski king Jan III had commissioned a villa further out that he called Villa Nuova, a name which morphed into Wilanów by the time it was inherited by August Czartoryski's wife Zofia. But it was set in formal gardens not to Izabela's taste. The parks she had seen in England had opened her eyes to other possibilities. But she was no follower of fashion and thought long and hard about what she wanted.

On 24 September 1770 she acquired the abandoned manor and village at Powązki, five kilometres from the centre of Warsaw. The village, which had dwindled to six decrepit cottages, sat in about a hundred hectares of land which had lain fallow for some time, cut through by a small river.

She began work there at the beginning of March 1771. Although she had engaged the services of Ephraim Schröger, an architect who had studied Roman remains in Italy and was now mainly designing theatrical scenery for the king, Izabela had planned everything herself. She began by planting 240 large lime trees and 3,600 saplings, and building a wooden cottage, which was ready by the end of the month, with a fully planted kitchen garden around it; it was to be functional as well as picturesque, but not Spartan. The poet Stanisław Trembecki would describe it as 'a precious stone in a wooden box'.[6]

'The house, which stands upon a gentle rise, has the appearance of a cottage, constructed like those of the peasants, with trunks of trees piled upon each other, and thatched with straw,' recorded Lord Herbert's tutor and travelling-companion William Coxe, '[. . .] we expected the inside to be furnished in the simple style of a peasant's hovel, but were surprised to find every species of elegant magnificence which riches and taste could collect. All the apartments were decorated in the most costly manner; but the splendour of the bath-room was particularly striking: the sides are covered from top to bottom, with small square pieces of the finest Dresden china, each ornamented with an elegant sprig: and the border and ceiling are painted with beautiful festoons.' What Coxe does not mention is that the bathroom was underground and was reached by a mechanical lift.[7]

Izabela's cottage was just a beginning. She had the river dredged, creating two islands linked by rustic bridges. The larger one was left 'wild', with walks winding through a wood, the smaller was dotted with cottages for Izabela's children, Mademoiselle Petit and other members of the household, each with its own garden.

That spring Repnin passed through Warsaw on his way back to the Turkish front having had a few months' leave, but it is not known whether he met Izabela or saw his son. Soon after that his successor, Volkonsky, was replaced by Baron Kaspar von Saldern, whose instructions were to destroy the influence of the Czartoryski. Quick-tempered and rude, he did nothing to improve the situation and was soon replaced as ambassador by Baron Otto Magnus von Stackelberg. Before he left, Saldern had such a violent altercation with Izabela's father that the latter had an apoplectic fit and died, on 11 December 1771. Her friend Helena Przeździecka, who had married Prince Michał Radziwiłł in April of that year, hurried over to the Blue Palace to console her. Their childhood friendship had grown into a companionship based on similar tastes in everything from clothes and interior decoration to more ambitious plans; Helena took a great interest in her project at Powązki, and in time would emulate her by creating her own very different bucolic refuge. Helena was, In Izabela's words, 'charming, amiable, good and original', and it was the last of these qualities which she found particularly endearing. 'My Goddess,' she addressed her more than once in letters. They both loved country pursuits, particularly going for long walks, happily trudging through mud and braving storms and downpours.[8]

It is doubtful Izabela grieved for long after her father's death. She had been far more affected by that, earlier in the year, of her great-aunt and mother-in-law Zofia. When Izabela failed to become queen her father lost interest in her, spending most of his time on his estate at Terespol with his mistress. And two weeks after his death she gave birth to a daughter, christened Franciszka, who did not survive childhood.[9]

Whatever Izabela's true feelings, her father's death was a godsend. She and Adam had overspent during the past few years, and the civil war had a disastrous effect on the family's finances; marauding troops of both sides regularly turned up at their estates demanding forage, and sometimes a pay-off. Fleming's death brought Izabela an inheritance of several large estates in Poland and Lithuania, as well as one adjoining the town of Borklo (now Borculo) in eastern Holland, which he had inherited from an uncle. They resolved to sell it, so they would have to go there, and as the political situation in Poland was drawing to a catastrophic conclusion, they decided to make a longer voyage of it.

They set off on 2 July 1772, taking with them their two daughters, Teresa aged 7 and Marianna 4, under the care of Mademoiselle Petit. The infant Adam Jerzy was left in Warsaw in the care of nannies. Aside from the two girls, they were accompanied by several servants, attendants, including the young poet Józef Szymanowski and Michał Zabiełło, and, as usual, their treasurer Blum. They travelled through Breslau, Meissen, Leipzig, Cassel, Düsseldorf and Amsterdam, reaching Borklo on 4 August. Izabela spent twelve days there making arrangements for the sale of the property. Since it was endowed with an ancient right to strike coinage, she had a gold two-ducat piece struck, with her head on one side and her arms on the other. Leaving Adam with her power of attorney, in mid-August she travelled on to Paris. But she did not linger there, and as soon as her husband joined her they left for London.

How long Adam stayed is not known, but Izabela meant to spend the autumn and winter there with her daughters. She attended to their education, teaching them to read and write and, in the case of the older Teresa, to play the harpsichord. She was also educating herself, by going to the theatre and to concerts. She was discriminating in the society she chose to frequent, showing independence of spirit and a disregard for fashion, seeking out like-minded women.

One, Lady Elizabeth Craven, was five years younger than Izabela. She was the daughter of the Earl of Berkeley and had been married to Lord Craven for five years. She was a free spirit with a literary bent – she translated and wrote plays, verse and later some travel books. When Izabela met her in London that autumn, she was having an affair with the French ambassador in London, the handsome, witty and musically gifted comte Adrien-Louis de Guines. She immediately warmed to Izabela. 'I was so much attached to [Izabela], and so delighted with her society, that I contrived to dine alone with her at my house in Charles Street, as frequently as I could; and we have passed many hours together *tête-à-tête*,' she wrote. 'She was one of the few women whose talents and manners suited me; her talents were very superior and her manners without affectation. She was a perfect musician and a fine painter; danced inimitably; had knowledge without pedantry, and never displayed her learning with ostentation.' According to her, Izabela was, just like herself, 'grave and gay by turns' and would confide in her 'anecdotes of her early days, which certainly did not intend should serve as a guard to the tenderness of heart and the unsuspecting mind which she discovered in me'.[10]

At some stage that autumn Repnin came to haunt Izabela. How and where they met is unclear. He had turned up in Spa in June, in poor health and short of funds. From there and The Hague, where he went next, he sent pitiful letters to his uncle Panin begging for financial assistance. A shadow of his arrogant Warsaw self, he cast himself as a victim, making out that he had renounced a brilliant career for Izabela's sake and incurred the wrath of Catherine, thus condemning himself to financial ruin and disgrace.[11]

'I had become the only thing Prince Repnin had left,' she wrote, falling for his line. Things only got worse when he grew jealous of Guines, who, while conducting his affair with Lady Craven, had begun courting Izabela, who was not entirely averse. 'I will admit frankly that I was flattered to be the object of his love, and I would have certainly loved him if he had not so exclusively loved himself,' she wrote.[12] Repnin expressed his jealousy in a manner 'so violent, so insulting' that Izabela took offence. His behaviour had made 'the ambassador appear the more pleasing', but whatever advantages Guines might have possessed were eclipsed by the arrival in London on 20 December 1772 of his nephew by marriage, Armand de Gontaut-Biron, duc de Lauzun.

Lauzun was generally thought to be the son of the duc de Choiseul by his own niece, as his formal parent, a soldier who had become a courtier to Louis XV, was thought to be impotent. 'It was therefore at court and, so to speak, on the knees of the king's mistress [Madame de Pompadour] that I spent the first years of my childhood,' Lauzun explained.[13] At the age of 18 he was married to the beautiful Amélie de Boufflers whom Rousseau eulogised in his *Confessions* and tried to seduce when she was only 9. But she left her husband cold. Known as '*le beau Lauzun*', he led a peripatetic love life, mostly with like-minded, though highly sentimental ladies. But on meeting Lady Sarah Lennox, who had been the first love of George III before she married Sir Charles Bunbury, Lauzun fell in love. He followed her when she returned to England but after giving birth to his child she had dismissed him. He went back to Paris in a state of desolation and not even an affair with Madame du Barry just before she became mistress to Louis XV could console him. He volunteered for active service and distinguished himself in the conquest of Corsica, leaving it in June 1769, two months before the birth of Napoleon. He had come to England now to distract himself following another unhappy love affair, hoping to see his daughter by Sarah Bunbury.

On the evening of his arrival in London, he was taken by Guines to a soirée at the house of Lady Barrington. 'A lady, better dressed and better coiffed than the English ladies usually are, came into the room,' he recalled. 'I asked who she was; I was told she was Polish, that she was the Princess Czartoryska. Of medium but perfect build, the most beautiful eyes, the most beautiful hair, the most beautiful teeth, a very pretty foot, very dark, strongly marked by smallpox and no longer fresh, sweet in her manner and inimitably graceful in her slightest movement, Madame Czartoryska proved that without being pretty one could be attractive.' He thought she might distract him from his late sorrows.[14]

Adam had also turned up, having just fulfilled a painful duty in St Petersburg. To put an end to the civil strife they had provoked, Poland's three neighbours, Russia, Prussia and Austria, had decided to partition the country, helping themselves to large slices of its territory. The only one of the three to benefit significantly was Prussia, no surprise since the crisis had been orchestrated by Frederick II. As a result of the partition, some family estates now lay within the Russian Empire and their continued ownership depended on making an act of submission to the Empress Catherine. One of these, August's Szkłów, produced an annual income of 300,000 złoty. As both August and Michał had antagonised Catherine, it behove Adam to go and do what had to be done. Returning to Warsaw on 26 October, he had set off for London.[15]

Izabela may have struck the 22-year-old Elizabeth Craven as sophisticated but she was only 27 and not up to dealing with the situation she found herself in. Alone in London with two young children, she was trailed by a miserable and jealous Repnin, being courted by Guines while he was still conducting an affair with her friend, and the object of advances by the seductive Lauzun. The arrival of a husband profoundly depressed by what was happening to his country and by the humiliating procedure he had endured in St Petersburg would have been of little comfort, and only served to underline the irregularity of her position. Having a lover was one thing; being at the centre of a love contest was another. On 31 December the *Bath Chronicle* reported that she had arrived in the city the previous day, accompanied by her husband, Repnin, Lauzun and his friend the Chevalier Henri de Fulque d'Oraison. It could not have been a comfortable trip, and back in London in January 1773 Izabela gave way to depression.

'I was ill, I wept, I could not say why for nothing in the world afflicted me,' she recalled. She began to think she would die in England. She was feeling so morbid one evening that she called for a priest, made her will and wrote letters to her loved ones before going to bed. They were staying with the Earl of Pembroke and the walls of her bedroom were lined with calico printed with bunches of poppies which, as she lay in bed and began hallucinating, appeared as death's heads, keeping her awake in agonies all night. Adam did his best to distract her and finally took her to see Benjamin Franklin at his lodgings in Craven Street. Though many of those who visited the renowned benefactor of mankind who had invented the lightning conductor were driven by simple curiosity, Adam may have had a specific purpose in taking her to see him.[16]

Franklin had for some time been interested in cures for 'melancholia' and other psychological conditions and had been experimenting with electric shock therapy and then music. Fascinated by the sound made by rubbing a wet finger over the rim of a wine glass, in 1762 he had constructed an instrument he called the 'armonica', which consisted of twenty-three bowls of varying diameters mounted on a horizontal spindle which the player could rotate by means of a flywheel attached to a foot treadle, and play by passing his fingers over the rims of selected bowls.

Izabela had no idea who Franklin was. 'In the carriage on our way to see him, my husband explained everything, but I was not very interested,' she recalls. 'I hardly knew there was another hemisphere. I did not understand about conductors, I was entirely ignorant of electrical machines, I had never heard the Harmonica.' She sat listlessly as her husband carried on a conversation in English which she barely understood. 'Franklin was not speaking to me, but fixing his eyes on me and taking my hands in his he said to me, in a tone of voice I shall never forget: "Poor young lady". Without knowing his language, I understood and felt touched and consoled. Then, opening the Harmonica he drew from it long sounds and seeing the way this affected me he continued with this music which I found celestial. Suddenly a torrent of tears relieved the chill which was stifling my heart. Then Franklin made me sit down and allowed me to weep for quite some time. He sat next to me with that kind and consoling attitude which is so good for those who suffer; after a quarter of an hour he saw me smiling to convey my gratitude. "You are healed" he said, and it was true, he had drawn aside the cloud which had enveloped me. I looked at the day and the world with pleasure once more. I felt a sense of well-being which had for a long time been alien to me. I believed in the future and no longer wished to die. At that moment I saw Franklin as a father, and I did not hesitate to embrace him.' He suggested she let him teach her to play the instrument, and she accepted eagerly. He gave her twelve lessons, and she never forgot what he had done for her. Her spirits had certainly improved, as Horace Walpole noted Izabela and Adam performing a lusty Cossack dance at a ball given by the French ambassador on 8 February.[17]

After taking leave of the king, Adam left London on 15 February 1773 making his way back to Warsaw via various German cities and Vienna. His travels were made bearable as he took with him not only an adequate suite of attendants and servants, nine in all, but also the wherewithal of comfort. This included three dozen silver plates, a dozen sets of silver tableware, two monogrammed damask tablecloths, six dozen napkins, a Meissen coffee set and the necessary kitchenware. He also travelled with a small library and all that was necessary for writing.[18]

On 16 March Izabela received a letter from him from Leipzig. 'You are charming to write to me so often,' she wrote back, 'your every detail I find interesting, everything in your letters delights me and my heart returns you all those feelings which you know so well how to express.' She informed him that she had suffered from headaches and insomnia over the past week, which prevented her from dancing a quadrille at a ball at the French embassy. Having had no news from Warsaw, she was anxious about the future of the country. 'Our misfortunes succeed each other and multiply. Nobody sees any happy days anymore; I can see that, and am convinced of it, yet I passionately desire to return.' She reported that Teresa was making progress and reading well in Polish and both girls had learned to dance 'very prettily' and were so excited at the prospect of going to a masked ball that they had pinned their invitations to their bedsteads.[19]

On 26 March she attended what Horace Walpole described as 'a grand ball' given by Guines in rooms decorated with arbours and bowers. The queen was present amid the 'terrible crush' and watched two new quadrilles, one themed on Elizabeth I, the other on the French king Henri IV. Izabela, dressed as Queen Elizabeth in a dress of blue satin with a white lace collar, took part in the first, along with Lady Sefton, Lady Melbourne and the sculptor Anne Seymour Damer.[20]

In her next extant letter, dated 31 April [sic], Izabela thanked Adam for sending a portrait of the now 3-year-old Adam Jerzy, which made her weep with joy. She had shown it around to universal approval, with one lady describing the child as a 'rosebud' and her new friend Lady Jersey as 'the little strawberry', and she herself was 'mad about it'. 'Milady Jersey whom you surely know is the woman with whom I have become most close,' she wrote to Adam. 'She is a charming woman who loves me very much. I will go with her to the country and from there I shall make my tour of this land.'[21]

Before she went to stay with Lady Jersey at Middleton Park in Oxfordshire, Izabela was swept up in a drama involving her other friend, Elizabeth Craven. Having caught her in flagrante with Guines, her husband had acted 'in a manner that shames humanity and furiously degrades the English in my eyes'. He had challenged Guines to a duel and snatched his sick wife by force 'from her bed, in barbaric fashion to confine her in a country house, having dismissed all her servants and replaced them with others'. Izabela could hardly contain her indignation. Guines had persuaded Lauzun to go down to the country to make contact with the captive, but nothing had come of it, and it was Izabela who undertook to breach the walls and bring her solace.[22]

She also buoyed up a far from happy Adam, who had been on another humiliating trip to St Petersburg to make the necessary obeisance to Catherine. The long journey along the Baltic coast was tedious at the best of times, but with the springtime thaws and frosts it took twenty-two uncomfortable days, and he was in despondent mood when he got back to Warsaw on 6 June. Seeing his country dismembered and bound into a greater degree of dependency on Russia than before, he was tempted to sell up in Poland and emigrate. Izabela would not hear of it.

'You ask me, my dear friend, whether I would agree to sell everything at home and to establish ourselves here, or in France, or anywhere else,' she wrote. 'I will tell you frankly what I think of that. I have already told you, and I repeat it again, that out of inclination, or perhaps out of habit I am strongly attached to Poland, and that it is always there that I would choose to live as long as there would be the shadow of a possibility. If the misfortunes and the destructions force us to expatriate ourselves, we will at that moment have to choose a country according to the circumstances which will then exist.' She pointed out that he was too good a son to leave Poland while his father was still living, and it would be sad to leave behind so many relatives and friends. 'What is more, my sweet friend, we can still do some good at home, so why not try? If not to the country in general, then to many people in particular. It is a blessing to have the means to do it. [. . .] remember that you have a son, and that you may have another. [This suggests that, given she was resisting the advances of Repnin, Guines and Lauzun, there lingered a possibility of Adam siring one.] Form them, educate them and you will not be bored for a moment. I have another plan in my head which I will lay before you in detail when we see each other. At present, my friend, we must first think of paying our debts and not make any new ones.' She urged him to reduce his household, and there was some scope for that.[23]

The accounts for 1772 show fifty-nine servants in the Blue Palace, not counting the stable staff. The accounts for 1773 show seventy-two on the payroll, some in French livery, some in Polish dress, some in hussar uniforms, and the pages sporting ostrich feathers in their hats. 'The fewer people one has the better one is served,' she argued. At the same time, she was busily shopping for things he had requested, mainly books, but also a piano, and investigated a machine for pulling up trees.[24]

She assured him that he would approve of her plans, without saying what they were. One can only guess that they centred on Powązki. From Middleton, she set off on a tour of the country houses of friends and acquaintances, principally to see their parks and gardens. She planned to meet up with Adam towards the end of June at Spa, where they would spend a couple of months before going on to Paris.

What Izabela had not taken into account as she made her preparations to leave England was that Lauzun had fallen in love with her. A few days before her departure Guines gave a dinner for her in the pleasure gardens at Vauxhall. In the course of the evening she mentioned that she was sending her children and servants on ahead and would meet up with them at Dover. As she would be travelling alone, Guines and Lauzun vied with each other to accompany her. Lauzun wrote declaring his love and his desire to devote the rest of his life to her.

'Nothing on earth could have surprised me more than what I have just read,' she wrote on receiving his letter, 'but what does not surprise me and will never surprise me is the sincerity and sensitivity of your soul. There are insurmountable obstacles between us, and I swear that M. de Guines has nothing to do with them. I must not, I cannot have a lover, but you inspire in me an attraction which will last as long as I live; whatever places we inhabit, whatever happens to you, I demand that you keep me informed; my tender friendship gives me that right. We cannot go to Dover together but call on me before my departure.'[25]

Guines then proposed they both accompany her, which infuriated Lauzun, but Izabela managed to slip away without telling either of them. When he found out, Lauzun hurried to the stables, saddled up the first horse to hand and was soon on the road to Dover. His horse ran out of stamina at Sittingbourne, and after sending off a letter full of despair he returned to London and spent the evening gambling heavily.

# 6

## *Dangerous Passions*

The Chevalier d'Oraison was struck by how unhappy Izabela looked when he saw her pass through Brussels on her way to Spa. And although the society gathered at Spa was brilliant, her mood would not have been lightened by the arrival of Repnin on 3 June. Another unwelcome arrival at Spa, a little over a month later, was Branicki.[1]

With astonishing lack of judgement, the king had sent him on an unofficial mission to Paris to obtain the support of France. Not only did Branicki fail to play on the widespread sympathy in Paris for Poland, he managed to antagonise the new foreign minister, the duc d'Aiguillon. He fell into the company of the duc d'Orléans and indulging in debauchery with him encouraged delusions of grandeur. 'Without the king's permission,' wrote Stanisław Augustus, 'he left France to go to Spa, to join the Princess Czartoryska, née Fleming, whose lover he was trying to become, and would go on trying for many years after, always without success.'[2] Twelve days after Branicki, Lauzun turned up, and, only six days after him, on 30 July, Adam appeared on the scene.

They spent August and September at Spa, and if Lauzun is to be believed it was an eventful stay. He dramatized and presented the facts in a self-serving manner in his account, but there can be little doubt as to the gist of the tale he tells. And the violent mood swings he describes Izabela going through ring true. Franklin may have cured her fit of depression in London, but she remained in a state of extreme agitation that summer and was often unwell. She was torn between strong feelings for Lauzun, her sense of obligation towards Repnin, and her duty to her husband and children not to cause overt scandal.

She had treated Lauzun with coolness on his arrival and he responded by seeming indifferent, treating Repnin with cordiality and courting two Irish ladies, Mrs St Leger and her daughter. He was polite with Izabela, and gladly lent her a light phaeton he had brought from England, which she enjoyed driving. But when he heard Branicki making disparaging comments about her, he challenged him to a duel, which was only stopped by the intervention of Lady Spencer, who was on her way back to England from a European tour with her daughter Georgiana, soon to become Duchess of Devonshire.[3]

His defence of her honour touched Izabela, and he claims she even grew jealous when he offered Miss St Leger the cup his horse had won in a race. As the social Season had come to an end, he considered accompanying the two Irish ladies back to England. But when he did get an opportunity to speak to Izabela in private he reduced her to tears with an account of the tortures he had gone through when she left London, and old emotions revived.

'We must stop, and never resume such a dangerous conversation,' she said, insisting they cease seeing each other. But they did meet. 'It would be useless, M. de Lauzun, to try and hide from you how much I love you,' she told him only a day later, warning of the 'dangers' that would result from their continuing to meet. She told him she could never make him happy without disgracing herself. 'You do not know with what excess I am capable of loving you, and all the misfortunes that can stem from such a passion, and all the remorse which will devour me ceaselessly,' she went on. They vowed to keep their feelings under control. 'We meant well,' writes Lauzun, 'but we did not know ourselves to what extremes we loved each other.' She seems to have suffered a fit of some kind, and he went to Leyden to consult the renowned Dr Gaube, who reassured him that there was nothing wrong with her and suggested a diet.[4]

Lauzun would not keep away and even attempted to consummate his love. She was shocked and rebuked him indignantly, but then felt guilty for having allowed him to think she was willing. He claims to have fallen ill with remorse, which only deepened her feelings for him, as did his refusal to fight a duel with a jealous Repnin, on the grounds that it would cause a scandal and dishonour Izabela. It was a little late for such delicacy; the goings-on at Spa had given rise to gossip, which by the time it reached Poland accorded Izabela as many as four lovers and the ability to 'make them come and go with a wink'. After a face-to-face explanation the two rivals agreed that Lauzun would allow Repnin to take Izabela, as long as it was to some other country.[5]

Repnin did not take Izabela anywhere, as she had no intention of leaving her husband or her children. What Adam thought of the goings-on, and indeed how much he knew of them, will never be known, but they do not appear to have affected their relationship. At the end of September or the first days of October 1773 they went to Paris. They took separate lodgings, he at the Hôtel de Varsovie, she at the Hôtel de Chartres. This was presumably dictated by practical considerations, as they had differing agendas in Paris and while Adam had a few attendants and staff, Izabela had two children, Madeleine Petit, a couple of maids, and a new French one, Madame Parisot, whom Lauzun had found for her. And if Adam was having dishes delivered by a *traiteur* (particularly large quantities of oysters – eighty-six dozen in December alone), Izabela's was, as the accounts suggest, a self-catering establishment.

Adam was engaged in meetings with the defeated leaders of the confederation of Bar, several of whom had turned up in Paris still hoping for French support. They included her aunt Aleksandra's husband Michał Ogiński and Kazimierz Pułaski, who had at one time been in the service of the Familia and needed financial assistance. Adam provided this, which enabled Pułaski to survive in Paris until he could set off for America, where he would join the rebels. Adam also examined the two young cadets, Kościuszko and Orłowski, whom he had sent to study in Paris.

Izabela was presumably taken up with the education of her daughters, which probably included visiting the monuments of Paris and Versailles. A deal of walking is suggested by the fact that during her four-month stay she had eighteen pairs of shoes made. She combined her own taste for the theatre with the urge to educate her daughters and attended performances at the Comédie Française and other theatres. Marianna never forgot one evening at the theatre when they were spotted by Marie-Antoinette, then still wife of the Dauphin, who invited them into her box.

Izabela avoided the *'grand monde'*, as she was by now better educated than most and resented 'that je ne sais quoi which all the French have [in their manner] in order to make foreigners feel that they believe themselves to be superior to them'.[6] She also avoided Madame Geoffrin, who took umbrage. Yet she must have gone out into society, given the surviving tailor's bills, for quantities of dresses, including harlequin and other fancy dress, masks and hats.

How much she saw of Lauzun is unclear. He had been called to Paris as his regiment was on guard duty at Versailles and other royal palaces, but he also seems to have gone to England, as he had a horse running at Newmarket on 4 October.[7] He was back in Paris by the end of the month, convinced that nothing could come between him and Izabela and that their 'destiny' must be 'fulfilled'. He called on her at the Hôtel de Chartres on the evening of 5 November.

In his melodramatic account, she told him that she was his and demanded he take her, but when he did he realised she was taking no pleasure in the act and shedding tears. She pushed him away, bemoaning her own wickedness and the boundless misery she had brought upon herself. He left and passed the night in torment. When he called on her in the morning, he found her unconscious with a trickle of blood flowing from her mouth, and, seeing a small box lying beside her guessed that she had taken poison. He swallowed the rest of its contents and lost consciousness but then woke up vomiting blood. Although he was still in poor shape he went to Fontainebleau to do his duty and there received a letter from Izabela in which she declared her undying love and said he should never have obeyed her when she told him to leave, begging him to come back and die locked in her arms.[8]

How all this could have been going on, given she was attended by three maids and accompanied by her two daughters and Madeleine Petit, is difficult to imagine. The events are recorded in the language of the most sentimental novels of the day, and it may be that Lauzun was carried away by literary ardour, but he was an intelligent and sensitive man who would hardly have made up such things about a woman he respected as well as loved, simply for the gratification of some fantasy, particularly as his memoir was not intended for publication. What is equally surprising, and barely credible, is that the characterful and resilient Izabela should have given in to despair to the point of attempting suicide. The only explanation, if Lauzun's account is true, is that she was still suffering from depression.

They continued seeing each other and in the last days of January 1774 she conceived his child. In February, she sat for a portrait by Alexandre Roslin, in which she seems self-possessed, if somewhat pensive, and even a little impish. At about the same time, she commissioned two portraits of Marianna from Marie-Geneviève Navarre and one of Teresa by Aleksander Kucharski. Before leaving Paris she also purchased many items for Warsaw and Powązki, such as rolls of painted wallpaper, along with a writing table and a travelling bidet.[9]

How much Izabela saw of Adam in Paris is also unclear. Alongside his political involvement with the émigré Barians and contacts with the French ministry, he pursued his own literary and educational interests, but it seems likely that he and Izabela took certain decisions jointly. One was to recruit a young painter as their resident artist. They settled on Jean-Pierre Norblin de la Gourdaine, a pupil of Francesco Casanova, who would serve them for decades and put down roots in Poland.

Izabela left Paris on 9 April 1774. Adam was unable to leave with her, as he had been detained at the last moment, so Lauzun obtained leave and accompanied her to within a few miles of Warsaw. As they parted, she told him she was pregnant with his child, and would give it to him, so he could have the most precious part of herself.[10]

Soon after arriving in Warsaw she moved into her cottage at Powązki, where only a couple of weeks later she was woken in the night by Madame Parisot admitting Lauzun, who had obtained three weeks' leave and come to spend them with her. Before leaving again, he swore that he would return for the birth of their child. In the interim, he made plans for what he hoped would be a future together in Warsaw.[11]

Like many in France, Lauzun was alarmed by the partition of Poland and the extent to which it had enhanced the power of Prussia. He composed a memorandum pointing out that it lay in the common interests of Russia and France to reverse this; he argued that Russia did not need the territory she had acquired, Austria could be persuaded to give up hers by her ally France, and Prussia could then be forced to cough up its part. He sent the memorandum to Adam, who passed it on to the Russian ambassador, Stackelberg, who sent it to St Petersburg.

Towards the end of September Lauzun set off for Warsaw once again, but was delayed by Izabela who wrote telling him to hang back in Strasbourg, then in Frankfurt. It seems the normally understanding Adam was not pleased by Lauzun's presence in Warsaw, possibly for political reasons. But as the date of her child's birth drew near at the end of October 1774, she wrote to Lauzun telling him to come. He arrived the day she went into labour, and Madame Parisot supposedly smuggled him into Izabela's bedroom in the Blue Palace and hid him in a closet behind her bed, where he claims to have spent the next thirty-six hours agonising over her screams, only emerging once she had given birth. The child was christened Konstanty Adam Aleksander Tadeusz on 28 October 1774.[12]

Izabela hid Lauzun with friends in the country, but as Adam did not want him hanging about she sent him away. After a spell in Dresden, he went to Berlin, where he flirted with one of the queen's ladies-in-waiting, Countess von Hatzfeldt. Gossip travelled fast, and he soon received an icy letter from Izabela telling him not to bother to come back ever again. But in January 1775, he was summoned to Warsaw by Adam, who set up a nocturnal meeting with Stackelberg. He had received a favourable response from Russia and requested a further memorandum, copies of which were sent to St Petersburg and Versailles. Lauzun received a gracious letter from Catherine and powers to negotiate, and a similarly encouraging one from France's new foreign minister, the comte de Vergennes, summoning him to Paris. Vergennes was interested in anything that might diminish Prussia and keen to develop France's trade with Russia. Lauzun's project included the option of persuading Stanisław Augustus to abdicate and retire to be King of Lorraine like his predecessor while the younger brother of Louis XVI, the comte d'Artois (the future Charles X), took his place on the Polish throne, which would have satisfied a long-standing Bourbon ambition.[13]

Something unusual was taking place: Lauzun's project was eminently sensible and would have benefitted both France and Russia, yet it was being driven, and undermined, entirely by the amorous designs of four

men. It had originated in Lauzun's desire to get himself posted as
France's ambassador in Warsaw so he could continue his romance with
Izabela. It had been taken up with enthusiasm by Stackelberg for similar reasons; although Izabela's friend Helena Radziwiłł had married for
love only three years earlier, she was now intimate with Stackelberg,
and he yearned for a posting as Russian ambassador in Paris, where he
hoped she might join him. This would have suited Repnin, who wanted
to resume his former position in Warsaw. Stackelberg was determined
he should not, as it might upset his agreement with Lauzun to keep
Repnin away from Izabela.

The plan was scuppered by Branicki, who was himself lusting after
Izabela and wanted Lauzun out of the way. He had lately developed
close ties with the Russian court and had put it about that Lauzun was
working against Russian interests. In the end, the project was dismissed
by Panin, who had been informing Prussia all along, but not before it
had caused a stir in every court between Versailles and St Petersburg
and nearly upset the existing system of alliances.[14]

Lauzun had not been welcomed by Izabela when he returned to
Warsaw in January, but he managed to convince her that his flirtation
in Berlin had meant nothing, and Izabela forgave him, 'with that gra-
ciousness that was inseparable from her every act,' he writes. 'I wished
to resume my former rights, but she refused absolutely.' He tried to
revive her love by various means, including flirting with another
woman, but only succeeded in arousing the jealousy of Branicki, who
challenged him to a duel. The king came to hear of it and forbade it, at
which point, in March 1775, Lauzun was summoned back to Paris by
Vergennes.[15]

He spent his last evening in Warsaw with Izabela at Powązki but
although they held each other in a long embrace before he could tear
himself away, that was the end of the affair. They continued to corres-
pond, but her letters grew shorter and less frequent, and the only news
reaching him was gossip about her and other men, principally Branicki.
'I wrote to her in strong language, but my protests were poorly received,'
he records. 'Profoundly hurt, I replied with desperation and indignation. I dared to demand my child; I did not wish, I wrote, that he should
be brought up among my enemies, but I was denied. We quarrelled and

ceased writing to one another.' 'I remained faithful to the princess,' he wrote, but he was soon courting Marie-Antoinette.[16]

'How delightful they are, those first moments of love, when dreams and hopes have not yet been upset by reflection,' Izabela would write.[17] The cult of sublime yet destructive feeling permeated European literature of the day, and she may well have been affected by the spirit of the times, but although she had lived through some dreadful moments, she emerged stronger emotionally from the experience and more focused on what she identified as her priority, the upbringing of her children, which coincided with her plans for Powązki.

Her desire for a country retreat had been superseded by another, more original and ambitious, and above all more practical. Other bucolic playgrounds which became fashionable in the 1770s, such as the duc d'Orléans' Monceau, Marie-Antoinette's Petit Hameau, Stanisław Augustus' Łazienki, Elżbieta Lubomirska's Mokotów and other such retreats outside Warsaw were stage sets for sensual amusement, crafted landscapes enhanced by Greek or Roman temples and relics designed for uplifting reflection or playgrounds full of bath-houses, Chinese pavilions, Turkish kiosques, and grottos. Powązki was meant to provide a life in harmony with nature, in the most realistic sense – Marie-Antoinette might well walk about with a shepherd's crook surveying cosmetic lambs, but Izabela became a real shepherdess.

Her visits to English country houses had revealed the possibility of bringing the landscape up to the house, but she had found those parks too contrived and arid. For her, to be truly picturesque a landscape must be alive, and it was the human element that made it live. But it was not enough to settle families of peasants in cottages, to provide the folkloric figures in the landscape and the hermit who had become de rigueur. The inhabitants of the landscape must tend it in useful ways. This did not rule out classical ruins, but they must be integrated into the life of the place; the picturesque ruin of a Roman amphitheatre at Powązki served to stable the horses, the hermitage housed a watchman who doubled as a guide, and except for the odd column or urn, every structure served a purpose, and most were in the rustic style. Coxe admired the 'romantic bridges, rudely composed of the trunks and bent branches of trees' linking the islands to each other and the meadows around. A Swiss visitor noted that even the massive trunk of an ancient tree had been hollowed out, fitted with a concealed door, and furnished with a day-bed made out of branches. The mill was functional as well as ornamental, the ponds produced fish, the hives honey, the orchards fruit, the kitchen gardens vegetables, a herd of cattle milk and beef, a farmyard chickens, ducks and geese – both for personal consumption and for sale. With time, she would build a brickworks, producing not only bricks but floor and roof tiles. A Prussian aristocrat was enchanted by Powązki after a visit to Elżbieta Lubomirska's Mokotów, where the multitude of temples, grottos and cottages struck him as meaningless and ultimately exhausting. 'The merit of [Powązki] is the perfect image of nature, which is not thwarted here,' noted the prince de Ligne in his book on the great gardens of Europe.[18]

That Izabela had taken her two little daughters along on her travels was unusual at the time and it is probable that after Rousseau's *La Nouvelle Héloïse* she had gone on to read *Émile*, for she had taken the upbringing of her children upon herself. She treated them as human beings from their earliest childhood and enjoyed their company. Powązki provided the ideal setting for her to live with them, to bring them up to love nature and the simple things in life, and to develop their characters.

Each was given their own cottage, all of them rustic on the outside, but with a different interior, and a sign outside decorated by Norblin with a name and an emblem. Teresa's had a basket of white roses, with the word 'Kindness', Marianna's a chaffinch with 'Gaiety', Adam Jerzy's oak leaves with 'Steadfastness'. Izabela's had a hen with her chicks. The children worked their own kitchen gardens, helped the labourers at harvest time, fed the chickens and tried their hand as shepherds. Behind the idyll lurked a patriotic character-building purpose: by teaching them to love the countryside, she meant to imbue them with a love of Poland, and by making them enjoy working in their gardens she meant them to learn to love work itself.

Powązki was also a great open-air stage. Izabela was highly visual and liked pictures which represented human action, feeling and morals, and she began putting on live tableaux or balletic scenes illustrating them, both with the aim of educating her children and for general entertainment.

She welcomed a wider circle of friends at Powązki, including the king, and foreigners passing through Warsaw never failed to visit. They were entertained with picnics, eaten sitting on the grass while shepherds' pipes might be played in some hidden spot. They would be taken on a tour, served tea and as the light faded there would be illuminations of the main features and music made by hidden players. There might be a ballet, a play or tableaux vivants performed by Izabela and her children who were skilful actors, enthusiastic dancers and good musicians, along with other members of the family and household.

Such festivities did not disturb the essentially pastoral and familial nature of the place. Adam Jerzy would remember stays at Powązki as the happiest time of his life. 'We only rarely received people from outside,' he wrote, 'but living together, our mother for her children and we for her, we nevertheless staged amusing scenes. It was a never-ending Eclogue, a real picture of bucolic poetry.' They rose early and breakfasted with Izabela. They would then do some gardening. Lunch would arrive on a donkey with two panniers, and they would have it in a different spot each day. On Sundays, they would walk to mass at a local church.[19] Izabela may have lapsed from the strict observance of her grandmother Eleonora, but her faith was increasingly important to her, possibly as a result of the emotional and psychological turmoil of the past couple of years, and certainly because of the uncertain future she and above all her country was facing.

# *Nature and Motherhood*

T he Poland Izabela returned to in May 1774 after nearly two years abroad was a very different place from that she had known in the 1760s, when the start of the new reign augured a bright future. Russia, Prussia and Austria had robbed the Polish-Lithuanian Commonwealth of almost one-third of its territory and nearly two-fifths of its population. More significant were the implications; although it had been in decline, its sovereignty had not been in question, but that had been violated and what was left of the country turned into a Russian dependency. The English diplomat Nathaniel Wraxall, who arrived in Poland in 1778, felt that 'there is strong reason to believe that the final dissolution of Poland cannot be very remote'.[1] The French philosopher Abbé de Mably was also convinced this 'sinister event' was unavoidable. 'Why, I ask you, should Europe, in an effort to prevent a second partition of Poland, do what she did not do to prevent the first? It patiently suffered your decline, and it will patiently suffer your fall,' he warned the Poles.[2]

As he lay dying in August 1775 Izabela's grandfather said his one consolation was he would not live to see this.[3] His death cast a pall over his brother August, who withdrew from political activity. 'The reign of the Czartoryskis is over,' declared the Russian ambassador on hearing of Michał's death. 'My orders are that they should never recover the influence and power they enjoyed in the past.'[4] Stackelberg was small and plump, cunning rather than clever, full of self-importance and, like Repnin, unable to resist the urge to treat the most distinguished Poles and even the king as he would not dare to treat an equal at home.

Many resigned themselves to the new state of affairs and toadied to him. To Izabela and others the disaster of the partition acted as a spur to resist. Since they could no longer try to reform the state, they would work on the nation. The Familia was now led by Stanisław Lubomirski and his son-in-law Ignacy Potocki. Adam was its figurehead. He sat on the military department of the governing council and supervised the army of Lithuania. As well as fostering the Cadet Corps he was active in the newly founded Commission of National Education, choosing text-books to be published or translated, setting the curriculum and examining results. He also devoted much care to the newly founded National Theatre and drew up plans for a National Museum.

On Michał's death Izabela inherited Wołczyn, several other estates and sixty-three villages, some of them now in Russia, and in the summer of 1776 Izabela and Adam made a progress through what was left of the Grand Duchy of Lithuania to nurture the Familia's influence in the area. Meaning to turn Wołczyn into a base for this, they redesigned the the-atre and the open-air stage in the park, the orangery and the Chinese pavilion, and dredged the canal. There was regularly a table for sixty and another to accommodate supplementary guests. There were ban-quets, illuminations of the park, dancing and theatricals, sometimes provided by itinerant troupes, sometimes by the family and assorted guests. Izabela also staged animated tableaux, which might range from illustrations of historical events to bucolic representations of peasants reaping and threshing. In season, there was also hunting and hawking to entertain visitors.[5]

Their court was enriched by the poet Franciszek Dionizy Kniaźnin and the playwright Franciszek Zabłocki, both of whom had joined the Jesuit order shortly before its dissolution in 1773 and found employ-ment as Adam's secretaries. In addition to his valet Boissy and his physician Dr Goltz, Adam had acquired for his personal service one Circassian, two Turks, one Greek and a black man of unspecified ori-gins, all of them dressed in colourful, supposedly ethnic costumes.

Adam himself had taken to wearing traditional Polish dress when visiting his estates, canvassing and attending the Sejm, as this went down well with the poorer *szlachta* who conflated French dress with courtly corruption and the garb of their forefathers with traditional values. In his book on the Polish constitution Rousseau stressed the importance of this costume as an element of national identity, and by extension of civic virtue. The Familia's policy now centred on cultivating those previously regarded as irredeemable backwoodsmen. This involved a rapprochement with Franciszek Ksawery Branicki, now Grand Hetman, overall commander of Polish forces, who had a following among conservatives and minor *szlachta*.

He also had influence in St Petersburg, having courted Panin and the favourite, Prince Potemkin. He had helped in negotiations over the Czartoryski properties incorporated into Russia, and Adam had grown fond of him. According to the king, he was amused by Branicki's swashbuckling style and his 'flamboyantly courtly though ineffectual' wooing of Izabela.[6] How ineffectual it was is debatable; Izabela's last daughter had been christened Franciszka, which was a departure from the usual practice of giving names of family forebears. And at the end of December 1777 she became pregnant again, and would give birth to a daughter, christened Zofia on 26 September 1788. Although Lauzun, too, maintained that Branicki's attentions were 'always poorly received' and Izabela had a more sympathetic admirer in Kazimierz Rzewuski it seems likely Branicki was Zofia's father.[7] Izabela was two months short of her thirty-third birthday and the attentions of a handsome man would have been flattering, and persistence can be winsome. Accommodating Branicki would also have been politic, and she was now shaping the Familia's political profile.

Izabela had come a long way intellectually since her meeting with Rousseau over seventeen years earlier, and it was largely under his influence. Thanks to her neglected education and childhood spent largely in solitude in the country, she had never imbibed the empirical and rationalist spirit of the Enlightenment and followed her own feelings and impulses. Her reading of Rousseau encouraged her trust in feeling as a guide, in intellectual and moral as well as in emotional matters, and gave her the confidence to trust her instincts, by convincing her that 'feeling' was the most noble and moral motive in human action.

Her notebooks contain quotations along with her reflections on them from authors as varied as Aristotle and other Greek philosophers, Pliny, Virgil, Homer, Tacitus, Bacon, Pascal, Tasso, Milton, Shakespeare Pope, Sterne, Buffon, Voltaire, Goldsmith, Fielding, Goethe, Ossian, Hafiz, along with the Talmud, Necker on economics, and many more. These provoked reflections on subjects as varied as the beliefs and actions of the ancient Greeks and Romans, on the religion of the Ethiopians, the history of places as varied as Sicily and Scotland, on war, despotism, the plight of the downtrodden, the natural world and its wonders, and many other topics. It is not always clear which of these notes are her own thoughts and which merely paraphrases of passages in the books she was reading. But there can be no doubt she took in and reflected on everything she read.[8]

In 1780 she was elected a member of the Berlin Academy of Arts, which suggests that she was being taken seriously outside her own country. The naturalist Georg Forster, who had just completed the circumnavigation of the globe with Captain James Cook and fellow naturalists Joseph Banks and Daniel Solander, was surprised, when he called at the Blue Palace, at the degree of learning displayed by this princess, who received him in her negligee. Yet she was no bluestocking. 'Her usual manner was to appear simple and as if fearful of exposing her ignorance, only, when drawn out, to deploy with apparent reticence some of her inexhaustible resources, keeping others in reserve which nobody suspected, and to strike her greatest blows just as she was leaving the stage on which she had shone, only to reappear on another with the same *éclat*, leaving behind memories and regrets,' according to Wirydianna Radolińska. In this way she never offended the ignorant by a show of learning.[9]

Her instincts chimed with those of a younger generation who dismissed the Voltairean rationalism of their fathers in favour of a Rousseauistic view of the world. In political terms, this meant a rejection of the pragmatic programme pursued by the king in favour of a more mutinous, heroic one based on the conviction that will could conquer where calculation failed. The king and the Familia had exchanged roles; while the chastened monarch had been forced into a more pragmatic policy of regenerating the country in ways that did not challenge Catherine's dominion, the Familia now adopted a more rebellious stance, and Izabela assumed a position all her own, as the *beau idéal* of patriotic Polish womanhood. This fitted with Adam's role of father figure to a generation, the alumni of the Cadet Corps. When Tadeusz

Kościuszko incurred the wrath of the powerful father of a girl he had attempted to elope with in the summer of 1775, Adam spirited him away and furnished him with funds to travel to Paris, where he would enlist to fight for the American rebels.[10]

Wołczyn was too far from Warsaw for a political headquarters, and the summer of 1778 was the last Adam and Izabela spent any length of time there. In the spring of that year August had made a preliminary distribution of his estate, as his properties were now in two countries. Most lay in the part of Poland taken over by Austria and renamed Galicia. The two notable ones still in Poland were Wilanów outside Warsaw, which he gave to Elżbieta Lubomirska, and Puławy on the Vistula, which went to Adam. Originally a castle perched on a bluff overlooking the Vistula, defended on the landward side by walls, earthworks and moats, the seventeenth-century Sieniawski palace at Puławy had been torched by Charles XII during his invasion of Poland and rebuilt in the rococo style in the 1730s by August's wife Zofia. The house itself was not particularly large, but it was approached by an avenue of limes over ten kilometres long, a forecourt of impressive proportions, a bridge over the former moat, through railings with an ornate wrought-iron gateway and a vast *cour d'honneur* with a large basin and fountain at its centre. This, and the two wings flanking the forecourts, made it seem more substantial than it was, and the double stairs to a platform at first-floor level, at which one entered the house, lent a sense of scale.

So did the vast room taking up the whole length of the façade overlooking the Vistula, whose walls and ceiling were covered in gold leaf and painted after cartoons commissioned from Boucher. There were two grand apartments and other great rooms on the same floor, one with panelling by Meissonier. The inventory made when Adam came into possession includes mostly French furniture, sixty-nine family portraits and three seasonal changes of 'garniture' for some of the rooms. But while the house did have palatial elements, its character was more that of a spacious country villa. Yet the wings flanking the two large forecourts provided up to 130 sets of quarters, some for up to three or four persons, to accommodate guests, members of the household and staff. And the kitchens were capable of catering to a minor court. On a normal day in November 1780, Izabela and Adam sat down to dine at a table for thirty, with Marianna, Madeleine Petit and the more important guests and members of the household. The younger children dined at a table for seventy-four, while a third table was set for less privileged guests and members of the household, bringing the total of people served to 230.[11] On her deathbed in 1771, Zofia had enjoined Izabela to cherish Puławy, and Izabela would not fail her. 'I identify myself with Puławy,' she later jotted in one of her notebooks.[12]

She still loved Powązki and would visit it frequently, to look to her gardens, her pigeons, her chickens and her vegetables. But it had served its purpose in her scheme and was too restricted to fulfil the next stage. Yet its chief function, as a setting for a life lived in nature, had to be grafted on to Puławy, which provided her with ample scope to develop three passions which had come to dominate her life and give it meaning, and she promptly set about transforming the formal gardens.

Izabela's love of nature was visceral. She was fascinated by it and would spend hours in its contemplation, watching a river flow, listening to the sound of birds, watching the rain fall. She saw in it the hand of God and found calm and solace in it. To her delight, she found that Rousseau's reflections on Nature in *Les Confessions* mirrored her own, and after rereading them several times, she copied them out in her scrapbook.[13]

The spectacular position and surroundings of the house on the bluff overhanging the majestic Vistula demanded a more grandiose conception than the homely landscape of Powązki. The dominant element, Izabela decided, were to be trees, which in her view enhanced architecture. She would plant thousands, always choosing native varieties, considering exotic ones unnatural in the present setting, but she also loved self-seeded and even deformed ones.

Here, too, her landscape was to be peopled, with peasants labouring fields, shepherds herding cows, fishermen working the river and a resident hermit. While the lie of the land demanded grandeur, she would create secluded gardens in which the family could gather for lunch or tea, as well as hidden walks and enclosed spaces for quiet contemplation, often adorned with a monument, be it a simple stone with an appropriate inscription or a bust of the Swiss poet Salomon Gessner, whose pastoral *Idylls* she admired.

She also admired the French poet Jacques Delille's *Les Jardins ou l'art d'embellir les paysages,* which she had the 14-year-old Marianna translate into Polish, with the help of the resident poet Franciszek Karpiński. But she followed her own whim and wrote to Delille questioning and taking issue with some of his ideas (he would include a description of Puławy in his 1801 edition of the work). Her vision remained an entirely personal one, and in 1805 she would publish her own thoughts on laying out gardens.

It was characteristic of Izabela to involve her daughter in the enterprise at such an early age; she owed to Rousseau the conviction that there was more to motherhood than giving children life and feeding them, and she had started early. 'My Dear Friend,' she had written to the then 13-year-old Teresa in 1779, instructing her to take the old green English carriage and drive down to Puławy, bringing the barely 9-year-old 'Master Adam' with her. Her letters brim with motherly love, but also companionship. 'The sadness of having left you and of not being able to spend the whole day with you all is a privation for me that nothing can compensate,' she wrote having had to go to Warsaw for a few days, leaving them behind in the country. She retails current gossip and describes how frightened she was when a stalker who had been persecuting her for days had finally managed to break into her bedroom at midnight before being thrown out by one of the servants. In another letter she tells Teresa about a burglary at Powązki, where a lot of china had been stolen thanks to the guards being 'as lazy as pigs' and discusses dresses for a forthcoming ball; both Teresa and Marianna, then 11, received visitors in a ladylike manner and went to balls. 'Adieu, my dear friend; I know how much and tenderly you love me, it is part of my happiness, all the dearer to me as this feeling will lead you to fulfil all my hopes for you', she ends one letter. 'Your heart, your way of thinking, warrant that you will put all your effort into making yourself what only depends on you to become.' While she treated her children as equals and reasoned rather than punishing them, she did expect much of them, and Adam Jerzy remembered being strongly rebuked by his mother when at the age of 9 he failed to recite from memory a long passage of Racine faultlessly.[14]

Izabela had become pregnant again in the summer of 1779. There is no evidence as to who the father might have been. One possibility is Kazimierz Rzewuski, with whom she had a close affinity. The child, a daughter christened Gabriela, was born in the Blue Palace in early January 1780. It had been a difficult delivery and the child would die six months later. On 10 January Izabela was in bed recovering from her birth when in another room of the Blue Palace Teresa, who was playing with her friend Konstancja Narbutt, approached too close to the fireplace. When her dress caught fire, she panicked and rushed out of the room, which fanned the flames. The painter Norblin, who happened to be playing piquet with Mademoiselle Petit in the next room, grabbed a coat lying on a chair and managed to put out the flames, but it was too late, and the girl died in agony three days later.

In view of Izabela's condition, the news was kept from her. When she asked to see her daughter she was told it might be dangerous for the girl, so Izabela wrote her a note, then another, and, growing suspicious she insisted on being allowed to get up. At that point the house physician Dr John told her the truth, whereupon she had a fit which paralysed one side of her body. She was only able to walk with the help of crutches until newly fashionable electrical therapy restored mobility to her leg. A trace of the disability may have lingered; one diarist noted a slight defect in her walk which she disguised by leaning to one side, hand on hip, 'which gave her an easy but graceful poise'.[15]

Adam had been on a diplomatic visit to the Radziwiłłs at Biała, and it was only when he boarded the ferry at Warsaw and enquired after local news that he was told by the ferryman who had not recognised him that one of Prince Czartoryski's daughters had died in a fire. He rushed to the Blue Palace and, on having the news confirmed, collapsed in tears.[16]

Izabela never got over the loss. Whenever the death of a child came up in conversation she would burst into tears and was so overcome she had to walk out of a play in which the heroine's daughter dies. 'Thursday, the day of the week on which she died, was for many years a day of mourning, of pious meditation for us,' recalled Adam Jerzy. Teresa's cottage at Powązki was moved from the 'village' to a secluded spot in a little wood and maintained as a shrine. 'A temple of regret' in the words of the prince de Ligne, who visited shortly after. 'Every day, Princess

Czartoryska waters with her tears the little garden of the home of her unfortunate daughter who perished in flames,' he wrote.[17]

Nearly twenty years later, on 15 October, Teresa's name day, Izabela wrote of how she dreaded that day, which had been one of joy, of flowers, celebrated 'with the intoxication of a mother who idolised her child' but was now horrible. 'It is You who gave her to me, my God! It is you who took her back!', she had written on an earlier anniversary of Teresa's death, 13 January. 'Subject to Your decrees, to Your holy will, I have survived that terrible misfortune! But a mother's pain must touch Your mercy; sixteen years have passed without quenching my tears! O God, O my Father, O my benefactor, grant me at least the happiness of my other children! May the pure and loving heart of my Teresa obtain from the breast of her Creator what her mother dares request.'[18]

Teresa had probably been Izabela's only surviving child by Adam, but while her death affected both of them deeply, it did not loosen the bonds between them. If anything, they were growing stronger, even though they spent much of the time apart. While she worked on the grounds at Puławy and enjoyed frequent trips to Warsaw and Powązki, Adam was often away, visiting friends and political allies.

In early May 1780, he set off on a tour of inspection of family properties in Podolia which he combined with a visitation of the schools in the area. It was conducted in the manner of a royal progress. Escorted by a squadron of Cossacks from his Ukrainian estate of Granów, he was received with honours at country houses along the way, where local gentry would gather on hearing of his approach. He enjoyed the flattery of the men and the petting of the women, with whom he liked to spend hours in saucy banter. He also enjoyed playing the benevolent monarch, as when he reached Brzeżany, a huge Renaissance castle built by the Sieniawskis, with frescoed ceilings and damask-covered walls adorned by a multitude of portraits, vast depictions of Polish victories and Italian religious paintings.

When the estate steward presented, in chains, several peasants and their families who had fled his less than benign administration, Adam declared they were free to go wherever they pleased and gave them money for their journey. As they begged to be allowed to stay if only he would rid them of the tyrannical overseer, he dismissed him and ordered new cottages to be built for them. While such gestures might smack of vanity, Karpiński, who was present, noted that he had known few men as aware of the sufferings of the poor.[19]

In April 1781 Adam left for Grodno to preside over the tribunals of the Grand Duchy of Lithuania and would remain there for much of the next two years. His term in this office was widely praised, and it was noted with approval that in one dispute he adjudicated against his own father. Towards the end of the second of these two terms, on 4 April 1782, his father died. 'I never saw a son more moved by the death of his father than the prince,' noted one of his secretaries, 'disconsolate, he wept for several days; even women, whom he loved, could not console him, and he would not even talk to them.'[20]

August had been widely regarded as the last of a kind, and even Stackelberg declared that, with him gone, there was nobody left to whom he would doff his hat.[21] His remaining estate was divided between Adam and his sister, with his share valued at sixty million and hers at twenty-five million złoty (about £3.5 million and £1.4 million in today's money).[22] She inherited Łańcut and twenty-two smaller estates, Adam got Sieniawa, Wysock, Oleszyce, Jarosław and Wiązownica in Galicia, Międzybóż, Granów and a number of Ukrainian estates still within the Kingdom of Poland, as well as his father's Lithuanian estates, some of them now in Russia.

Adam and Izabela were now in full possession of the Blue Palace in Warsaw, and they made themselves more at home there. He extended his library, she redecorated her rooms. Each of the four children had their own apartment with their complement of servants and their tutors in adjoining rooms. The staff consisted of half a dozen chambermaids and a dozen *frotteurs*, and three servants described as 'cripples', while Adam was attended by Ali the Turk, Osman the African and a couple of black pages.[23]

Adam and Izabela were now in possession of property in three different countries. In February 1782 the Emperor Joseph II had appointed Adam to command a new Imperial Noble Guard, made up of Polish gentry from Galicia. He duly went to Vienna, having kitted himself and his servants out in the Polish dress which he proposed as the regiment's uniform. When he arrived, the emperor also put him in command of a regiment of infantry with the rank of general, and proposed investing him with the Order of the Golden Fleece. Adam declined as it would require giving up either the Polish White Eagle or the Russian Saint Andrew. Joseph proposed granting him a dispensation to wear all three orders, but Adam declined, judging it irregular. He was treading carefully: with properties in Poland, in Russia and in Austria, he had the status of a *sujet mixte*, owing allegiance to the monarchs of all three states. This entailed a degree of contortion: while he kept Stanisław Augustus informed of what was going on in Vienna, Joseph gave him a cipher for the reports he was to send him on the activities of 'the neighbour' as Austria's secret agent in Warsaw, with the code name 'Abbé Sartori'.[24]

Izabela did not accompany him to Vienna. She was enjoying life in Warsaw, where she could see her many friends, particularly Helena Radziwiłł. She had recently begun work on an ambitious project, the construction of a vast complex of Greek and Roman temples, symbolic tombs, ruins and cottages forming an 'Arcadia' not far from her country home at Nieborów. Izabela was fascinated and the two exchanged ideas and tips, as well as elements that might fit into each other's schemes. But Nieborów was too far for frequent visits, and Warsaw lay between the two. On 10 February there was a spectacular torchlit skating party given for Helena and Marianna by Kazimierz Rzewuski. Handsome and cultivated, like Izabela an Anglophile, he was more than good company, and as he was rich and single he had plenty of time on his hands, much of which he spent with her and her family.

That summer, Izabela and Adam set off on a grand tour of their newly acquired estates in the southeast of the country, in part to inspect them, in part to canvas support for the forthcoming Sejm. The party consisted of Adam, Izabela and their two sons, accompanied by a swarm of attendants and servants, which grew along the way as nobles from the area they passed through joined it. The route had been planned by Adam and the marshal of his court, Borzęcki, with stops for the night at their own or others' estates along the way. As there was not room for the whole party in even the grandest of the country houses, some of which were palatial, and as the further afield they ventured the scarcer such houses, nights were often spent under canvas.

One of the court functionaries escorted by a couple of Cossacks rode a day's march ahead to prepare the next stop and ensure the necessary victuals, fodder, firewood and other necessities were on hand. He would be followed by eighteen covered wagons each drawn by seven horses bearing, respectively, the kitchen, the larder, the bakery, the cellar, the pastry cooks, confectioners, the coffee-makers, the housekeeping store, the pantry, a physician and a chemist, the farrier, the luggage and the family's wardrobe. This convoy was escorted by an officer and a couple of soldiers on horseback and followed by three grooms mounted and dressed in the Turkish style leading six camels draped with oriental embroidery and decked out with tassels and bells, bearing the library packed in trunks. Behind these came three large carriages and a number of brakes containing Adam's physician Dr Goltz, two chaplains, Major Orłowski, Adam Jerzy's governor Colonel Stanisław Ciesielski, the poet Kniaźnin, the librarian and mathematics master L'Huillier, an assortment of other attendants, including Adam's secretaries, one for foreign correspondence, one each for Lithuanian, Podolian and Mazovian affairs, and one for current business, and, in a separate break, his barber. Last came Adam and Izabela, in a carriage drawn by six horses, with two lackeys on the box and several more walking alongside, escorted by outriders in Asiatic garb, armed with bows and arrows and fourteen mounted noble attendants on richly caparisoned horses. Adam would sometimes take to his horse, and he was always followed by two attendants in Hungarian dress and Ali and Osman. This caravan was escorted by fifty Granów Cossacks and was swelled with other carriages and riders as locals joined.

The places chosen for the night were usually picturesque spots by a river. Dinner would be served in a large tent of crimson damask, accompanied by French, Hungarian and Rhine wines, champagne and English beer. After dinner, ice cream and lemonade were served, Anastasius the Greek produced coffee, while Ali and Osman brought pipes and anyone who wished to read could take a book from the cases borne by the camels.[25]

At Lublin, Adam visited the main school, where he was treated to eulogies in Polish and Latin, spent some time talking to the boys and then decreed they were to have three days' holiday. At Międzybóż the young courtiers and Adam Jerzy staged a mock battle with the Cossacks. A highlight of the trip for Izabela came at its extremity, when they reached the Polish border fortress of Kamieniec Podolski (Kam'yanets'-Podil's'kyi). The commander's daughter-in-law, the stunningly beautiful Zofia Witt, a Greek born in Constantinople, suggested a visit to the Pasha commanding the Turkish fortress at Chocim (Chotyn) across the border.

Although it had once been a Polish outpost, the Turkish town that had grown up around it after its capture struck Izabela by its oriental aspect, its glistening minarets towering above the houses brightly painted in different colours, with their wooden galleries bedecked with flowers. These, she noted, were occupied by men reclining on sofas 'smoking and letting themselves go to a kind of lazy indolence' which she assumed to be their national character.

The party was received by the Pasha, an old man with a noble face and black eyes dressed in fine robes with a golden dagger at his belt, reclining on a sofa and holding a little girl who was playing with his long white beard. 'I was arrested by this picture as I entered,' recorded Izabela, 'it seemed to me I was seeing Time playing with Childhood.' The Pasha was gratified when, having enquired why she had stopped and stared, he was told she had been overawed by the beauty of the scene, and he had stools brought in for the gentlemen and cushions for the ladies. He then pointed out that the men must cover their heads in his presence, which caused some difficulty: the current fashion for those wearing French dress was for tiny flat tricorns which were not worn on the head but carried under the arm. The men had no option but to balance these on their heads and sit stock still to stop them falling off. 'Seeing our gentlemen sitting on their stools with these would-be hats on their heads, I burst out in a fit of uncontrollable laughter which soon took over the whole company,' Izabela wrote, 'even the Pasha laughed.' As they were served lunch, the Pasha, whose religion forbade him to eat with infidels, retired. Janissaries carried in a large round low silver table, placed cushions around it and brought quantities of dishes, which they immediately removed to make room for others, without allowing anyone to partake of them. Mrs Witt explained to the non-plussed Izabela that the janissaries were allowed to eat the leftovers, and as the Pasha was not present to give the customary permission they clearly thought they could have a feast at the expense of the infidels. 'At that, I decided to act,' writes Izabela, 'and, seizing a heavy stout spoon with a long handle which was lying on the table, I lay in ambush. They had just brought in a chicken with rice and as soon as it was on the table I saw a huge dry hand stretch out to take it. Making use of the weapon I had seized, I applied a vicious blow which made the janissary let go, and we fell on the chicken and rice, leaving not one grain. Encouraged by my gratifying success, I did not let go my spoon and we dined very well in perfect security.'

The Pasha was delighted when he heard of the incident, but when Izabela asked to see his horses he refused, explaining that the look of a Christian cast over them might be harmful and he loved them too much to expose them to such danger. 'Apparently loving his women less than his horses, he offered to have me admitted to his harem,' noted Izabela, who accepted with joy. She was struck by the beauty of his favourite. She had just given birth and was unwell so Izabela offered to bring her own physician to see her, but when the Pasha discovered that she had given birth to a girl and not the desired boy, he would not allow it, and Izabela heard a couple of days later that the infant had died. She felt remorse and regretted her intrusion into a world to which she did not belong.[26]

# The Conquest of Berlin

A dam's tour of Podolia may have been a triumph, but his return to Warsaw was less glorious. He had assumed he would inherit his father's post of Voivode of Ruthenia and his colonelcy of the royal foot-guards, and took it personally when the king awarded both to others. His sister had broken with her royal friend and Adam joined her and those opposed to his policy at the Sejm of 1782. While Izabela supported him from the spectators' gallery, she remained on friendly terms with the king, continuing to frequent the Royal Castle to take part in amateur theatricals. The episode nevertheless alienated the Czartoryskis from the court, and they would henceforth spend more time at Puławy.

There, Izabela set about creating an environment and a way of life based on her own vision of how it should be led. It was to be her personal contribution to the Familia's political programme; she meant to set an example that would show Polish society how to regenerate the nation. Fundamental to this was education, and in common with her husband she began with that of her children.

She had brought her two eldest daughters up herself, sharing with them her own educational journey. She had also taught Adam Jerzy to read and write and schooled him in French and its literature. But as the boy was to be the head of the clan, he must be intellectually prepared. Adam carefully selected tutors, such as the physiocrat Pierre Samuel Dupont de Nemours; the Swiss mathematician Simon L'Huillier, later a professor at the universities of Tübingen and Geneva; the classicists Gottfried Ernst Groddeck, recommended by Herder, who would spend twenty years at Puławy doubling as Adam's librarian before moving on to the university of Wilno, and Niels Iversen Schow, later professor at Copenhagen. They joined the in-house Puławy poets Franciszek Dionizy Kniaźnin, Franciszek Karpiński, Józef Szymanowski and Julian Ursyn Niemcewicz, who taught the children Polish language and literature, under the overall supervision of Colonel Stanisław Ciesielski. The younger son, Konstanty, born at the end of October 1774, followed these studies with less rigour. Adam would test his sons on their progress and organise debates to develop their oratorical skills and discuss various forms of government and political systems with them. They rose early and began the day with fencing lessons with their French *maître d'armes* Ferdinand Durpin and while their curriculum was tight, they also hunted, with greyhounds and fox hounds, and took music lessons from a Parisian *maître de musique* by the name of Patonart and dancing lessons from another Frenchman, Louis-Aimé d'Auvigny, formerly *maître de danse* at the opera in Paris and later at Stuttgart.

Izabela was more concerned with their spiritual and emotional development. 'Religion is the prime mover of everything; it makes man act usefully, love with feeling, bear suffering, find solace in hope and think great thoughts,' she noted in one of her albums, and she wanted her children to feel the same. 'I do not wish to force you to fulfil the minor rules and rituals, which are meaningless,' she wrote in one letter to Adam Jerzy, 'but I wish and demand that throughout your life you honour religion, and not allow yourself to mock it in any way. As to the Lord God, I am sure that your heart will command you to love Him, as your reason will find proofs of His wisdom and omnipotence at every step and in everything that surrounds you.'[1] If anything, Adam Jerzy was too serious, and his tutor Dupont de Nemours would later remark: 'I have never seen a child who showed more goodness, sensitivity, high-mindedness than you did while still so young.'[2]

Izabela also devoted much attention to Marianna, who followed some of the same lessons as her brothers and was turning into an interesting and talented young woman, playing leading dramatic roles by the age of 15. In 1782 Izabela had commissioned her portrait from Angelica Kaufmann, but since the artist was then in Naples, she sent her a sketch drawn by herself along with a description of the girl's looks

Izabela around the time of her marriage, a lost miniature by an unknown artist.

Adam about four years earlier, pastel by an unknown artist.

The firework display in the gardens of Wołczyn following the wedding.
The 'Temple of Friendship' erected for the occasion features
a sculpture of Pylades and Orestes.

Jan Andrzej Morsztyn, comte de Chateauvillain, with his daughter Izabela, by Hiacynthe Rigaud, 1693.

This poor portrait of Adam's father August Czartoryski by an unknown artist does little justice to his renowned elegance and charm.

August's wife Zofia Sieniawska, depicted here in her hunting dress, was no beauty but probably the greatest heiress in Europe.

Izabela's grandfather Michał Czartoryski, the brains of the Familia, in his youth.

Izabela's father George Detlof von Fleming as a young man.

Michał's wife, Eleonora von Waldstein, is depicted in this over-door panel with a view of the newly completed wooden main house at Wołczyn, before the addition of the stone wings and *cour d'honneur*.

The most passionately destructive of Izabela's loves, the duc de Lauzun, drawing by Louis Auguste Brun.

Izabela's cousin and first lover, Stanisław Poniatowski, before he was elected king.

The empress Catherine's much-hated man in Warsaw, Prince Nikolai Repnin, on whom Izabela was forced.

Izabela in the 1760s, a self-confessed 'coquette', painted by Per Krafft for the king's private study.

The Blue Palace, Izabela and Adam's Warsaw home, detail of a painting by Bernardo Bellotto.

A watercolour by Jean-Pierre Norblin de la Gourdaine
showing a party at Powązki, Izabela's rural retreat.
Izabela's wooden cottage can be seen on the hill.

Painted in Paris by Alexandre
Roslin in February 1774, this
portrait shows Izabela at a
moment when she was making
life-changing choices.

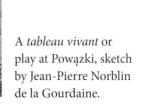

A *tableau vivant* or
play at Powązki, sketch
by Jean-Pierre Norblin
de la Gourdaine.

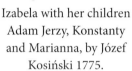

Izabela with her children
Adam Jerzy, Konstanty
and Marianna, by Józef
Kosiński 1775.

Izabela and Adam's
daughter Teresa, pastel
by an unknown artist.

Marianna, pastel by an
unknown artist.

A locket containing portraits of Adam Jerzy, Zofia and Konstanty,
with locks of their hair, by Jan Gottlib Jannasch.

Jan Klemens Branicki, the most persistent of Izabela's admirers and possibly Zofia's father. Study by Giovanni Battista Lampi for a portrait now lost.

Kazimierz Rzewuski, the most enduring of Izabela's loves and a close friend, by Anton Graff.

A skating party at Powązki given by Rzewuski in honour of Marianna and Helena Radziwiłł in 1782, by Jean-Pierre Norblin de la Gourdaine.

Izabela in the 1780s,
by Jean-Pierre Norblin de la Gourdaine.

and character. The resulting portrait, showing her *en trois quarts* laying flowers at the foot of a garden monument to Minerva, is surprisingly characterful considering how it arose. She was pretty and both Kniaźnin, who was teaching her poetry, and Karpiński, with whom she translated Delille's work on gardens, fell in love with her.

Izabela did not bestow as much care on Konstanty, an independent-minded child now 10 years old, and the 5-year-old Zofia would later complain that she was left to the ageing Mademoiselle Petit, whom she loved dearly but found wanting as far as education was concerned. She taught Zofia French by rote with no reference to grammar, and mathematics, limited to addition and subtraction. For the rest, she gave her books to read while she herself often dozed off. For history, Zofia ploughed her way through the Old Testament and the histories by Charles Rollin which had been used by her mother. She was taught no modern history and only a smattering of European geography. The Catechism she read was covered with caricatures drawn by Marianna and lacked many pages, which had been torn out. But Mademoiselle Petit did teach her to pray and planted in her a deep faith that would mark her whole life.

Izabela's apparent neglect seems out of character. 'It has to be said,' Zofia wrote in a later memoir, 'that I was excessively neglected even in the matter of cleanliness, as I was only made to take a kind of bath every Saturday evening; on that day I would be washed from head to foot, but that was all for eight whole days, and I still have painful memories of my hands covered in ink from Saturday to the Monday week.'[3] It is only fair to say that both Izabela and Adam were often away from home during the years of which Zofia writes, 1786 to 1792. There is a note of self-pity to Zofia's memoir which is absent from the accounts of Izabela's other charges, who included not only her children.

Several years earlier, Izabela had taken in the daughters of friends who had either been orphaned or whose parents had fallen on hard times, such as the two Narbutt sisters. Others joined them and soon Izabela was looking after a dozen or so young girls, who were treated as part of the family, as were the similarly bereaved boys Adam and Izabela took in. 'It is impossible to enumerate the young men and ladies, the entire families brought up in their house, set up in the world by their care, with a touching charity, a paternal solicitude which doubled the benefit,' recorded one woman, by no means an admirer of Izabela.[4]

This extended family was marshalled by Izabela according to her own method of character-building, in which expression of feeling and performance played a seminal role. There were two theatres at Puławy, one inside the house, the other an open-air amphitheatre on the Kępa, a peninsula created by a backwater of the Vistula at the foot of the bluff on which the house stood. Troupes of actors would occasionally be brought in, but mostly it was the family and household who took the stage. Kniaźnin produced translations and adaptations as well as his own works, some in heroic Greek mode with choruses, some in the form of operatic comedies, for which the resident composer Wincenty Lessel provided the music. The repertoire was broad, including Shakespeare, still not widely performed outside England.

Almost obsessively active herself, Izabela inculcated in her children and her other charges the habit of purposeful activity when not reading or writing. At Powązki, this had centred around physical work on the land and animal husbandry. At Puławy, it was focused on more creative pastimes that would stretch the imagination, such as designing and making costumes and sets for plays and other entertainments such as themed or fancy-dress balls. When news of Montgolfier's ascent in a hot-air balloon reached Puławy in 1782, Marianna and the other girls spent weeks pasting together pieces of paper under the direction of the mathematics teacher L'Huillier to produce their own version. The resident artist Norblin assisted in these activities as well as giving drawing and painting lessons. He was joined in 1783 by Aleksander Orłowski, the son of an innkeeper at Siedlce, where Izabela found him doodling on the walls. Struck by his talent, she brought him to Puławy and paid for his studies. In 1784 they were joined by another of Norblin's pupils, Jan Rustem.

Puławy attracted neighbours, such as the Mniszechs at Dęblin only fifteen kilometres away, Igancy Potocki at Kurów, a little further, the Kicki family at Ryki, and Aleksander Lubomirski of Opole Lubelskie, a dull man with a stunningly beautiful and vivacious wife, Róża Chodkiewicz, known as 'the little Rose of Czarnobyl' (Chernobyl) after her father's estate. Izabela's aunt Aleksandra Ogińska frequently drove over from Siedlce. Only fifteen years Izabela's senior, she had much in common with her niece. Her husband, Michał Kazimierz Ogiński, was a distinguished soldier and musician; he had perfected Erard's harps and, at the request of Diderot, written up the instrument for the *Grande Ency-clopédie* before fighting for the Confederation of Bar. After a short exile in France he returned to Poland, but they lived apart. She rebuilt Siedlce, inherited from her father Michał Czartoryski, in neoclassical style and turned the formal gardens into an Arcadian landscape park.

She, too, had taken in a bevy of young ladies. Fun-loving and active, she was keen on amateur dramatics and dancing, and being a good shot herself, in winter held shooting parties. Although they were separated by about 100 kilometres, the two households visited each other regularly, and although she loved going to Siedlce herself, Izabela was occasionally annoyed by the propensity of her husband and Adam Jerzy to become infatuated by one or other of Ogińska's protégées.

Izabela was no prude, but her Puławy had nothing of the rococo licentiousness of earlier days. Its literary output was purely lyrical, reflecting the vision which inspired her. Szymanowski disowned the salacious satirical poetry he had written in his Warsaw days, while in the preface to an edition of his new works Kniaźnin begged his readers to forget he had composed erotic verse in his youth.

Under Izabela's influence Puławy had become, in the words of one poet, 'the capital of homely virtues, charm and culture'. Reflecting her patriotism, 'Everything there was Polish, everything national'. According to him this meant that anyone who 'breathed the air of Puławy' was easily distinguishable from the rest of society. 'There may have been flirtation, romanticism and exaltation in the women, a little light-heartedness and flightiness among the young,' he goes on, but asserted that it 'did not overstep the bounds of dignity'. He could not encompass 'how many public virtues, how many domestic ones, how much humanity, how much charity, how much sacrifice, how much dedication, how much beneficence to the peasants, to cripples, to poverty, to orphans, to the unfortunate' were to be found on the 'charmed isle' that was Puławy.[5]

Izabela's love of Puławy did not signify a complete break with her past life. She spent the first months of 1784 in Warsaw and, when spring came, Powązki. She redecorated her room at the Blue Palace, hanging a portrait of her father next to the fireplace and some drawings on the other walls, furnishing it with a large table with a small bookshelf fixed to it, a cupboard and her harpsichord. She was reading the letters of Madame de Sévigné, taking Italian lessons and, despite suffering from searing pains in her right arm, which Dr John was treating with vesicatories (unguents that caused blistering) that hurt even more, she was working at her drawing under the guidance of the painter Franciszek Smuglewicz.

Nor did she reject the pleasures of the city, dining out, at the Castle with the king where she noted the dishes produced by his Italian chef Paulo Tremo, with her grandmother Eleonora and other relatives and friends, among them Helena Radziwiłł. During the carnival she went to balls, at court, at the Russian embassy and at various palaces, on one occasion dressed as a nun, and had a terrible hangover on the morning after Shrove Tuesday. She went to the theatre and the ballet, and to performances of the operas of Paisiello, who was in Warsaw, by the renowned soprano La Todi. She was present at the ascent of a hot-air balloon, from the courtyard of her grandmother's palace, and of another larger one which she watched with the whole of Warsaw massed on the banks of the Vistula.

Although she complained of having seemingly 'incurable' debts, she bought presents for Marianna, often referred to as Marynia, including a new writing set, engravings and a small box, as well as various gifts for others at Pulawy. She was also scouring the city for a tambourine and was frustrated by the delays in the delivery of a harpsichord. She even sent her some rare mushrooms, with advice on which sauce to eat them with.

She wrote to her daughter every two or three days. 'Adieu, my dear friend,' she signed off one letter. 'It is too little to say that I love you, that is a word every mother says to her child. But the fact is I love you much more than I love myself, much more, truly, than my own life, I feel you are a part of my soul and that nothing on earth could ever replace my dear, my good, my kind Marianna.'[6] Her letters are full of information and gossip, related in a sprightly mixture of Polish and French. Her opinions are clearly expressed, whether on a new painting by Smuglewicz, the bust of herself commissioned by the king, which she found very ugly, and despite suffering from frequent migraines she maintains the enthusiastic tone of a young girl. On 24 February she announced that Kazimierz Rzewuski had given her a new dog, 'which is the loveliest thing in the world'. This was just as well, as her old Fidèle would die at Puławy in April.[7]

Visits to Powązki, where she dined with Helena Radziwiłł, brought back happy memories. The thaw had caused some damage, the gatekeeper had died and the cashier Blum had been fired for stealing, so there was plenty to do. She improved and remodelled, borrowing a marble cupid by Edmé Bouchardon from the king to place in a choice spot and building a cottage for her French maid, Madame Parisot, which was referred to as 'Paris' and drew the family by her excellent cooking. By mid-May Powązki was at its best, with roses and lilac in flower at her windows, and Izabela only wished Marianna were with her to make things perfect.[8]

One of the pieces of gossip Izabela had sent her was a rumour circulating in Warsaw towards the end of January that there had been a revolution in Russia and the Empress Catherine was dead. As it happened, a different rumour had reached St Petersburg, and this one concerned Marianna herself.

It was that Prince Ludwig of Württemberg-Montbéliard, a handsome young man of 27, was about to get married in Warsaw. This was of interest in the Russian capital since the prince's sister, Sofia Dorothea, had married the Empress Catherine's son and heir Grand Duke Paul and was now the Grand Duchess Maria Feodorovna. Her father was the ruler of the principality of Montbéliard, a fief of the Holy Roman Empire lying between Switzerland and France belonging to the junior branch of the house of Württemberg.

In the first days of February, while visiting his sister in St Petersburg, his eldest son, Prince Friedrich Wilhelm, received a certain Mr Vidal, his brother Ludwig's *homme d'affaires*, who handed him a letter. We do not know its contents, but in his reply, dated 6 March, Friedrich Wilhelm wrote that he had dismissed the current rumour of his younger brother's 'quest' as 'the whim of a young man eager to get married', which he thought ill-advised. But having heard from Vidal 'the extreme state' of his finances and that Ludwig saw 'the marriage in question as the last available means' of avoiding the consequences, and that since he had been assured that their parents did not oppose it he was prepared to accept 'the Princess in question' as Ludwig's wife. He clearly considered it a mistake, but his tone was cordial. 'Adieu, my dear brother,' he signed off, 'may you find the happiness you seek, may it be constant and durable; I will join in it with great eagerness on account of the feelings with which I am, my dear brother, your faithful brother and friend.'[9]

The Grand Duchess expressed the fear that Ludwig would not wait for the emperor's approval, while 'Czartoryski will never give him his own daughter without the consent of [the emperor], who seems to me to wish to have nothing to do with this business'. Ludwig had implied that their parents did not oppose the projected marriage, but she suspected they had not been informed. She was right, and his behaviour would have consequences.[10]

Their mother was a niece of King Frederick II of Prussia, and Ludwig was currently serving in the Prussian army. Maria Feodorovna was married to the heir to the Russian throne, and their father was a vassal of the Holy Roman Emperor Joseph II. Certain niceties had to be observed, and Ludwig was overriding them.

He was in bad odour with his parents on account of his dissolute life; anticipating that they would not approve of his plan he kept them in the dark but tried to make out that they did, even to the King of Prussia, to whom he had written asking for his blessing. On 6 April Frederick II wrote from Potsdam saying he would be delighted to oblige provided Ludwig had obtained the approval of his parents, and to give him leave to go to Puławy to deliver on his 'solemn promises', but suggesting he ought to consider whether he had the financial wherewithal to support a wife. In answer to two further letters from Ludwig asking for some kind of endorsement, Frederick replied that he had nothing to add. On 26 June, he categorically refused to write to the Czartoryskis in support of Ludwig's plan to marry their daughter.[11]

There is no evidence that Ludwig had made any 'solemn promises' to Marianna, or that he had even met her. And it is impossible to establish when he first went to Poland or when Adam and Izabela became aware of his intentions. According to the Grand Duchess's close friend the baronne d'Oberkirch, Ludwig's parents did know and objected on the grounds that as they belonged to a reigning dynasty and the Czarto-ryski did not, it would have to be classed as a morganatic marriage, which Adam baulked at, and only allowed it to go ahead at the insist-ence of the young lovers. It is true that in a letter to Marianna brimming over with tenderness dated simply 'Siedlce, the 6ᵗʰ', Adam expresses his delight 'in anticipation of the happiness of your future ties'. But he was a stickler for form unlikely to have behaved in such a way, and the bar-oness's evidence is unreliable in other respects.[12] On 15 September the French chargé d'affaires in Warsaw reported to his superiors in Paris: 'The Pr of W in the service of the king of Prussia has in the past few days become engaged to the daughter of Pce Adam Czartoryski.'[13]

Although that too is only dated 'the 9ᵗʰ', a letter from Madeleine Petit to Marianna is more informative. It not only tells us that Marianna is engaged, but also that she is 'happy and contented with the choice she has made'. The old retainer concurs, having seen the fiancé during his visit to Puławy and is measuring herself up for a dress for the impend-ing nuptials.[14] Marianna had admitted to her that she found the young man's excessively theatrical and passionate courting technique, what she termed his '*Céladonisme*', somewhat ridiculous; when he turned up at Puławy, Ludwig allegedly went down on his knees before Adam beg-ging for his daughter's hand and making wild expressions of love. Madeleine Petit reassured her that he would soon shed his extravagant behaviour and pompous manner, and adopt the '*le ton de notre pays*'.[15]

From Warsaw on his way back to Berlin at the beginning of Septem-ber, Ludwig wrote an effusive letter to Adam saying how much he liked and respected him, enjoyed his stay at Puławy and loved the daughter Adam had entrusted him with.[16] He seemed to most people to be sin-cere. 'He has just come back from Warsaw, where he got engaged to the Princess Czartoryska, the charming, beautiful and in addition the rich-est heiress in Poland,' the Prussian royal chamberlain Count Asahverius von Lehndorff noted in his diary entry for 18 September. 'Of course, he is absolutely enchanted by her. He is a fine-looking man, a real Hercu-les, but a terrible spendthrift, who will need all Prince Adam's ducats.' Ludwig would not stop boasting 'about the millions which he will receive as a dowry', but he thought him 'a good and handsome boy'. Ludwig left for Poland again a couple of days later.[17]

There had still been no communication between the parents of the engaged couple. The only letter Adam appears to have received was from Prince Ferdinand, youngest brother of Frederick II. As well as being Ludwig's great-uncle, he was his uncle by marriage, Ludwig's mother being Ferdinand's wife's sister. On 20 September he wrote to Puławy expressing his satisfaction at the news of the engagement and affirming that Ludwig would make Marianna very happy 'as I have known him from his childhood, and have always found a good heart in him, a matchless honesty and frankness in his character'. He went on to say that the wedding should not be delayed as he had been reliably informed the Grand Duchess, who loved Ludwig more than her other siblings, was eager to see it take place as soon as possible.[18] They married on 28 October at Siedlce.

This sequence of events is perplexing. As Ludwig's sister the Grand Duchess had surmised, normally Adam and Izabela would never give their assent without the approval of the groom's family and possibly of the emperor, with whom Adam corresponded on cordial terms; the emperor addressed him as 'Mon Cousin' and eagerly accepted health tips and remedies from him.[19]

Even more puzzling is the later evidence that Marianna was opposed to the match. 'I have to admit that she married her husband with a physical and moral repugnance so great that she could never approach him without a violent shudder,' Izabela would write a decade later. 'You will say that we were wrong to force her! Alas! You are right, and that wrong is indelible! But the P. of W. seemed to us to be a good man, kind and honest and our daughter's repugnance seemed to us mere childishness.' Elsewhere, Izabela later confessed that although they had meant well, she could not understand with hindsight how the marriage had come about, as they had all found him repellent.[20]

By the time she wrote this there were good reasons why hindsight might have distorted her vision. It seems unlikely that Izabela would have dismissed the feelings of her 16-year-old daughter and 'dear friend' so lightly. Nor would someone as instinctive as her have suppressed her feelings of revulsion. And from Madeleine Petit's letter it is clear Marianna was quite happy about it to the last moment.

The only explanations of this flouting of conventions that spring to mind are that either Adam and Izabela were blinded by eagerness to acquire dynastic ties with two reigning houses, or that something had occurred which made it impossible to extricate their daughter from the engagement. The first seems unlikely given the family's standing and Adam's keen sense of propriety – and not being able to stage a grand royal wedding would have defeated such a purpose anyway. The second might have had something to do with Marianna's repugnance, and might even have been its cause if, in a fit of '*Céladonisme*', he had compromised her in some way.

Ludwig's parents were not pleased when they heard of the marriage. Grand Duchess Maria Feodorovna's efforts to placate them and persuade them to accept the fait accompli had little effect. Ludwig's elder brother Friedrich Wilhelm informed him that in view of their parent's anger he was withdrawing his support, and Ludwig himself would not dare to face his parents for another sixteen months, despite the urgings of Frederick II.[21]

Ludwig commanded a regiment stationed at Treptow (Trzebiatów) in Pomerania, whither he brought his bride. She was followed by frequent letters from Izabela assuring her that she would be very happy and giving her advice on housekeeping, servants, accounts and the other things a wife was expected to deal with. Marianna wrote saying she was finding life difficult, to which Izabela replied that was only to be expected, and that if she persevered she would be richly rewarded. Marianna took her advice and put on a brave face. 'You fulfil my hopes when you tell me how happy you are with your husband,' Izabela wrote, 'love him, look after him, make him happy, be his first, his most tender friend.'[22]

Adam paid back a sum of money Ludwig had borrowed from Prince Ferdinand, but he and Izabela were horrified when they discovered the full extent of his debts. They were in no position to pay them off at once, and after looking into the matter Adam concluded that Vidal had been cheating him and advised Ludwig to dismiss him, hinting that he would not pay anything until he did. But in other respects Izabela at least appeared to find no fault in her son-in-law. 'He is my son, I love him as my own child, and I want to see him happy,' she wrote to Marianna.[23]

The day after the wedding, Marianna had written a dutiful letter to

Frederick II expressing her respect and signing off as his 'devoted niece', and at the end of December Ludwig took her to Berlin, where they were met by Izabela, who felt bound to support her. She came without Adam, accompanied only by two of her protégées, the sisters Aleksandra and Konstancja Narbutt, the painter Jan Rustem and a couple of servants.

The day following her arrival Izabela was introduced to the king's younger brother Prince Henry, who took an instant liking to her, then to the queen, who invited her and Marianna to dine on 1 January 1785. On 5 January, complaining of the discomfort of squeezing herself into the requisite dress, she attended a court reception, accompanied by Ludwig and Marianna. According to Count Lehndorff, they made a beautiful couple, with Marianna showing every sign of adoring her husband.[24]

On 9 January Izabela was bidden to Potsdam by the king. She had been eager to meet him and anxious at the delay in the invitation, but she was apprehensive nevertheless; he was already being called Frederick the Great. On reaching Potsdam she was met by the queen's lady-in-waiting Julie von Voss, who ushered her into an audience chamber, which she expected to find full of people and where she hoped to be able 'to hide in the crowd'. 'Instead of which when I entered I found myself alone with Mme de Foss and as I walked through the door another opened opposite and the king came in alone. "This is the Princess Czartoryska whom I have the honour of presenting to Your Majesty" she said, and, turning on her heels, she went out, leaving me alone with what I thought of as the most terrifying man on earth, whom I considered to be well above anything I had ever known, in wit and knowledge. I became so confused that if I had left immediately, I might have sworn that the king was six feet tall. He took me by the hand and in a kindly tone of voice said "But I am old, I have poor eyesight, permit me to take you up to the window and turn you to face the light so I might examine you at leisure." Still holding her hands he went on: "You have given us an angel. I met her yesterday. Her happiness concerns me more than I can say." Hearing these words I raised my eyes and found the courage to look at the one who had called my daughter an angel. I was surprised to see before me not a colossus as I had thought, but a small man, smaller than myself, a little misshapen, in a worn uniform stained all over with snuff, with the most beautiful blue eyes, a kind though piercing look, and something reassuring about his whole person.'

Seeing that she was still nervous, he went on. 'Your angel will always find a friend in me. She has married my nephew, but I wish to be frank with you. Those two beings are not made to go well together; she's an angel, and as for him . . .' He went on to say that it could not last. 'In any case, she must always come to me when she feels the need.' He went on to speak of other things, of Poland, which he had just carved up, and of its king. He asked whether the king wore a military uniform, insinu-ating a lack of valour in Stanisław, to which she replied that he often wore the uniform of the Cadet School. 'That is good,' he replied, 'because he is still a king at school.' Izabela was revolted by the cheap jibe at the expense of her country and its king, her cheeks stung and her eyes filled with tears, and she shot back: 'Sire, you have given him a cruel and undeserved lesson.' He did not reply and but went on. 'I have often said that Poland should be governed by its women. That would be much better. I know several of them and you confirm my opinion in every respect.' [25]

By evening word of the welcome she had received was all over Berlin and she was the centre of attention. 'The princess Czartoryska, a very distinguished lady, charmed one by her wit and her amiability,' noted Prince Ferdinand's 14-year-old daughter Louise. 'The whole of Berlin was in a state of excitement at the presence of these two princesses, there was talk only of parties and pleasures. Our evenings were filled with gaiety.' [26]

The king held a dinner for Izabela at Potsdam at which they dined off gold plate, served by pages and '*coureurs*' in velvet liveries dripping with gold thread and tassels, assisted by hussars in brilliant uniforms. The king placed Izabela opposite himself and spoke only to her; they dis-cussed at length how Richelieu and Mazarin had rebuilt France. [27]

Izabela spent another five weeks in Berlin, fêted by the king's brothers who fell over themselves to please her, by his minister Count Podewils, the French marquis de Jumilhac, who confessed to never having met anyone like her, the comte de Ségur, on his way to take up his post as French ambassador in St Petersburg, and what Lehndorff described as 'a swarm of admirers'. [28] This is not surprising. Izabela's natural manner provided a contrast to the stiffness of the Berlin court and society. She joined in all the entertainments, be they balls or amateur dramatics, choreographing dances and composing songs and verses for special occasions. She also displayed her knowledge as well as her charms at dinner and would sit down at the piano afterwards to play and sing, sometimes late into the night. Not everyone was charmed, however. Wirydianna Radolińska claims people laughed behind her back. 'Her dress, her way of entering a drawing-room, her bearing, was quite unlike that of anyone else,' she noted. 'To all of these advantages she added that of being a great *grande dame* and effortlessly eclipsed all the women of her day.' When, at a fancy-dress breakfast given by Prince Ferdinand, Izabela and her two Narbutt protégées appeared in Cossack dress and executed a dance which delighted the men, the ladies expressed in loud whispers their view that she was a shameless show-off. But nobody took much notice. Lehndorff noted that wherever she went, this 'Sarmatian Princess met with friendliness and all kinds of little attentions', and not just on account of her personal charms. 'She's certainly a very lovable creature, but I think she is a clever woman who knows how to win over all sorts of people and thereby influence them.'[29]

Izabela attended sessions of the Prussian Academy of Arts of which she had been a member since 1780 and which would promote her to the higher status of Honorary Member a year later. She had Prince Henry show her his collection of porcelain, his gallery of paintings and his engravings, and she pored over his edition of Buffon's *Histoire Naturelle*. He even had his own pet parrot brought out to show her, and apparently gave it to her.[30] She visited notable gardens and discussed planting with the director of the royal gardens. She took the Narbutt girls to the Academy of Painting and to the galleries of private residences. She met the Abbé Bastiani, one of Frederick's intellectual coterie, known as *le philosophe de Sanssouci,* who gave her a medal for her collection. An avid collector of memorabilia, when she was shown around the king's study at Sanssouci while he was at lunch, she purloined one of his pens. On Frederick's desk, she saw not only letters from Voltaire, sheaves of accounts and some musical manuscripts, but a bowl of cherries, with a note in his hand reading: 'there were 32'. He must also have counted his pens, as he found her out.[31]

As she prepared to leave Berlin her admirers planned a week of farewell parties. On 8 February, Shrove Tuesday, Prince Ferdinand gave a masked ball at which his three children and those of other royal princes executed a ballet as an interlude. The ball resumed, but an hour later another interlude opened with 'Cossack music'. Izabela and her two girls, as well as Marianna, Ludwig and four other dancers, all dressed as Cossacks, performed another ballet. Izabela then declaimed some verses she had composed in honour of her hosts, and presented the king's designated successor Frederick William with a sabre which had belonged to King Jan Sobieski, Prince Henry with a kerchief which she had painted, and Prince and Princess Ferdinand with Turkish embroideries. 'The whole company was enraptured by the Princess and her enchanting nature,' recorded Lehndorff, 'especially as she was sensitive enough to sing a few verses in honour of the assembled spectators, thanking them for all the kindness she had been shown.'[32]

On 13 February Izabela called on the queen to say goodbye. The following day Prince Henry organized an elaborate entertainment in her honour. In one of the rooms he had erected a temple, with the inscription: 'To the Friendship of Princess Czartoryska', with an altar attended by several 'temple priests' and two children representing the gods of Love and Friendship. Izabela was led into the temple by Princes Frederick William and Henry and the two gods recited verses in her honour after which they handed her gifts from the two princes. They concluded by saying that Berlin was her second fatherland to which she would ever be bound by bonds of love.[33]

The next day it was the turn of Prince Ferdinand, who threw a surprise party for her. The guests had been instructed to wear costumes they might have worn at Powązki, which had been described to them, and he had filled his great hall with replicas of the cottages there. On arrival Izabela was led in by the three royal princes to the accompaniment of folk songs. She was moved to tears and enchanted by the music. They then all sat down to dinner. Two days later, after dining with Prince Henry, Izabela climbed into her carriage and set off for Belgard whither Ludwig and Maria had gone a few days earlier.

She spent two months with them, doing her best to iron out the problems that had arisen in their marriage, which were largely caused by Ludwig's attitude to his parents-in-law. From the moment he reached Berlin he had begun denigrating them, claiming they had promised to pay his debts and then reneged on it, calling Izabela miserly, arrogant and cold towards him, and accusing her of setting his adored wife against him. But his complaints met with scorn.[34] It could not have been a happy two months for Izabela, and, to distract herself she shook up the local Junker society by giving a ball at the beginning of April for 180, a rare event in Pomerania.

On 2 May 1785 she was back in Berlin dining with Prince Ferdinand, with whom she would go to stay at Rheinsberg a few days later. In the meantime, she was making the most of her days in the Prussian capital. 'I come and I go, I rush to see all the things I did not see the first time,' she wrote to Marianna. She visited the famous Berlin porcelain factory and bought a coffee cup for Adam.[35]

One day, she went to watch a parade and was impressed by the turn-out of the troops, and by the king, on a white horse, in his threadbare uniform. He spotted her and sent an equerry over to invite her to join him. He greeted her with 'affectionate politeness'. 'I was pleased, I was flattered, I felt a little surge of pride,' she admitted. When the last of the regiments had filed past, the king summoned its colonel, Prince Charles Ferdinand of Brunswick. ' "Prince," he addressed him in a bantering tone, "I am pleased with you and your regiment, and I wish to reward you. Here is the Princess Czartoryska. I entrust her to you; take her back to Berlin with your regiment, form a square around her carriage and escort her all the way to the [Hotel] City of Paris where she is lodging." ' He then bade her an affectionate farewell and, mounting his horse, rode off. His orders were carried out with much merriment, half of the regiment in front of her 'triumphal chariot' into which she had climbed bursting with laughter, the other half behind, and Brunswick and his officers riding either side. 'The band was making an unbelievable noise, and I, dying of mirth, made my entry into Berlin to the astonishment of the bystanders.'[36]

On 13 May she arrived at Prince Henry's huge palace of Rheinsberg, which he had turned into an artistic and musical centre. Izabela spent two weeks there, taking part in amateur dramatics with her host and other members of the house-party. 'The shows here are charming,' she wrote to Marianna on 25 May, 'I am having great fun.'[37] The following day she accompanied Prince Henry to the castle at Boitzenburg, to see its baroque gardens being transformed into English-style parkland.

Back in Berlin, she had lunch with the minister and mining expert Friedrich Anton von Heynitz, who showed her his mineral cabinet and presented her with a small collection of samples. But she did not linger, as she was worried by news she had received from Warsaw. On 11 June she spent the evening at Prince Ferdinand's and sang duets from French operas with the marquis de Jumilhac, and two days later left for Warsaw.

# 9

## *Political Egeria*

On 17 January 1785, while Izabela was in Berlin, Warsaw was shaken by the news that the king's chamberlain Franciszek Ryx and General Komarzewski had been arrested for conspiring to murder her husband. A woman by the name of Dogrumov claimed they had bribed her to seduce Adam and poison him. Suspicion was cast on the king as the instigator.

Instead of dismissing it as the intrigue it clearly was, Adam believed her allegations. Egged on by Elżbieta Lubomirska, who was blinded by her hostility to the king and by her son-in-law Ignacy Potocki, he took the matter to court. The case fell apart when the hearings revealed the farcical nature of the attempts by the woman and her accomplice to extract money from both sides. She was punished and the court ruled the matter should never be mentioned again.

Too embarrassed to admit his naivety, Adam left Warsaw in dudgeon. To sever his last connection with the king he resigned his command of the Cadet Corps, and henceforth spent much of his time in Vienna. Izabela would accompany him on another trip to London in October 1785, when she impressed Mary Berry by 'her 'fine figure, tall and upright, with a certain *air de reine* when she entered the room'.[1] But she was soon back at Puławy. She was concerned with the state of Marianna's marriage, which was not a happy one. From the surviving correspondence it is difficult to trace its ups and downs, since many of the letters have erroneous dates added later or none at all, while most of Marianna's have been lost. To complicate matters, mother and daughter used code words, some of them impenetrable.

Marianna tried to make the best of things, supported by her parents, who paid for the redecoration of their residence at Treptow and sent her furniture. She kept herself busy by reading and writing, drawing, writing music and setting verses to it, and by transforming the formal gardens into a landscape park. She tried to reassure her mother that she was happy, and in one letter painted a picture of 'two people made to love each other and to live together', which delighted Izabela, who felt that all would henceforth be well. But some of these exchanges were clearly meant to cheer each other up.[2]

'You may well try to seem contented with your lot, but we have the misfortune here of not being able to believe you,' Madeleine Petit wrote to Marianna in May 1785, only six months after the wedding, 'and that is no small torment for those who love you.' She urged her to open her heart to her mother if she felt she could not continue and to put an end to it before her health gave way.[3]

Their relationship was bedevilled by Ludwig's sense of insecurity. Although Adam did pay his debts, it was never fast enough as Ludwig kept adding to them. This only increased a dependency on his wife's family which fuelled his resentment of them. He claimed they looked down on him and that even Mademoiselle Petit did not accord him due respect. He was jealous of Marianna's relationship with her mother; when she grew homesick and expressed the wish to visit Puławy, he accused her parents of trying to lure her away from him. He resented Adam's insistence that he get rid of Vidal and bridled when he sent a man to Berlin to sort out his affairs. Attempts to placate him with presents merely aggravated the situation.

When Ludwig did finally go to face his parents at Montbéliard in the spring of 1786 his satisfaction at being forgiven by them was cancelled out by his annoyance that they only did so because they took an instant liking to Marianna; they were charmed by her and took their 'chère Zizi', as they called her, to their bosom. This provoked complaints that his parents-in-law did not do enough for him and that Marianna was treated better at Montbéliard than he at Puławy.[4]

Ludwig could be delightful one moment and violently abusive the next. According to the Empress Catherine, he put Marianna through 'hell', beating her if she did not perform menial tasks such as pulling off his boots and washing his shirts. He once dragged her out of bed by her hair and she was only rescued from serious injury by the entrance of the doctor. He would later beg forgiveness and promise to improve his ways, on one occasion crawling on his knees to where Adam was sitting and kissing his feet in tears. And when the baronne d'Oberkirch brought them together with his parents they were like 'two young turtle-doves', so in love it was a pleasure to watch.[5] Some of his letters are so effusively affectionate that it is difficult to dismiss them as humbug. There were times when Izabela warmed to him and expressed a tenderness also beyond conventional pleasantry. Such violent mood swings suggest that he might have suffered from some personality disorder. And while Ludwig was clearly unstable, Marianna was probably not the perfect foil for him. Her intellectual superiority and wider cultural horizons would only have exacerbated his feelings of insecurity, as would her attractiveness to other men. Some passages in her mother's letters could be interpreted as admonitions on that score, and suggest she was not an entirely innocent victim.

Izabela sent motherly advice, avoided telling her daughter about some of Ludwig's worst outbursts against Adam and herself, and swept things under the carpet. Encouraged by his returns of affection and winsome ways, she deluded herself that he would settle down with time, and when he brought Marianna to Warsaw and Puławy she had found him so delightful that she could not imagine a better son-in-law.[6]

In view of Ludwig's jealousy at their closeness, she often wrote not to Marianna but to her companion Teresa Tokarska, and Marianna replied through Madeleine Petit, both using code words and aliases. She also recommended that Marianna write in Polish and be sure to have two letters on her desk, one bland one in French, in case her husband should come into the room and insist on reading it. She also advised her to burn her own letters and to sign nothing. She admitted that her daughter's situation was 'certainly not pleasant and occasionally unhappy', but urged her to take comfort in the fact that she had nothing to reproach herself with, and that since it was her destiny to be with Ludwig she must put up with it, keep busy and not say anything about his behaviour, even in confidence; it seems Ludwig was trying to blacken both Marianna and Izabela in his sister the Grand Duchess's eyes.[7]

Izabela's attitude seems out of character given her close friendship with and concern for the wellbeing of her children. But in the absence of evidence it is impossible to establish what was really going on in her daughter's marriage, and she kept hoping that their relationship would stabilise. She had other things occupying her mind, and she was anxious about her son Adam Jerzy.

He was 16 years old and alarmingly introverted. His father wished he would be 'more cordial and accessible', and Izabela urged him to 'try to vanquish those moments of ill humour which overcome you from time to time without reason'. 'My friend, it is so easy to capture hearts and so good to be loved, that one must do everything to achieve it. My dear Master Adam, I often say this to you, and will continue to say it, as I wish you to be happy,' she had written a couple of years earlier. But she was annoyed by his moping when he fell in love with one of Ogińska's protégées at Siedlce, and, rather than let him be, she encouraged his religious leanings. 'My friend, the irrefutable truths of religion, the conviction that there is a Being who watches over our happiness or measures out punishment to us, are essential to us,' she wrote to him. 'They are the foundation of everything.'[8]

She was also increasingly absorbed by the political aspects of the world she had created; by the mid-1780s 'Puławy' had come to signify more than the place itself and was equated with a life of virtue. And the highest virtue in the Poland of the 1780s was love of country and service in its cause. In aiming to create a new model for society based on an idealised chivalric past, Izabela was not only inspiring people, particularly the young, to be better citizens, she was drawing them into what was essentially a political cause. She had always loved her country, and after the partition she became an ardent patriot. The amateur dramatics and pageants she staged were a vehicle for the expression of her patriotism and a means of instilling it in others.

The Familia had been among the first to abandon the Sarmatian *kontusz* in favour of French dress, which was associated with the Enlightenment, but it now played on the strength of feeling against what were seen by many of the poorer *szlachta* as foreign imports by adopting it again. Izabela encouraged everyone at Puławy to wear Polish dress, which had the effect of setting its wearers apart ideologically from the king's entourage, who mostly dressed in the French manner. Adam happily followed her in this; on New Year's Day 1786 he caused a sensation in Vienna by parading with his suite in the richest and most flamboyant possible version of Polish dress.[9]

The year had begun quietly for Izabela, with her husband in Vienna, various other members of the household away and Mademoiselle Petit sick. 'So we are only eight at table with all the children, and six in the evening,' she reported to Marianna. She was redecorating her apartment and installing a fireplace in it, building a new hermitage and placing stones with poetic inscriptions in the gardens, going for walks, skating on the backwater, embroidering, reading and writing 'prodigiously'. Between advice and encouragement concerning her marriage, she informed Marianna that she was studying Greek history with Adam Jerzy and that Kniaźnin had written a play for which Lessel was to provide music.[10]

The play in question, *The Spartan Mother*, was a musical drama with choruses in the Greek manner. The text may have been by Kniaźnin, but Izabela had provided the idea and supervised the writing, as she would the production. The heroine is a woman of Sparta who, when her city is threatened by the Thebans, sends her elder son out to fight the invaders. When he returns from the field of battle covered in blood, she urges him to go back into the fray, and take his younger brother with him. She loves them dearly but is ready to sacrifice them for the sake of their country, which she holds even more dear. They return victorious and make offerings to Mars. In the grand finale, the whole population of Sparta comes together in an expression of unity. The message was clear: action, even if desperate, is preferable to reasoned compromise, heroism trumps reflection, and the nation should stand united.

The premiere took place in mid-June 1786 in the large riding school at Puławy, with Izabela and her sons in the leading roles. The set, painted by Norblin, represented a colonnade at the end of which was a temple of Mars. Including the chorus, some sixty actors took part. The audience, drawn from Warsaw and Lublin as well as the surrounding countryside, numbered over 500. Aleksandra Ogińska had come from Siedlce, where she had held a meeting of those opposed to the king's policy. Three Potockis married to Elzbieta Lubomirska's daughters, Stanislaw, Ignacy and Jan, were also there.

It had cost her a great deal of effort, Izabela admitted to Marianna, but she felt it had been worth it. 'Everything breathed chivalry and the love of Motherland,' wrote Ignacy Potocki. 'This truly national entertainment produced emotion and civic enthusiasm.' It was so well received that it inspired a number of literary works in the same vein, and there were calls for it to be staged all over the country in order to arouse patriotic zeal. There were less edifying reactions, including a lampoon by the poet Stanisław Trembecki in which he urged Polish women to give all their illegitimate sons to fight for the Motherland.[11]

The euphoria following the performance of *The Spartan Mother* was punctured by Adam's failure to get elected to the next session of the Sejm. He and Izabela had made a long tour canvassing through south-eastern Poland, but he lost to the king's candidate. Puławy and the court were now openly antagonistic. When Adam and Izabela went to Warsaw in November a crowd of supporters drove out in their carriages to meet them and escort them into the city. According to one diarist their audience with the king lasted only seven minutes, after which they proceeded to a banquet given for them by Branicki, who was by now no friend of the court, and would attend another given by the Russian ambassador Stackelberg. Hardly Spartan.[12]

Politics seems to have brought Adam and Izabela closer than ever. 'With every day your mother becomes more attractive to me, and to all those around her,' he wrote to Marianna in January 1787, 'it is extremely rare to combine so much intelligence with so many qualities, nobody could have more tact, better judgement, or to make better use of them, she behaved wonderfully during the [Sejm].'[13]

Adam Jerzy had left on an educational tour abroad under the care of Colonel Ciesielski. They set off with Aleksandra Ogińska, who was going to Carlsbad to take the waters, and their road lay through Kraków, Prague and Weimar, where they parted. Accompanied by a small court, she travelled on to Carlsbad, while Adam Jerzy remained in Weimar. He called on the poet Christian Martin Wieland, who struck him as distinctly unpoetic in a bonnet which looked like a night cap, and the philosopher Johann Gottfried von Herder, both of whom were correspondents of his father. He was invited by Goethe to a small gathering to which he read the work he had just finished, *Iphigenia in Tauris*, and Adam Jerzy was impressed by the beauty of the man as well as his work.[14]

Izabela followed his progress avidly, demanding frequent reports and dispensing advice, with a tenderness that softened the repeated admonitions to open up and allow his excellent qualities to shine. She was planning to travel across Germany herself, as it was high time she met Ludwig's parents. She had written to his mother, thanking her for her kindness to Marianna, and received effusive replies, in which Dorothea Friderika of Württemberg had written, 'Never have [such feelings] come more easily to me, never have I felt less merit for cherishing someone who is so worthy of love', adding that she loved Marianna as though she were her own child.[15] But as Izabela was about to set off for Montbéliard, higher powers intervened.

The Emperor Joseph II had left Vienna on a journey which would take him through Galicia and Ukraine to Kherson, to meet Catherine II, who was making an imperial progress down the Dnieper to inspect new Russian conquests. Having reached Lwów (Lviv), which he renamed Lemberg, Joseph suddenly decided to make a detour and visit Puławy. Izabela was taken aback when she heard of it and, unimpressed by the implied honour, baulked at the idea of hosting the emperor. The house was not prepared and there was no time to make the necessary arrangements. At Adam's suggestion, they immediately set off in the direction of Lwów, feigning not to have received news of his proposed visit, and headed him off on the road between Zamość and Tomaszów. He was annoyed and bid them wait on him at Lwów, whither he would return after his tour of the Zamość area.[16]

When they did meet him he was in better mood and 'extremely friendly' towards Izabela, whom he favoured with a call every day. 'He speaks well, but talks too much,' she noted. He promised to send her bulbs and seedlings from the gardens at Schönbrunn and invited her to join him on a tour of Italy. On one occasion, he asked her what she thought of Catherine and said he himself did not think much of her, describing her as 'ridiculous', but swore her to secrecy, saying he wished to remain on good terms with Russia. A sense of uncharacteristic modesty prevented her from writing down the things he told her, 'shaking with laughter'. 'He is strange, this emperor Joseph,' Izabela concluded. He trusted in her discretion and when he heard she was going to Montbéliard, he begged her to go on to Paris and deliver a package to his sister the queen, in person and 'without witnesses'.[17]

After she had formally taken her leave, he suddenly decided to call on her late at night, when she had already retired to bed, and as he arrived unaccompanied in a cab, the Cossack guarding her door refused to let him in. Joseph identified himself but the man did not believe him and an altercation ensued. Roused by the commotion, Izabela came downstairs and assured the man that this really was the emperor, but he was not convinced until Joseph gave him ten ducats.[18]

It was not until July 1787 that Izabela left for Montbéliard, taking with her the Narbutt sisters, the elder, Konstancja, now married. Before setting off, she left instructions for Konstanty and Zofia to each be given a beekeeper's hut and a plot of land to turn into a wood. Her route lay through Vienna, where the emperor entrusted her with a package for his sister. Ludwig had solicitously given her directions as to which roads to take and which posting stations were the most efficient, for which she thanked him in a letter from Frankfurt am Oder on 3 August. Six days later she was in Leipzig and on 15 August in Frankfurt am Main.[19]

From there she had meant to head for Montbéliard, but on being informed that Ludwig's parents were away, she went to Manstein, where she found 'a thousand pretty things to see', and from there to Düsseldorf to see the art gallery. At Gotha she looked for a good edition of the Greek tragedies for Marianna, but found only poor translations. As Ludwig's parents had still not returned to Montbéliard, in mid-September she decided to go to Paris, where she had instructed Adam Jerzy to join her from Treptow, where he had spent time with Marianna and Ludwig.[20]

Elżbieta Lubomirska had a number of people staying in her apartment in the Palais-Royal, including her son-in-law Stanisław Potocki and the painter Maria Cosway, who had come over to carry on her affair with Thomas Jefferson. So Izabela and her party were put up by Franciszek Rzewuski, brother of her great friend Kazimierz. She was in a strange mood. 'I am overcome with emotions, fears, anxieties and regrets,' she wrote to Konstancja Narbutt, now Dembowska, who had succumbed to homesickness and gone back to Poland. 'Paris bores me,' she added. She was delighted by one opera performance, but found the theatres not as good as in the past, she went around galleries and looked at the work of various artists, did some shopping, drove out to Moussan to have lunch with the duc d'Orléans, but spent most of her time with other Poles. 'Paris amused me but did not seduce me,' she wrote to Marianna on 29 October, the eve of her departure. She had only stayed so long in order to carry out the emperor's errand, and it was not until the 27th that she had been able to see Marie-Antoinette alone.[21]

When she reached Trianon, 'the queen received me very warmly in a cabinet which, seen by candle-light seemed charming,' Izabela records. 'I said so to the queen during a pause in the conversation. "You find this cabinet charming," said the queen, "because you are seeing it by candle-light; in daytime it is very sad, as the windows give onto a small service yard and they have bars on them. When I see those iron bars it makes me feel sad, because it looks to me like a prison." Poor queen, what a presentiment! What the package contained I do not know. Judging by the manner in which it was entrusted to me and by that with which it was received, it must have been important.'[22]

Before leaving, she installed Adam Jerzy with Elżbieta Lubomirska, who had engaged the services of the Abbé Scipione Piattoli as tutor to her nephew Henryk, and Izabela hoped her son would benefit from his learning, as well as the wisdom of Stanislaw Potocki and the worldliness of Lubomirska herself. She urged him to come out of himself and take greater interest in others. His father was going through a difficult period, she wrote, and their hopes were centred on him, Adam Jerzy; he must work, look, listen and learn. He was to take lessons in fencing as well as English, music and drawing. She warned him to be wary of people and keep away from *esprits forts*, and to remember that God was the source of all that was good. The 17-year-old boy would not disappoint: '[In Paris] he was regarded as a prodigy for his vast and deep knowledge in everything, by the Duke de La Rochefoucauld, Marmontel, Condorcet, and all the men of great talent to whom I introduced him,' Jefferson's friend Philip Mazzei wrote to James Madison.[23]

Izabela left Paris without regret, not minding if she never saw it again. Accompanied only by Aleksandra Narbutt and one maid, she set off for Montbéliard. Her arrival at the castle, a fortress perched on a rocky outcrop overlooking the town, was marred by the coachman she had employed in Paris; being an annoyingly 'methodical' man, he had locked her carriage door, which thwarted the enthusiasm of the prince, who had come out followed by servants with candles and sprung forward gallantly to open it and had to wait for him to clamber down from the box and fumble for the key in various pockets while they exchanged pleasantries through the window.

The Württembergs greeted her warmly as the mother of Marianna, whom the princess referred to as 'ma Zizi, ma délicieuse petite amie'.[24] 'Your mother-in-law is a rare woman,' Izabela wrote to her daughter. 'The Prince is also an excellent man.' To Ludwig, she wrote that she loved his mother and found every day she spent with her a new reason for liking her. 'There are no better people on earth,' she wrote to Konstancja Dembowska. She found the castle 'very comfortable' and enjoyed her stay, particularly as her hosts had 'forgotten that etiquette ever existed'. They embraced her as enthusiastically as they had her daughter, even the youngest member of the household, their 4-year-old granddaughter Catherine, 'Trinette', referred to Izabela as her 'petite maman'. When it was time to leave, the princess insisted on accompanying her, first to Strasbourg, then on to Stuttgart and Hanau, to visit the landgravine of Hesse-Cassel. Before they parted, they drew up a 'contract' in which they bound themselves to exchange gifts, of drawings, embroidery, seeds, shrubs, liqueurs and cheese. 'Oh, my good, very dear, very sweet friend,' Dorothée wrote after they had parted, referring to her in their subsequent and very tender correspondence as 'My Princess, my dear Isabelle'.[25]

Although she had left Adam Jerzy in the care of others, Izabela did not forget him and wrote frequently. 'Your character is very sound and strong, your soul beautiful, your heart tender; you have sense, ability and the will to work,' she wrote from Montbéliard. ''You only lack the ability to give consistency to this and courtesy to be amiable and loved.' Her letters brimmed with loving yet strict lectures wedged between snippets of news of her doings, urging him to 'live for others too', and to 'contribute to the good of society, to the happiness of those who love you'. From Strasbourg where she had paused to buy books – 'I cannot resist this temptation; I feel I am gathering friends in whose company I shall spend many a pleasant moment, because they are faithful friends who will never fail us' – she did not fail to remind him to change into Polish dress when he went home.[26]

She reached Berlin on 29 December 1787 and was well received by Frederick William and his queen, and by her old friends. 'I was embraced like society's darling,' she recorded, and although she suffered from headaches and her eyes hurt, she was in good spirits. Before leaving for Berlin she had written to Puławy telling Konstancja Dembowska to send her favourite pretty black-eyed Cossack boy who danced well to meet her there and given precise instructions on how he was to be kitted out – in black Cossack pants, a red jacket (to be run up from an old dress of hers), belt and hat.[27] 'The presence and charm of [Izabela] greatly enlivened the carnival,' noted Prince Ferdinand's daughter Louise. 'She organized fêtes and surprises for the King which amused him very much.' At a grand party given by Frederick William at the end of the carnival, she choreographed a quadrille on the theme of a fashionable opera, in which all the royal princesses took part. 'The sumptuous costumes surpassed everything we had seen,' wrote Princess Louise, noting that Izabela was exceptionally well received and even courted, despite her age.[28] But she was exhausted by the social whirl and longed to be back at Puławy. Ludwig and Marianna, who had come from Belgard, apparently happy, would join her there in the spring; he was planning to leave the Prussian service and move to Poland, where the couple could settle down under the eyes of her parents.[29]

But Poland was anything but settled in that spring of 1788. A generation brought up under the enlightened rule of Stanisław Augustus longed to break free of Russia, and as Catherine and her ambassador in Warsaw had consistently humiliated him he lacked the authority to restrain them. He complained that although she came to Warsaw twice in April, Izabela did not bother to call on him.[30] She was too busy playing her part in what had become a national movement.

'At that time there were two majesties, two capitals, two courts in

Poland,' wrote one contemporary, 'one in Warsaw with Stanisław Augustus, the other in Puławy with the Prince [Adam Czartoryski] and his wife, and this was in many respects the more impressive.'[31] The Puławy accounts for 1787 to 1790 list liveried staff of four butlers, twelve footmen, six *frotteurs*; six men in the pantry, five cellar staff; nine in the laundry; twenty kitchen staff, including four cooks under the chef, and two butchers; between two and four additional men under a French pastry chef and an Italian confectioner; a couple of Turks to make the coffee and prepare pipes; and forty stable staff, including coachmen, postillions, farriers, outriders, a wheelwright, saddlers and grooms, and they do not include non-servile staff such as the two doctors, musicians, poets, painters and priests.[32]

This allowed for large gatherings at which Izabela put on patriotic displays, including another performance of *The Spartan Mother*. In a version of her 'portrait' updated that year, she explained that love of her country had come to dominate her feelings. 'It is an aim to which I have harnessed my whole future. My husband, my children, my feelings and my character make this aim, this cult, so dear to me that nothing in the world could detach me from it.'[33]

Adam's urbanity was not always in tune with her exalted mood, and he once committed the faux pas of appearing at breakfast in one of his Austrian uniforms. On another occasion he drank too much champagne and made a gaffe when toasting one of their new political allies. Izabela intervened, saying: 'Go, husband, and have a sleep because you bluster when you get drunk.' This he graciously did.[34]

But he was taking no chances as he stood for election to the forthcoming Sejm; he brought a horde of up to three thousand poor *szlachta* to Lublin to vote for him. He provided them with victuals and a patch of land outside the city on which they sat around fires roasting oxen and drinking his health while their horses grazed around them, reminding one observer of a Tatar encampment.[35] Exhorted by Izabela, who at one ball danced with potential supporters until three in the morning, they easily ensured the election of Adam and his running mate Kazimierz Rzewuski.

The young generation of the Familia, who called themselves the Patriots, were led by Ignacy Potocki, but Adam presided over the proceedings and Izabela set the tone. She marked the opening of the Sejm on 6 October 1788 with a grand ball at Powązki, and the Blue Palace was where they gathered and potential allies were wined and dined.

The opening of the Sejm was accompanied by a surge of patriotic defiance and Izabela was in her element as gesture dominated the politics. In a fit of excitement, the deputies voted to raise the army to 100,000, for which the country had neither the men nor the money. The chair on which Catherine's ambassador reclined to keep an eye on proceedings and intimidate anyone who displeased him was ostentatiously thrown out of the spectators' gallery, which was taken over by Izabela, with her sons and other ladies, cheering patriotic speeches and jeering at voices of caution, waving their shawls to add effect. There was some justification for this truculence, as an opportunity had arisen for Poland to throw off the Russian protectorate.

In the summer of 1788 Russia's wars with the Porte and Sweden had prompted Britain, Prussia and the United Provinces to form the Triple Alliance to restrain her. The prospect of hostilities with Russia meant Britain had to secure an alternative source of grain as well as the timber and other materials essential to the Royal Navy, and only Poland could supply these. But as Prussia controlled the flow of these goods down the Vistula to the port of Gdańsk, the Patriots sought an alliance with Frederick William.

Given her recent experiences in Berlin, Izabela was optimistic, while Adam was sceptical and felt that Poland's other neighbour should be taken into account. But when approached by the Austrian minister with the proposal that they try to put together a pro-Austrian party, he replied: 'but whom can we find here who would side with the Emperor? Only Your Honour, myself and my dog.' That did not stop people suspecting him of hidden ambitions, some thinking he was hoping to replace the king, others that he aimed to put Ludwig on the throne. In September 1789 the French agent in Warsaw reported rumours that Adam was hoping to put his son on it.[36] There is no evidence that either he or Izabela considered it, but she was taking centre stage.

Her promotion of traditional Polish dress as a marker of patriotic virtues had caught on and assumed the status of a uniform for those swept up in the surge of national feeling. It entailed the abandonment of tied-back long hair, and when the marshal of the Lithuanian confederation in the Sejm, Kazimierz Nestor Sapieha, joined the Patriots, Izabela personally cut his hair in the Sarmatian style at a public ceremony at the Blue Palace to the sound of drums and trumpets. He was cheered wildly when he entered the chamber the following day.

At the ball on 4 May 1789 in honour of the Marshal of the Sejm, Stanisław Małachowski, which took place in illuminated gardens filled with 4,000 guests, decorated with images of him supporting a swooning Liberty and being crowned by the Motherland, it was Izabela who was chosen to place a 'civic crown' on his brow and recite a paean of her own composition in the name of Polish womanhood. Niemcewicz contributed a poem calling on the women of Poland to assert themselves in defence of the country, and pamphlets appeared urging wives and sisters to make their voices heard, to bring up their children as good patriots ready to fight and die for their country.[37]

Izabela's sons were too young to fight, and Adam Jerzy was being groomed for higher things. Ludwig, on the other hand, seemed a worthy offering to the Motherland. Given the expanding army's urgent need of experienced officers, his long tenure of a senior rank in the Prussian army would be invaluable. Adam obtained his naturalisation, the rank of lieutenant general and command of a division.

Izabela's ostentatious patriotism did annoy some, and even Helena Radziwiłł could not resist the odd sarcasm. But while it drew surprisingly little satirical comment in Poland, it would not have been viewed favourably in St Petersburg. Such considerations probably underlay Adam's decision that she accompany Adam Jerzy, who was to continue his studies in England.

She left Warsaw on 26 September 1789 with Adam Jerzy, his tutor L'Huillier, Major Orłowski, her maid Konstancja, and a couple of other attendants. She lingered at Puławy, only leaving that with regret, bidding farewell to its trees and glades, its nightingales and its river, as well as to Marianna, Konstanty and Zofia, commending them all to God. 'I have always had a great facility for enjoying anything,' she jotted down a couple of months earlier, and it would stand her in good stead over the next months. The weather was fine, and, finding the swaying and jolting of the coach tiring and the company unappealing, with

Adam Jerzy silent and Orłowski snoring most of the time, she walked beside it for much of the eleven-day journey to Vienna, her first stop.[38]

There, the party stayed with Elżbieta Lubomirska in the Esterhazy palace on Mölkerbastei which she was renting, having fled Paris at the outbreak of the Revolution. Relations between the two sisters-in-law had never been better than correct, while the social life of the imperial city left Izabela cold. 'I am much fêted here,' she wrote to Marianna on 9 October, but complained of suffering from 'spleen'. 'The local dry figures and coldly-polite receptions are not for my soul.'[39] She did not see the emperor, who was ill, but was warmly received by Ludwig's sister the archduchess Elizabeth, wife of the future Francis II. The ageing and increasingly eccentric chancellor, Prince Wenzel von Kaunitz, gave a dinner in her honour at which, to general amazement, he did not go through his usual routine of washing out his mouth in front of the guests. She was also made much of by the British whom she came across, who were excited at the political changes taking place in Poland.

From Vienna she travelled through Linz to Munich, and, as the weather continued fine, she walked much of the way, sometimes accompanied by Adam Jerzy and always by her dog Kozaczek. She had decided to make a detour through Switzerland to indulge a long-entertained dream of visiting the setting of *La Nouvelle Héloïse*. She also wanted to meet a man of whom she had heard and read much, the poet, philosopher and pastor Johann Kaspar Lavater. He had achieved fame and a remarkable following by his treatises on physiognomy, which argued that character could be detected from the study of people's features. What particularly attracted Izabela were his religious teachings: he advocated private spiritual development and self-perfection through the cultivation of feeling and what he called 'the religion of the heart'.

Izabela walked into Switzerland on a path running along the Rhine, and quickly fell in love with the country and its inhabitants, who charmed her with their 'bonhomie' and their 'frank and affectionate manner'. She made straight for Zurich, which she reached on 25 October, and that very evening called on Lavater. She had written to him and wanted to test his theories by visiting him before anyone could have told him she was in town, and he did not disappoint. When she appeared at his door, he looked hard at her features and declared that she was the person who had written to him some time before, and retrieved her letter from his desk.[40]

She saw much of Lavater over the next days. 'I am delighted by him more than I can say, and I am very sincerely drawn to him on acquaintance with his beautiful soul and his pure and consoling morality,' she wrote to Konstancja Dembowska, 'I don't know what I would not give to have a confessor such as him.' She made a full confession which prompted her to make resolutions for the future. She gave him money for his ministrations to the poor of his parish, and as he was in financial straits she offered to help him dispose in London of four paintings by Dürer which he wanted to sell.[41]

Lavater was greatly taken by Izabela and his letters to her brim with tenderness. In a neat minuscule hand on small cards contained in a beautifully bound case entitled '*Bibliothèque Czartoryskienne*' he wrote out for her instructions on how to behave in every situation. He also provided 'the incomparable friend Czartoryska' with a 'mixture of thoughts for travellers, which contains less that is new than is true'. 'I speak to you with as much trust as though you were my brother,' he prefaced his two hundred snippets of advice to remain always aware, open-minded, alert, trusting and observant while travelling, which should always be a quest for truth as well as sensation. He also composed a threnody on the death of her daughter Teresa which he published with the year of her death on the title page. 'Yes, I want to be the friend of Lavater for my whole life,' she reciprocated in the first letter she wrote after she left.[42]

On leaving Zurich, Izabela and her party made for Berne and thence the shores of Lake Geneva, on a pilgrimage to the sites made sacred for her by Rousseau. 'I have seen one of the most beautiful countries in the world,' she wrote to Marianna, 'I saw the lake of Geneva and its surroundings, amiable people, attractive women, educated men. I saw Vevey, Clarens, the rocks of La Melleraye, I saw superb landscapes and all that nature could gather in the way of beauty.' She visited the house of Madame de Warens at Vevey and was thrilled to find her cabinet left exactly as described in *La Nouvelle Héloïse*. She leapt at the chance of buying some letters by Rousseau and a portrait of Madame de Warens. She also added to her collection an object redolent of medieval chivalry; as she was driving through Moret near Fribourg, her coach broke down and while she waited for it to be repaired she visited the chapel built on the site of the battle in 1476 in which the Swiss had resisted the Burgundians, and from the ossuary she took a piece of what she assumed to be the bone of a fallen hero.[43]

As she was suffering from migraines, from Vevey she went to Geneva to consult the renowned Dr Tissot. Towards the end of November 1789 she doubled back to Montbéliard, where she would spend the next month and celebrate Christmas. The Württembergs were more enchanted by Marianna than ever and grateful for Adam and Izabela's understanding of their son's profligacy and generosity in bailing him out. The atmosphere was so relaxed that even Adam Jerzy began to 'unfreeze'.[44]

By 4 January 1790 Izabela was in Paris. The Revolution was still in its early stage but it had wrought much change and, having paid a few calls, looked at the shops and been to the theatre, she decided not to linger. She did see Lauzun, who like the rest of the aristocracy had given up his titles and was now General Biron. He had had a distinguished military career since they last met, capturing a colony for France in Africa, setting down rules for the humane treatment of prisoners of war and fighting with the Americans at Yorktown. He 'expressed the same feelings and great eagerness to come to London to see me,' Izabela wrote, 'but I adopted a very serious tone and put an end to the idea.'[45]

# England and Scotland

On 10 January 1790, after a sea passage during which she was 'cruelly sick', Izabela and Adam Jerzy reached London with their suite and Lauzun's friend the Chevalier d'Oraison, who had joined her party.

She quickly located 'a pretty house and a good cook, a pretty carriage', but was shocked at the expense of life in London. She bought a harpsichord and a guitar and engaged a music master. She set about learning English, shopped and paid calls, and went to the theatre, but was disappointed that Mrs Siddons was not playing and found the opera 'ridiculously bad'. She also visited nurseries to order seeds and shrubs, and hired an Irish gardener, Dionysius McClaire, whom she sent to Puławy. She would later meet another, James Savage, who impressed her so much that she took him on for three years on a salary of £70 per annum, three times the going rate in London. 'I have found all my old acquaintances and all my old friends,' she wrote to Konstancja Dembowska. 'I have not yet gone out into the *grand monde* and have spent most of my time arranging things so that my son should not waste his time.'[1]

Adam Jerzy had received precise instructions from his father: apart from learning English, he was to go to the theatre, listen to sermons, read and go into society, visit major cities and manufacturing towns, and stay in country houses. He was not to attend horse races and on no account go hunting, as this might end in his having a fall, breaking his neck and leaving to posterity only a cartoon of the kind for sale in the Strand entitled: 'The Polish prince who broke his neck chasing an

English fox'.[2] He began by spending several weeks studying the English constitution with the Lord Chancellor, the Marquess of Lansdowne. He attended a criminal trial and that of Warren Hastings, to one of the sittings of which Izabela accompanied him; she was impressed as much by the sight of the 3,000 people present as by Charles James Fox's eight-hour speech.[3]

When she did start going out into the *grand monde*, she found it 'boring beyond belief' and longed for a companion with whom she could laugh. 'I am not made to live far from those I love,' she wrote to Marianna. 'I need another heart, a listener, a friend, I need to share my life, my days, my moments with another.' But she must have gone out, as she was noticed by the Prince of Wales, who would remember her to Adam Jerzy over twenty years later. 'I'm being fêted, showered with friendship; but my heart is dead in the midst of all that,' she complained.[4]

She did have a companion in Lady Jersey and 'hardly left her house', which was free and easy unlike most, although even she was 'surrounded by frozen creatures'. That was not the case with her new friend Maria Cosway. 'She is a charming woman who sees many foreigners, who has many talents, and a great sweetness of character.'[5] One of the foreigners Izabela saw there was the deposed President of Corsica, Pasquale Paoli, soon to be welcomed back on the island by the Buonaparte brothers Joseph and Napoleon. Another she met at the Cosways' was the painter Philip James de Loutherbourg, who delighted, and terrified, her with his ghost stories. Both Maria and her husband Richard Cosway made portraits of Izabela, she in oils, he in pencil and watercolour, which was reproduced as a popular lithograph.

She took advantage of her stay in London to buy manuscripts by Pope, Locke and George Washington, a print of her husband's friend and correspondent Sir William Jones, images of Mary Stuart and other historical figures. At an auction she bought a carved powder horn associated with Henry VIII and a plaster death mask of Oliver Cromwell with other items that had belonged to him. From the sister of Captain James Cook she purchased his cutlass. As word spread that she was collecting such objects, people began to offer her paintings of famous people, pieces of armour said to have belonged to historic figures, a medallion with a lock of Elizabeth Woodville's hair and, in the case of Lord Fitzwilliam, a lace collar worn by Charles I.

If she found the social life difficult, it was the weather that really got to her; she complained of the grey skies and the cold, which gave her persistent headaches and attacks of spleen. But it was the news, which reached her on 5 March, of the death of Ludwig's sister the Archduchess Elisabeth, the 'angelic creature' she had so recently seen in Vienna, that distressed her most. Had it not been for the Channel, she would have left for Montbéliard instantly, to weep with her mother.[6]

She distracted herself as best she could, going to a concert in Westminster Abbey given by 700 musicians in the presence of the king and queen, and accompanying Lady Jersey to the launching of a 98-gun man-of-war. She visited the ship from stem to stern and thought it the most beautiful man-made object; she was moved to tears as she watched it slip into the water with hundreds of men on deck. She went to Richmond and to Twickenham to see Pope's house and sit under a weeping willow comforting herself by reading his verses (in French). People laughed when she mentioned what she had done, which struck her as odd, and although one did give her a casket made from a willow planted by Pope, to supplement the sprig she had picked herself, she felt no affinity with most of those she met.[7]

'I have grown terribly thin and I am in a bad mood,' she complained at the beginning of April. 'I am being sent lots of flowers by Englishmen, probably out of kindness, as I am neither pretty nor charming.'[8] She longed for the company of Marianna, whom she identified as 'another part of myself'. 'Sometimes I feel that when I breathe you are breathing with me, and that if you were taken away I would not be able to breathe at all,' she wrote on 16 April. 'God has created you with a character rare in a woman, tender in a daughter and invaluable in a friend.' Thinking of her children would restore her serenity, and then she thanked God for everything that had happened to her in her life. 'Fortunate in every way, all I can do is to ask that I should lose nothing,' she wrote.[9]

She admitted that there was much she liked about England. 'But there are two things to which I shall never accustom myself. The climate and the society. The one is excessively damp, the other superlatively cold. The one is bad for my health, the other for my soul.'[10]

She wrote to Lavater saying she longed to be able to go to Italy and pass through Switzerland to see him.[11] But she could not leave as she must accompany her son on his educational tour of the country – which she would transform into a magical sensory experience.

She left London on 28 May, accompanied by Adam Jerzy, L'Huillier, Orłowski, Oraison and a maid or two but without her dog Kozaczek, which had fallen ill. She was armed with a list of people and places she should visit, to which various acquaintances had added their recommendations. The first stop was Slough, where she was to visit 'Mr. Herschell le lunatique'. The lunatic was not at home, but they were allowed to examine his telescopes. They then visited Windsor Castle, where Izabela was particularly taken by the paintings, noting those by Van Dyke, Titian and Raphael. From there she went to see General Henry Conway's gardens at Park Place, near Henley, with their 'superb' grotto. At Oxford, she found the colleges beautiful and the libraries magnificent, but the students 'too free', and the distinction between gentlemen and scholars 'a very bad thing'.

She was not impressed by the park at Blenheim, thought that of Stowe had too many temples, and preferred Stourhead, though she considered the house there 'sad'. An early admirer of gothic architecture, she was spellbound by the cathedrals of Winchester and Salisbury. Stonehenge, where she picked up a fragment of stone and scraped some moss off one of the standing stones, set her dreaming of druids. A more modern note was struck at Portsmouth, where, after visiting the Isle of Wight, she took breakfast with Captain Chamberlain on HMS *Orion*.[12]

At Bath, she must have made an impression, since a week after her visit the *Bath Chronicle* carried an advertisement recommending 'C. MENGER, next door to the **White-Hart** inn, Stall-Street, and opposite the **Bear** inn, **TAYLOR** and **HABIT-MAKER** to their Royal Highnesses the **PRINCE** and **PRINCESS** of **CZARTORYSKA** and **FAMILY**'.[13] At Bristol she attended a public meeting by the dissenter and chemist Dr Priestley, and complained the weather was still foul. She had stayed at or visited several country houses, including Badminton, Chatsworth and presumably Wilton, given her connection with the Pembrokes, and was surprised to find the owners mostly absent. 'They disdain the beauties of spring and a part of the summer, not enjoying their superb country houses and only visiting them as the green foliage declines in order to hunt the fox.'[14]

She was reading Shakespeare in English, and at Stratford-on-Avon she lingered at his tomb to reflect on his greatness, and to scratch her name on it, before visiting the house in which she was told he was born. While listening to the patter of the current owner, who claimed descent from the bard, her eyes fell on a small chair which appeared to be fixed in the inglenook and was told it was where the great man used to sit, smoking his pipe, as he worked out the plots of his plays. Izabela decided she must have it. She agreed a price with the woman, but, according to her own account, when a workman arrived to remove the chair from the wall, the woman's deaf and dumb granddaughter flew at him, shrieking wildly, kicking and biting him. A clergyman was summoned to calm the child, and a bargain was reached whereby the legs were left and only the back was taken by Izabela. She claimed to have paid 200 guineas for it. According to other sources, she did not get possession and it was only a couple of months later that she sent Orłowski to purchase it, which he did, for twenty guineas. As she was leaving, Izabela marvelled at the fact that even after his death the great man's legacy enriched his descendants by way of the tourist trade. Little did she know that, according to another source, the old woman sold another sixteen such chairs over the next twenty years. Izabela also bought several small items made of wood from Shakespeare's mulberry tree, and left the place with a 'sweet and pleasant' sensation.[15]

She was drawn to sites and buildings redolent of historic deeds or people: at Warwick, the castle whose interiors evoked the age of chivalry, and the portraits, particularly Holbein's of Anne Boleyn, which set her dreaming; at Fotheringhay, the few stones that remained of the castle, which prompted meditation on the fate of Mary Stuart, one of which she added to her collection. Some of her quests ended in failure, as when she dragged her reluctant party on a long ramble in search of a supposedly picturesque cascade, and sometimes in farce. As they were taking tea in Cirencester, the innkeeper said there were ruins of a Roman bath nearby. 'I jumped up and beside myself with joy imagined a bath with mosaics, stones and a thousand wonders,' she related to Marianna. A guide was hired, and after a seemingly endless ramble they came to the ruins of a wall with an opening in it. The guide went in first, and as he bent over his breeches fell down, 'and all I saw in this Roman monument was the proudest arse I have ever beheld.'[16]

Always ready to see the comic aspect, she noted that Adam Jerzy had adopted the gestures and attitudes of the English, Orłowski insisted on speaking an English which nobody understood, while Oraison was 'charming, full of wit and originality', and, it seems, in love with her. L'Huillier was a bore and tactless, which annoyed the Frenchman and led to quarrels.[17]

Her itinerary was partly dictated by the curriculum Adam had set for their son and the recommendations of people she had met in London, which included the industrial wonders of the country. And while she craved sensuous communion with nature and the past, Izabela was also fascinated by modernity. 'We are going around the factories; it is a charming thing and touches on the miraculous how far industry and mechanics have been taken,' she wrote from Birmingham, where they spent four days.[18] They visited a button factory and Samuel Galton's gun works, where she was appalled to learn that he manufactured sub-standard ones to be sent out to Africa to be traded for slaves. It seems to have been the first she learned of the trade and was revolted. She noted down in her journal the chemical processes used in various factories she visited, describing in detail the smelting of iron ore, the new cotton-spinning machines she saw in Manchester and the methods used in coal mines. She visited Thomas Wilkinson's steelworks in Bradley and many other factories, in most of which she was led around by the owner. In Sheffield, she admired the knives and other implements produced in the steelworks.

In some cases, poetic sensation combined with the wonder of modernity, as in the case of the iron bridge over the Severn, completed only ten years earlier; she was overawed not only by that, but by the sight of Coalbrookdale on a moonlit night, its flaming furnaces looking like so many volcanoes. After visiting his factory at Etruria, she took a trip in 'Mr Wedgwood's boat' down the Trent and Mersey Canal, through a tunnel to Worsley. There, she managed to persuade the manager to let her go into the mine, and 'crawling on all fours' to where the coal was being hewn, she beheld 'the image of hell'.[19]

At Liverpool she visited the prison, at Manchester the hospital and the public baths, walking about town along streets deep in dung. But they were soon off northwards, where Izabela was struck by the beauty of the landscape, the ruined abbeys, ancient tombs, waterfalls and rocks, and went into raptures over York Minster. At Castle Howard they met with a 'charming reception' and over the next three days Izabela admired the house and its contents, particularly the Holbein portraits of historical figures, went riding in the park, was invited to cut her initials on a beech tree, and accepted the gift of two small dogs, one of which she named Kozio; judging by a seal she had cut in his image, which depicts him as a lion with a long upturned tail, he must have been some kind of Pomeranian.[20] She was overwhelmed by the kindness of the Howards, and the sympathy between the two families would endure for three generations.

They travelled on, through Darlington and Durham, whose cathedral Izabela thought mean and ugly, to Newcastle upon Tyne, and thence to Scotland, where she meant to scratch her name on the tombs of Fingal and Ossian, and 'to dwell with tenderness on the surviving monuments to Mary Stuart'. Her road lay through Edinburgh, Newbattle, Dalkeith, Hopetoun, Perth, Scone, and every castle, house, monument and ruin along the way. She revelled in the portraits of historic figures and was overwhelmed by the beauty of places such as Dunkeld. She dined with the duchess at Blair Atholl, as the duke was out shooting, and was carried up the mountain by Highlanders, who shared their humble fare with her while they 'sang Oscian'. They were fervent Jacobites and cursed the French for failing to support Bonnie Prince Charlie. Izabela was enchanted by these 'men without breeches' who not only refused to take money for the food they provided, but wanted to give her some, along with a couple of Highland ponies for her journey home.[21]

She bathed in Loch Tay before setting off for Killin, the goal of her pilgrimage, where she was disappointed to discover that what local tradition held to be the grave of the legendary Fingal was just a mound. But she never forgot with what reverence the Highlanders showed it to her. Much the same happened when she was later shown the rock under which Ossian was supposedly buried. She would later assert that imagination 'binds one to believe blindly that it is here and nowhere else that the bones of Fingal and Ossian lie'. She picked flowers at the spot for her collection before going on to stay with the Earl of Breadalbane at Taymouth Castle. She was in Campbell country, the land of her ancestors, and she was greeted warmly at Inveraray by Lady Louisa, who cooked traditional Scots dishes for her. 'I met with the most generous hospitality in Scotland, with a good and honest folk in the most beautiful places on earth,' she wrote to Marianna as she left the country.[22]

She took in Loch Lomond and picked up a shell on the banks of Loch Katrine in memory of the Lady of the Lake before going on to Glasgow and thence to Carlyle, staying at Hamilton Palace on the way. She paused at Penrith to see the lakes, going out in a boat and picnicking by the lakeside, where she carved Marianna's name on an ash tree and Adam Jerzy 'who always brings Greece into everything' seized a bottle of wine, and poured a libation into the lake before drinking the rest with Oraison.[23]

They stayed in squalid inns without beds and country houses such as Wentworth Woodhouse, whose interiors and paintings Izabela described at some length. From there, the party made for London, via Sheffield, Derby, Nottingham and Cambridge, reaching the capital at the end of August, delighted to be reunited with a fully recovered Kozaczek.

Adam Jerzy set about writing a report on everything he had seen and heard, before going to Bowood to stay with Lansdowne to resume his study of the British constitution. Izabela was pleased with his application, intelligence and general conduct. She felt he would be very useful to his country and noted with pride that Oraison, a democrat who feared the Revolution in France was taking the wrong course, kept saying: 'If only one brought up young men like this in France, things would be going very differently.'[24]

'I have seen a lovely country, a variety of nature, some superb landscapes, great agriculture, a free people, an industry carried to an unbelievable degree,' she wrote to Lavater on 1 September, but was disturbed by the resulting unemployment and misery. To her husband, she observed that although she felt Poland could do with more machinery, particularly the new frames for weaving and spinning, rapid mechanisation deprived people of their livelihood. At the same time, she admired the manner in which 'that class of people who are unable to look after themselves are looked after here'. 'I have never seen a country in which more effort is made for the convenience and pleasure of the people.' She nevertheless felt that while there was more of everything in England, 'we have more joys, more gaiety, a more beautiful climate and above all an everyday happiness which comes of our disposition and our character'.[25]

After a couple of days in London on one of which the Duke of Queensberry gave a grand dinner for her, Izabela went to stay with Lady Jersey at Middleton Park in Oxfordshire. Her husband was away 'hunting foxes which he never catches', leaving only her 'charming hostess' and her two daughters in residence, which suited Izabela perfectly. They went for walks, embroidered and made music.

Izabela had been hoping to get back to Poland at the beginning of October, but she did not want to leave Adam Jerzy on his own, lest he succumb to the fashion for heavy drinking popularised by the Prince of Wales and 'the Sect of Philosophers who believe in nothing'. At the same time, she was alarmed that Adam Jerzy wanted to cut short his studies and go back to Poland to join the army.[26]

While 'vegetating in the country' at Middleton, Izabela volunteered to decorate a small pavilion in the garden, and set about painting arabesques, which were much admired, particularly by the two girls, who joined in with enthusiasm. When it was finished, an 'altar of friendship' was placed in the room, and, with time, a poem above it likening Izabela to Raphael.[27]

'I'm very comfortable here. I am loved, I am looked after, I am showered with kindness, but I feel a sadness I cannot conquer, and terrible attacks of spleen,' she wrote to Marianna on 10 October. 'I have greatly gone off English country houses. They are superb but excessively sad, because of their isolation. One soon tires of lawns and trees when one doesn't see a living soul.' She loved her hostess. 'Wherever I shall be I will never think of Lady Jersey without emotion,' she wrote to Marianna, wishing she could take her back home with her to Puławy.[28]

Towards the middle of November she went to London, where she arranged for L'Huillier to accompany Lady Jersey's son, who meant to go to Geneva, and to meet Ludwig's younger brother Ferdinand, who had been sent to England by his mother in quest of a wife. 'Be a mother, a friend, a counsellor to him,' she begged Izabela. How much help she could be to the young prince is doubtful, but she took him to Middleton when she went back there for a short visit in December.[29] She and Adam Jerzy attended a ball at Blenheim, which Izabela found 'curiously boring', her only source of enjoyment was watching Lady Jersey's daughters being admired, as she had dressed and coiffed them herself, After that, they set off for Castle Howard for Christmas and the New Year. Although she loved the Howards, she was dying to go home. 'I can only find happiness in Poland,' she wrote to Marianna on 23 December.[30]

Back in London, she finally got to see Walpole's Strawberry Hill, with its 'Tribune', a chapel-like room crammed with paintings and objects, very much to her taste. She was accompanied by Stanisław Augustus' younger brother, who was Primate of Poland; he had come to purchase paintings collected for the king by Noel Desenfans (now in the Dulwich Picture Gallery), and she had given a dinner for him. Before leaving London, on 20 January she walked over to Hampstead with her son and a few friends to have tea with the Polish Minister at the Court of St James's, Franciszek Bukaty, and was delighted to be able to gossip with acquaintances from Lithuania who were visiting England. There was much talk of war in Europe, and it was not just her homesickness that made her long for home. 'I think only of Poland, and I say to myself, let them all come to blows, and perhaps we might get something out of it at the general peace,' she wrote.[31]

# Patriotism and Persecution

T he Sejm whose opening she had celebrated before she left in 1789
had enacted various reforms, and now some of its leading lights,
led by Ignacy Potocki and Stanisław Małachowski, were working with
the king on a new constitution, and by the spring of 1791 a project was
taking shape.

Poland had signed a treaty with Prussia, which had joined Britain
and the United Provinces in the Triple Alliance against Russia. Prime
Minister William Pitt's plan was to send an ultimatum to Russia to
make peace with the Porte and, if she refused, to send British and Dutch
fleets into the Baltic while Prussia, Poland, Sweden and Turkey confronted Russia on land. On 27 March a courier left for Berlin with the
ultimatum for endorsement by Prussia. At Spithead, Admiral Hood
hoisted his flag on HMS *Victory* surrounded by thirty-six ships of the
line and twenty-nine others. Frederick William began massing 88,000
men in East Prussia. But British public opinion and business interests
voiced opposition to war with Russia, and on 31 March Pitt despatched
another courier to Berlin requesting a stay of execution. With tears in
his eyes he confessed that this was 'the greatest mortification he had
ever experienced'.[1] That was nothing to the disenchantment Izabela was
about to experience.

She had left London in January 1791 with Adam Jerzy and her suite,
stopping in Paris, where she met Delille, then Vienna, where she had a
meeting with Leopold II. 'He has remarkable lungs,' she noted. 'He
shouts as he speaks, so loud one can hear him in the street. "You are

being tricked, you are being tricked," he greeted me in in a Stentorian voice, "Prussia is leading you along in order to crush you later."' He urged her to warn her husband, Małachowski and Potocki that Prussia was conspiring with Russia against them. She hurried on to Puławy, which she reached towards the end of April, and related what the emperor had told her. It seemed incredible the King of Prussia would renege on his obligations, and they could only hope it was untrue.[2]

The new constitution was passed on 3 May 1791, transforming the Polish-Lithuanian Commonwealth into a hereditary constitutional monarchy with a bi-cameral legislature and cabinet government. It was hailed by progressives all over Europe, with Edmund Burke describing it as one of the greatest acts of political wisdom in history, and, as Adam Jerzy reported from Paris, where Izabela had left him, many there saw it as an example to follow.

The new dynasty was to be founded by the 8-year-old daughter of the Elector of Saxony, Maria Augusta, marrying the Polish king's nephew, Stanisław Poniatowski. Adam was sent to Dresden to obtain the elector's acceptance and support, which, it was hoped, would add weight to the new arrangements. But the elector was afraid of sticking his neck out. Adam returned, in the words of one chronicler, with a fine set of Meissen porcelain and a valuable snuff box for himself, and nothing for Poland.[3]

The country was in a state of frenetic activity, as the bare bones of the constitution were covered with new institutions and procedures, and an army was trained. Two large encampments were set up, one at Bracław in Podolia under the king's nephew Józef Poniatowski, the other at Gołąb, not far from Puławy, under Ludwig Württemberg. Adam Jerzy, who had returned and joined the army, was attached to him as an aide-de-camp and Izabela made it her business to turn the encampment into a vast pageant of Poland's resurgence.

She may have been 46, yet she behaved with the same zest and desire as ever to be at the centre of things. And she was still making conquests among men, as Elise von der Recke, a German lady passing through Warsaw, noted with astonishment. 'In her person I find neither beauty nor grace,' she wrote in her journal. She thought Izabela 'instantly unpleasant', her bearing affected and pretentious, her gestures awkward and restless, and her courtesy wearisome, adding that 'as yet, I have not heard an interesting word from her'. She noted with disapproval that while all the ladies at one lunch wore ball-dresses, Izabela was in a brown riding habit of tight jacket and long skirt, and a man's broad-brimmed hat with a plume. She did relent a couple of weeks later, after attending a ball given by Izabela for the king, at which she found her 'exceptionally courteous and agreeable'.[4]

On 12 September 1791 the troops assembled at Gołąb in their new blue uniforms took part in the first of several ceremonies and exercises which Izabela choreographed or enhanced with chivalric and historical significance, stressing the connection between the present situation and the military triumphs of Poland's past, to inspire the soldiers with a sense of their place in history. The Puławy poets developed the symbolism, and Izabela herself contributed a hymn in which the troops featured as knights of old. She sang it herself to the soldiers, accompanied by her daughters dressed as *cantinières* and a bevy of young girls.

The officers were mostly graduates of the Cadet Corps and many of those drilling at Poniatowski's encampment rode over to pay their respects, among them Kościuszko. People from the surrounding countryside and from as far afield as Warsaw also visited, bringing victuals, gifts or money for the troops. Puławy throbbed with activity; tables were laid for more than two hundred and a hundred horses and sundry carriages were placed at the disposal of guests who wished to drive out to the camp. In the evening there were balls. But in the second half of the year the enthusiasm wore thin and turned to anxiety.[5]

Catherine had reacted to the passing of the new constitution with outrage: 'How dare they alter a form of a government that I had guaranteed!' she exclaimed. She was alarmed at the prospect of Poland becoming a well-ordered state and particularly by the new law granting freedom to all immigrants. 'What an idea!' she raged. 'That will lure most of the peasants of Byelorussia to Poland and deprave those in the rest of my dominions.'[6] On 29 July 1791 she instructed Potemkin to draw up plans for an invasion of Poland, to commence as soon as peace with Turkey had been signed.

She already had her useful idiots, in the shape of a group of conservative malcontents including Branicki, Feliks Potocki and Seweryn

Rzewuski, who had turned up in St Petersburg following the passing of the constitution, which they denounced as an assault on old Polish liberties. On 9 January 1792 the Treaty of Jassy brought to an end the Russo-Turkish war and Russian troops began their march back from the Balkans. On 28 February Catherine informed the Prussian and Austrian ambassadors in St Petersburg of her intention to invade Poland. Austria protested, but the death of Leopold on 1 March meant she could ignore it; his successor Francis II was an inexperienced 24 and his chancellor, Kaunitz, a weary 81. On 20 April Revolutionary France declared war on Austria, which concentrated their minds elsewhere.

Puławy was normally shrouded in gloom during January by the memory of Teresa's death. But in 1792 it was brightened by Marianna giving birth to a son, christened Adam Karol, though Ludwig had nearly killed her in a rage during the pregnancy. As usual, Izabela was full of cautions and advice on everything to do in such circumstances, from what breast-feeding mothers should eat to the exercise they should take.

On Maundy Thursday 1792 Izabela accompanied Zofia, who had been selected to make the traditional collection for the poor. She dressed her up as Mary Stuart, adorned with a gold medallion she had commissioned to commemorate the passing of the constitution. They first attended the ceremony of the king washing the feet of twelve paupers, after which Zofia accepted donations from him and all those present before being led off by Izabela to collect from door to door along the streets of the city. She was by all accounts so pretty that she collected several times the usual amount, to the delight of the Sisters of Mercy to whom she handed it over.

On 14 May Catherine's stooges gathered at the little border town of Targowica and formed a confederation to overthrow the new constitution. Russian troops poured into Poland, vastly outnumbering the Polish forces, which nevertheless scored a couple of successes in the south under Poniatowski. Things did not look so good further north.

Ludwig had been given command of the Army of Lithuania but delayed taking up his post and it was only when Marianna threatened him with divorce that he had left Warsaw, only to stop at Wołczyn, from where he wrote to the king claiming he had a 'cancerous' leg and begging for leave. By then, the king had been handed a packet of letters from Ludwig to addressees in Berlin in which he complained of being forced to take sides against Catherine and claimed he had been ordered by the King of Prussia not to accept the command. His sister was the wife of the heir to the Russian throne, which did make things awkward, but he was not a Russian subject, and at the time soldiers regularly served foreign sovereigns. The king had no option other than to let him go.

He had sent Adam to Vienna to put pressure on Francis and Kaunitz to make a stand and written to Frederick William requesting the military support guaranteed by the Polish–Prussian alliance, only to get the reply that as Poland had changed its constitution the treaty was null and void. As the Polish forces fell back, he wrote to Catherine asking for an armistice, but was informed that an armistice was not possible since the two countries were not at war and the only way to stop the fighting was for him to join to the confederation of Targowica, thereby abolishing the constitution.

When she heard of Ludwig's treachery, Marianna filed for divorce and went to Warsaw, where she took sanctuary in a convent. Izabela, who had begged her not to act hastily, went with her, taking along Zofia, who, having felt neglected during her mother's long absences abroad, recorded 'the extreme happiness of being with her, of living in the same room, of being at her side the whole day'.[7]

Ludwig, who was still in Warsaw, tried to make Marianna change her mind. 'I married you against my will, against my inclination, and under duress, so to speak,' she wrote back, 'and on the very morrow of our wedding I immediately conceived the hope of that some event would separate us one day.' He wrote to Frederick William to gain the assistance of his ambassador in Warsaw and went about telling people that he loved Marianna and she him, and that her action had been forced on her by Izabela. He lurked outside the convent trying to see her and even threatened to snatch her from it, before leaving for Berlin, where the king gave him the Order of the Red Eagle, 4,000 ducats and a commission in the Prussian army on the Rhine.[8]

Adam Jerzy fought on under new commanders, earning a decoration for his part in the engagement at Granne on 24 July. In the south,

Poniatowski had fallen back in good order, preparing to defend the approaches to Warsaw. He made camp at Kurów, not far from Puławy. Morale was high and he was planning to defeat General Kakhovsky's corps which was advancing on Warsaw. But at the end of July they learned that the king had acceded to Catherine's demands.

'I expected everything, but I did not expect baseness of this kind,' Poniatowski wrote to Izabela, who had returned to Puławy leaving Marianna in Warsaw. He rode over to Puławy on the evening of 30 July with Kościuszko, generals Mokronowski and Michał Wielhorski and, inspired by Izabela, that night hatched a plan to kidnap the king, bring him to the camp and fight to the death if necessary.[9] The plan was abandoned in the face of the king's lack of mettle, and Poniatowski, Kościuszko and the others, along with Adam Jerzy who had also come to Puławy, resigned their commissions in protest. Adam Jerzy left for Vienna, hoping to go on to England, to continue his studies.

His father had remained in Vienna, but Izabela determined to stay at Puławy, spending almost the whole time reading, 'hoping to oppose the wisdom of centuries to the sufferings of the present'. 'We are besieged,' she wrote to Dembowska when General Kakhovsky turned up with his corps of 20,000 men, 'this is the seventh day I have not crossed the threshold, as wherever you look there are only Russians.' She was appalled by the devastation they caused, flattening ripening fields, ploughing up her nursery and helping themselves to cattle, horses and victuals from the peasants. She treated the Russian officers who had installed themselves at Puławy politely, but when Branicki and Seweryn Rzewuski turned up she would not let them into the house, instructing the staff to tell them that 'she could reach an accommodation with enemies, but would never and did not know how to accommodate traitors'.[10]

In September Marianna went to Łańcut to meet her father. She was anxious he might not approve of her decision to divorce Ludwig, but when he joined her there from Vienna, she found him 'extra well' and as merry as could be, given the circumstances. She was less pleased with Łańcut itself, which was full of French émigré aristocrats, and resented the fact that the conversation centred around the horrors of the revolution in France rather than the misfortunes of Poland. This was not surprising, since Elżbieta Lubomirska's friend the princesse de Lamballe had just been murdered and her head had been paraded through the streets by the Paris mob. And Marianna would no doubt shed a tear herself when she heard the news that their neighbour, the little Rose of Czarnobyl, had been guillotined for having helped the Princess of Monaco escape from prison.[11]

At the beginning of October, Adam and Izabela, along with such of the family who could make it, gathered at Sieniawa. The house had not been inhabited for some time and was almost derelict. Little remained of the formal gardens laid out in the 1720s, the orangery, the fig house, the pineapple greenhouse, the maze and other features, only an over-grown orchard and avenues of venerable trees. The house itself was a single-storey structure, with two apartments, one either side of a huge central drawing room. Nearby were two wooden buildings, one for guests, the other for staff. 'We settled in quickly, and the main house became comfortable,' recorded Zofia, 'my parents were accommodated in some ease, while for the rest of us it could not have been worse, in a wooden outbuilding without beds, without furniture, but people arrived, we all did our best to console each other, we lived in hope, and a pleasant frivolity gained the upper hand, we amused ourselves, we recovered our gaiety.'[12]

They were joined by Kazimierz Rzewuski and other friends and vis-ited by locals eager for news. On 28 October, Kościuszko turned up. Adam embraced his former pupil with tears in his eyes. It happened to be Kościuszko's name day, and Izabela would not have been herself if she had not arranged a ceremony to mark it and he was solemnly crowned by the ladies with a garland of oak leaves from trees planted by King Jan III at nearby Wysock. Patriotic speeches were made, a pan-egyric composed by Izabela's chaplain Father Koblański was read out and the possibility of carrying on the fight with a national insurrection discussed. No doubt embarrassed by the solemnity, the hero played with the children. The following day brought news that delighted everyone – the Prussians had been soundly defeated by the French at Valmy.[13]

Izabela and Adam accompanied Kościuszko to Lwów where they persuaded the Austrian governor to provide him safe conduct out of Austrian dominions. Adam then went back to Vienna, where he joined

Adam Jerzy. In the hope of warding off reprisals on the family's property, they signed depositions which they handed to the Russian ambassador, Count Razumovsky, swearing that they had been drawn into the anti-Russian agitation against their will.[14]

Izabela returned to Puławy with Marianna and Zofia. There were Russian troops everywhere, the king was a virtual prisoner, friends were being persecuted, property was being confiscated or just plundered. Catherine treated what was left of the country as conquered territory and instituted a reign of terror against all those who had taken part in the reforms and the war. Those most actively involved slipped away, to Dresden and thence some of them to France.

'I have great need of encouragement, my Darling, as the times are cruel,' Izabela wrote to Helena Radziwiłł. 'Puławy is not what it was, there is too much misery about and that disfigures everything [. . .] I no longer feel the same pleasure or the same feelings about this place which is so dear to my heart. I don't even feel like planting any more; sometimes looking at my trees tears well up in my eyes and I find myself thinking that any day now someone will come and destroy them. [. . .] Oh my Darling, I feel so bitter! I'm terribly afraid that if nothing changes we shall have to leave this country and our Motherland. I shall miss Puławy, miss friends, miss my family. But it is impossible to bear what they are doing to us. From poor Puławy, the 12 dec. In the year of misery 1792'.

'I have spent eighteen months in the horrors of war, never sure of what the morrow might bring, ceaselessly terrified by the horrible sight of the desolation, misery and despair all around and by the loss of my Motherland which has fallen victim to bad faith and the prey of tyrants,' she wrote to Lavater six months later. 'God is just, God is good, I find it impossible not to hope that one day our misfortunes will be avenged! In the meantime, one has to resign oneself and worship His decrees in silence.' Without Adam or her son at her side, she felt alone and weighed down by the unhappy end to Marianna's marriage, for which she blamed herself.[15]

Expenses had had to be reined in, and there were now only around forty-five staff on the payroll. Another half a dozen incapacitated ones were retained out of charity, and the house accounts list numerous payouts to paupers, peasants, old people and the handicapped, and the artists Norblin and Orłowski were still on the payroll.[16]

But friends gathered, small parties were held, plays were staged and a degree of gaiety returned. As might be expected, the theatricals were attuned to the circumstances – one featured ladies in shackles which fell away as the distant sound of gunfire by patriotic insurgents heralded liberation. This was not mere fantasy, for plans were afoot and Izabela was involved in passing clandestine correspondence from Warsaw to Ignacy Potocki in Saxony, where the hardcore of the Patriots lingered waiting for an opportunity to act.[17]

After a short trip to Warsaw, perhaps connected with Marianna's divorce, which Ludwig's parents and Frederick William were contesting in the hope the couple could be reunited, Izabela and her two daughters moved to the safety of Austrian territory at Sieniawa. The move was politic, as she had already received an anonymous letter clearly meant to implicate her and Ignacy Potocki in subversion.[18]

In January 1793 Catherine decided to reduce the size of Poland further, awarding herself and Prussia generous slices of its territory. This put paid to any idea that something could be saved from the wreckage through accommodation with Russia. The Patriots who had congregated in Dresden began to think in more radical terms and on 24 March 1794 Kościuszko proclaimed a National Insurrection and ten days later his improvised forces defeated a Russian army at Racławice. Two weeks later the citizens of Warsaw rose and expelled the Russians and the king joined the Insurrection. But despite some victories, it was doomed; Prussia joined Russia, destroying Powązki in their assault on Warsaw, and Austria sent in troops to guarantee herself a share in what was now a foregone conclusion: a final liquidation of the Polish state.

On 10 October Kościuszko was defeated, wounded and taken prisoner at Maciejowice, near Podzamcze. At the beginning of November, General Suvorov breached the defences of Warsaw's right-bank suburb of Praga and initiated the butchery of some 20,000 of its inhabitants, mainly Jews. Warned that the rest of the city could expect the same fate, the Polish forces abandoned it, and the Insurrection petered out soon after. In January 1795 Russia, Prussia and Austria agreed a final dismemberment of the country and the king was carted off to Grodno, where he was placed in the custody of Repnin, who had been appointed governor of the newly conquered territories.

The outbreak of the Insurrection had found Izabela at Sieniawa, Adam Jerzy in England and her husband in Vienna, where she went to join him, taking Zofia with her. Terrified by news of the revolutionary horrors taking place in Paris, Viennese society felt no sympathy for Polish patriots. 'At Vienna men and women pointed their fingers at me, while avoiding me as though I were a criminal,' Izabela recorded. She received anonymous letters accusing her of 'crimes' such as distributing Phrygian bonnets to the peasantry, 'which were so silly and ridiculous that one would have to be an Austrian to think them up'.[19]

The Austrian and Russian courts were convinced she had a hand in preparing the Insurrection and the Prussian minister in Warsaw assured Frederick William that she and her husband had actively supported it. Rumour circulated that they had given Kościuszko money (which was probably true) and that one of their sons had been at his side. Catherine saw Izabela as a prime mover. In 1786, after the first performance of *The Spartan Mother*, Stackelberg had reported that 'her children have in their room a picture of Hannibal swearing eternal hatred of Rome', whose symbolism was obvious. On hearing of the outbreak of the Insurrection, Adam Jerzy had indeed left England hoping to join the fight, but had been arrested by the Austrian authorities in Brussels. In prison in St Petersburg, Kościuszko's interrogation included questions on Izabela's involvement in planning the Insurrection, and on her supposed plans to marry him to one of her daughters. Catherine had been shown forged letters in which Izabela insulted her and conspired against Russia.[20]

The consequence was described by Colonel Engelhardt, serving under General Derfelden, whose corps marched through Puławy. 'Derfelden had orders not to spare the Czartoryski estate, so Puławy was sacked and utterly devastated, the gardens and park of this beautiful spot, which rivalled Tsarskoe Selo, along with the richly and tastefully decorated palace were laid waste, prints, pictures were torn down and shredded; the library of 40 thousand volumes was destroyed in such a way that nobody would afterwards be able to find one entire work,' he wrote. Another recorded his shock at seeing paintings by Rembrandt and Rubens cut up. In addition, Catherine ordered all Czartoryski estates lying within her grasp (around three-quarters of all their possessions) to be sequestered and offered for sale to anyone considered loyal to Russia.[21]

Adam asked the emperor to intercede on his behalf, and Francis instructed his minister in St Petersburg to do so, in the meantime making him a generous loan. He also approached Razumovsky, the Russian ambassador in Vienna, who facilitated the despatch of one of Adam's agents to St Petersburg to pacify Catherine, but the envoy was not received. Adam also wrote to Repnin, who replied saying there was little he could do given Catherine's determination to punish them.[22]

As she contemplated the loss of most of her property, Izabela comforted herself with the thought that the wealth and status they had enjoyed would be replaced by 'sweeter and more solid joys'. Adam considered accepting the loss rather than pleading for the return of his property, but their many creditors would be ruined if he did, and he felt he could not sacrifice their wellbeing to his personal honour.[23]

Eager to help, Repnin suggested they send their sons to him at Grodno; if he could prepare them appropriately and obtain permission for them to go to St Petersburg, Catherine might be induced to relent. Izabela was terrified they might be imprisoned or, worse, turned into Russians. Repnin reassured her that although they might have to take service, either at court or in the army, this in Russia was a loose concept, allowing for long periods of leave during which they would be able to travel.

After much hesitation, Izabela agreed to let them go. In December 1794 Adam Jerzy and Konstanty left Vienna and made for Grodno, not knowing whether they would ever be allowed back and by no means happy with what they saw as an ignoble mission. On the way Adam Jerzy wrote a poem, 'The Polish Bard', in which he gave vent to his feelings of despair and bitterness at having to go and pay homage to the enemy of his country 'for a piece of land' and 'a little coin'.[24]

Izabela was desperate, and on 19 January 1795 poured out her feelings to Repnin. 'Until recently, my dear Prince, I was a happy woman, a happy mother, a happy friend, enjoying a life full of pleasure, happy in my memories and my hopes,' she wrote. 'I have lost everything, I have seen everything shattered. And now I come to the moment where I must see my husband and my children deprived of their entire fortune and their existence, with nothing left but immense debts and the misery that must necessarily follow so many misfortunes. I will not go into the details of the painful and poignant sufferings we have had to endure; I will spare Your sensibility, but I swear that I have often wished to die and life means nothing to me.' She assured him she had known nothing of the planned Insurrection other than the rumours everyone had heard, and that she would never have left all her belongings behind at Puławy if she had.[25]

Described by one lady who passed through Grodno as 'a slightly stooping figure' but not looking old, Repnin had suffered disappointments and had begun to seek solace in religion. He still nurtured fond feelings for Izabela, reminiscing about past times, asking about her dog, remembering a tune from the old days, even the wine they had drunk together, and in a moving letter he thanked her for trusting him.[26]

He groomed her sons for their task, explaining how they must behave towards everyone, beginning with Catherine's current favourites, the Zubov brothers, and did what he could to spread a good opinion of them in St Petersburg. He assured Catherine that the story of their being made to swear 'eternal hatred to Russia' by their mother was untrue.[27] He made them swear an oath of submission on their own behalf and that of their parents, and when he reported this to Catherine she relented. In April 1795 the sequestration was lifted from the Czartoryski estates which were provisionally placed in trust, and she instructed Repnin to send the boys to St Petersburg. Izabela was desperate to see them before they left, but Repnin warned her that would be dangerous.[28]

They reached St Petersburg on 12 May. Adam Jerzy was horrified by what he found there; having been brought up in the cult of liberty, he gazed upon the antithesis of his ideals of good government as Catherine reigned over her servile court. They had to court Valerian Zubov to gain access to his all-powerful brother, Catherine's current favourite, Platon, who behaved like a spoilt child, enjoying the prostration of the petitioners waiting on him as he made his morning toilette. They found it difficult to hide their feelings, and the knowledge that Kościuszko and many other Poles were imprisoned in the same city did not help. And if Adam Jerzy did not know it before, he would have now been made aware of his real paternity, as it was well known in St Petersburg and his resemblance to Repnin was openly commented on.[29]

In spite of his role in the Confederation of Targowica, they warmed to Branicki, whose high standing with Catherine permitted him to show his contempt for the Russians, whom he openly mocked. 'His eminently Polish lively wit and sharp observations made his conversation interesting and enjoyable,' Adam Jerzy recalled. When they asked him whether they should stoop to kissing the hand of Catherine as instructed when they were presented to her, he replied: 'Kiss her anywhere she wishes, as long as she gives you back your property.' They did kneel and kiss her hand, at the beginning of June. She remembered meeting their father when he was their age, and if her son the Grand Duke Paul was cool his wife treated them as in-laws and expressed her hope that their sister might yet be reunited with her brother.[30]

By the end of the month they had been admitted to the circle of Platon Zubov and had once more met Catherine, who bestowed gracious words on them. But Repnin warned Izabela and Adam to remain on their guard, to watch what they wrote in their letters to the boys, which he insisted on reading before sending them on, and on no account use any kind of code.

On 7 September 1795 Adam Jerzy reported that he had been invited to dine at Catherine's table. From then on the two were fêted and invited to dinners at the Tauride Palace, balls at the Hermitage and other palaces, and amusements of every kind. But they were not out of danger. Izabela received a letter purporting to be from some well-wisher in St Petersburg informing her that her sons had been well received and were behaving perfectly to the satisfaction of the empress and the court, without having made any compromises and still carried in their hearts an eternal loathing of Catherine and all things Russian. Realizing that this was another provocation meant to be read by the Russian police, she was terrified for them.[31]

An Ukaz was published donating estates confiscated from Poles who had taken part in the Insurrection to Russian generals and courtiers, including one of Adam's. Adam Jerzy and Konstanty were informed that they would be awarded some of the sequestered estates, but none were returned to their parents and no mention was made of their sisters. They were simultaneously commissioned, Adam Jerzy in the horse guards, Konstanty in the Izmailovsky foot guards. This did not entail onerous duties; Adam Jerzy was only required to mount guard once in the course of the year. At the start of 1796 they were made gentlemen of the bedchamber, which drew them into the rituals of the court, which Adam Jerzy found pointless and humiliating. But everything changed for him in the spring of 1796.

The eldest of Catherine's grandsons, the Grand Duke and future Tsar Alexander, had from the outset treated the Czartoryski brothers with respect, and one day invited Adam Jerzy to take a walk with him in the grounds of the Tauride Palace. As soon as they were alone and out of earshot, Alexander began pouring out his feelings; he was ashamed of the partitions, abhorred Russian policy, had prayed for the cause of Poland during the recent Insurrection, loathed the court and admired the attitude of Adam Jerzy and his brother.

He had been brought up by the Swiss philosopher Frédéric-César de La Harpe with liberal views which he could not share with anyone in Russia, and expounded to Adam Jerzy his dreams of transforming Russia. He saw in him not just a kindred spirit, but also a man who had during his studies in England acquired first-hand experience of the workings of constitutional monarchy. Alexander even asked him to compose a manifesto he could issue when he came to the throne one day, announcing how he intended to transform the country.[32]

Adam Jerzy was elated, and 'vowed a boundless friendship' to Alexander. It seemed to him that with Revolutionary France having rejected the Terror, the idea that Russia might be reformed by a liberal tsar held out the promise of a brilliant future for Europe, and for Poland. They spent long evenings enthusiastically refashioning the world, and Adam Jerzy introduced into these clandestine talks two others who shared his views: Paul Stroganov, who had spent the early years of the Revolution in Paris and been imbued with its ideals, and Nikolai Novosiltsev, who had joined him there for a time.[33]

Catherine II died in November 1796, and on ascending the throne her son Paul freed Kościuszko and all the Polish prisoners in Russia, making cryptic comments which suggested he aimed to restore the kingdom of Poland. He appointed the Czartoryski brothers aides-de-camp to his two eldest sons, Alexander and Constantine. In 1797 Izabela received a letter from the new empress Maria Feodorovna, who wrote how happy she was that her sons had been attached to her own.[34]

The past three years had not been easy for her. She hated Vienna, where she and Adam had been constantly invigilated by the police on account of their supposed revolutionary connections, but above all she missed Puławy. 'I had founded hopes for centuries of happiness on it!' she wrote on 12 January 1795. 'My flowers, my grassy swards, and my walks have been destroyed, my children are far from me and are not happy! My friends have been scattered, ruin and misfortune are their lot! My books have been pillaged and I still do not know with what I should replace the hope that has fled so far from me!'[35]

## 12

## *Czartoryska the Indestructible*

I t was not until Catherine, Frederick William and Francis II had
agreed their final carve-up of Poland that Izabela could come home
to Puławy, now under Austrian rule. She arrived late on the moonlit
night of 21 June 1795, with Zofia, a maid and Father Koblański.

'Seldom in my life have I beheld such a sorry sight,' she recorded.
'When I drove into the court, I was overwhelmed by dread at the emp-
tiness, the sense of abandon, and the silence. Looking at the palace
standing empty, with no doors or windows, I could not hold back my
tears. One could see the cold light of the moon though the whole building. Alighting from the carriage I met a hajduk whose face was still
etched with fear and misery.' The caretaker opened up a room in one of
the outbuildings which still had a window and a door that shut. She,
Zofia and the maid lay down to sleep on piles of hay, while Father
Koblański bedded down in an adjacent closet.

'This morning at dawn I went out into the garden. My spreading
trees, flowering shrubs and scented flowers sweetened the bitter sight of
the devastated and half-ruined house.' At the centre of the great court,
filling and overflowing the round fountain pond, was a huge mound of
broken furniture, shredded tapestries and oriental rugs, heads, hands
and legs of broken statues, smashed looking-glasses, porcelain, crystal,
Chinese vases, pieces of armour, cooking pots, astronomical telescopes,
globes, bronzes, paintings with their canvas slashed to ribbons, broken
violins, guitars and harpsichords. Caught in the branches of trees and
bushes all around were illustrations torn from Adam's fine edition of

Buffon's *Histoire Naturelle* – while the greater part of the archives and library had been carted off to Russia and many books had been stolen by individual officers, what they could not take they shredded.[1]

The only room which had been spared was the great chamber, because, Izabela assumed, the gilded panelling and the Boucher putti suggested to the Russian soldiery that it was a chapel. As well as gashed panelling, torn upholstery and shards of porcelain and glass, every room was marked with their traditional signature, the walls being smeared with excrement. Their purpose had nothing to do with looting: all the wine, spirits, oil, fruit, smoked meats and fish, coffee, sugar, salt and other stores had been poured out or scattered. Having devastated the house, the soldiers had moved into the grounds, cutting down trees and uprooting saplings. They were only stayed by a messenger from the emperor's ambassador in Warsaw forbidding further destruction of an Austrian field marshal's property. They moved on to other buildings in the park, then to looting churches and peasants' cottages.[2]

Izabela set in motion the cleaning of the house and the clearing of some of the debris, and within a week made a couple of rooms habitable. 'Moments of serenity, evenings of miraculous beauty, calm days and the knowledge that I am at home and that nobody will remove me from it are sweetening the sadness of life,' she recorded, after taking breakfast in the garden with Father Koblański and Zofia, now 17 and 'in the flower of youth'.[3] Other habitués of Puławy began to drift in, including, with time, Adam.

One can only marvel at Izabela's resilience, but Lavater did not. 'You have lost a great deal,' he wrote in a letter she received in September 1795. 'I hope you will have gained by the loss. You have suffered much, I congratulate you. We can become *more alive* only through misfortune. Poland is gone, but Czartoryska is there, and will always be' – the sheer energy of her soul made her 'indestructible', he affirmed. In reply, Izabela complained that she had written many times but received no reply. 'I sought consolation in your piety, in your healthy, pure and simple morality,' she wrote. 'Our losses, our misfortunes have drained our tears,' she continued. 'We no longer shed any and, accustomed to our privations, we thank the Supreme Being for what He has left us [. . .] Religion is the surest source for an oppressed soul. It consoles [. . .] and makes everything bearable. It binds man to his creator, the present to eternity and misfortune to hope.'[4]

A portrait painted a few months later, early in 1796, by Kazimierz Wojniakowski depicts Izabela in her increasingly casual country attire of turban and shawl, and while she has abandoned the enhancements of fashion and her hair has greyed, she looks remarkably youthful and exudes a dreamy serenity.

The physical task of clearing up and restoring Puławy was beset by problems of a practical nature and worries about her family, some of which she lists in a letter to Helena Radziwiłł, each followed by 'And that is not all!' The first is that she had no money, thanks to their banker, Cabrit, not delivering the revenue from the Podolian estates to Puławy and taking it instead to Warsaw, which was now in Prussia. Meanwhile, she had to pay taxes in Vienna and give handouts to starving peasants at Puławy, not to mention restoring or even running the house. A happy interlude was provided by Repnin, who, having been promoted to field marshal, was discharging all Poles drafted into the Russian army, and sent some sixty back to Izabela's estates.[5]

Izabela was now an Austrian subject and had to go to Kraków to swear an oath of allegiance to the emperor. She felt revulsion at the idea of performing this 'disgusting' act, and contrived to dodge the formal ceremony. Another consequence of the new state of affairs was the necessity of obtaining passports to travel around the partitioned Polish lands. The bother involved would have been bad enough without the pettiness of the officials, particularly the Austrians. In one case, the Prussians would not let a person stay in Warsaw and the Austrians would not let him travel on to Puławy. On another occasion the whole process descended into farce: Izabela summoned her regular dentist, Lefevre, from Warsaw, but the Austrians refused to issue him with a passport, so she had to meet him at the frontier, and her tooth was pulled between two sovereignties. Despite the pain, Izabela could not refrain from giggling at the sight of the people queuing either side of the frontier gawping in amazement at the operation.[6]

Such restrictions were often dictated by vindictiveness: Ignacy Potocki, who had been Marshal of the Sejm which passed the constitution in 1791, was confined to his estate at Kurów, less than twenty kilometres away, but was forbidden to drive over to Puławy for dinner. All the Czartoryski connections in Vienna could not breach this bureaucratic dungeon in which a sick man who had never been a threat to the Habsburg monarchy was confined. These travel restrictions were more than a nuisance to Izabela, as they obstructed her wish to revive Puławy as the family home, and the only one of her children she had at her side was Zofia. Her sons were in St Petersburg, while Marianna was trying to rebuild a life for herself as an independent woman following her divorce.[7]

The divorce was being contested by Ludwig, supported by his entire family. The most sincerely distressed were his parents, and particularly his mother, who was desolate at the prospect of never seeing Marianna or Izabela again. Ludwig himself made despairing appeals to Izabela and Adam and sought the support of his relative the Duke Elector of Württemberg to help bring 'this poor straying soul' back to him and make her happy, and to intercede in Russia to prevent the Czartoryskis losing all their estates, as this would rob his son of his inheritance. 'It would give me such pleasure to repay the bad behaviour of that family with good, honest action and to find ways of helping them,' he wrote, 'the only vengeance that as a good Christian I may allow myself.' The duke obliged, writing to both Adam and Marianna, who replied that she would do anything in her power to oblige him but had spent 'the best years of her life in tears' and did not wish to prolong the experience, and begged to be allowed to keep her son, whom Ludwig was also claiming.[8]

She was enjoying her freedom and did not lack suitors, causing Izabela some anxiety. Helena Radziwiłł, who had for some time been dreaming of sealing her friendship with Izabela with a marriage between their children, now suggested Marianna marry one of her sons. The proposal did not elicit much enthusiasm when Izabela mentioned it to her daughter, who said she was too old, and at this point in her life did not know her own mind. Zofia, who might have provided the same link, declared that she did not wish to marry yet.[9]

Izabela blamed herself for Marianna's unhappiness and worried about her future. She urged her to be careful of her reputation, advised her not to go to balls alone, particularly masked balls, and warned her against allowing her feelings to run away with her, as Marianna was reportedly flirting with a number of men. Izabela was particularly worried when the debonaire Józef Poniatowski, whose sister had bought a house at nearby Nałęczów, began courting her, warning her that he was only interested in conquests.[10]

Izabela was overjoyed when, in the summer of 1797, Adam Jerzy and Konstanty arrived. They only had three months' leave, and as they had been forced to keep their letters bland, they had a great deal to impart. Izabela and Adam listened with excitement as their sons told of their relations with the grand dukes and of Alexander's views on Poland, but feared that these clandestine exchanges might be denounced and lead to dire consequences. They would have been a great deal more anxious had they known of another relationship into which Adam Jerzy had entered.[11]

His friend Grand Duke Alexander had been married in 1793 at the age of 15 to Princess Louise of Baden, then only 14, who duly became the Grand Duchess Elizabeth Alekseievna. Alexander found it impossible to develop a relationship with her, and, encouraged by him, she found solace in the arms of Adam Jerzy, who fell in love with her. A similar arrangement existed between Konstanty and Alexander's brother the Grand Duke Constantine, to whom he was attached, and whose wife he too comforted.

They left Puławy before their three months' leave was up and resumed their posts at the Russian court. Courts are fuelled by a mixture of envy and fear, none more so than that of St Petersburg, particularly following the accession of the unaccountable Paul I. The young Czartoryskis were seen as interlopers and their intimacy with the grand dukes was deeply resented. They had to practise extreme caution, and Adam Jerzy passed all his private papers to Alexander, who hid them away from prying eyes. To make matters worse, Constantine did not like Adam Jerzy, with whom he had frequent arguments, one of which ended up in a violent fight, with them rolling about on the floor trying to strangle each other. But he was devoted to Konstanty. 'I love Kostuś like a brother,' he declared on meeting his father.[12]

Izabela was determined to bring Puławy back to life, and by the late autumn of 1797 there were parties and theatricals taking place. Guests included Helena Radziwiłł's younger son, Walenty. His elder brother, Antoni, had in the previous year married Louise of Prussia, the daughter of Izabela's friend Prince Ferdinand, and Walenty came to ask for Zofia's hand in marriage. Izabela told him the decision was her daughter's. 'You will understand that after the misfortunes of my elder daughter the second must be allowed to choose for herself,' she wrote to Helena while Zofia took her time to consider the proposal. 'May God grant that at least one pair of ours should be joined,' she wrote in the interim, 'one more bond between us would add another conduit for my happiness.' 'Adieu, my little soul – adieu, you, the best thing on earth, adieu, my good, my best, my exquisite, sweet and beautiful,' she signed off. But when Walenty did return in the spring Zofia refused him, to the dismay of both Izabela and Helena; he was disconsolate and would never marry.[13]

Izabela and her husband had considered various candidates for Zofia's hand, including Elżbieta Lubomirska's adopted son Henryk, which would bring Łańcut, Wilanów and other Czartoryski estates back into the fold, but they settled on Stanisław Zamoyski, whom she married on 20 May 1798. He was the younger son of the former Chancellor of Poland, Andrzej Zamoyski, who had been a key member of the Familia, and a Czartoryska from a different branch of the family. Stanisław's elder brother, Aleksander, was the incumbent of a vast entail, but Stanisław only had the estate of Podzamcze, not far from Puławy, which suited Izabela.

She longed to see her sons marry and provide heirs to carry on the family name, but they were entirely dependent on the whim of the tsar. Although he found their way of thinking and political views suspect, Paul was well disposed to them; he returned more confiscated land and gave both of them the rank of lieutenant-general. Yet when, in August 1798, Konstanty applied for unlimited leave, he flew into a rage and ordered him to be sent to Siberia. Characteristically, he then relented and allowed him to go, awarding him the Order of Saint Anne for good measure. Konstanty duly returned to Puławy, and was given an estate of his own, Międzyrzecz.

Adam Jerzy remained in St Petersburg, but when, on 23 August that year, the Grand Duchess Elizabeth gave birth to a daughter who was dark like him and not blonde like Alexander, Paul erupted into a rage. His first reaction was to send Adam Jerzy to Siberia but realizing that this would be seen as confirmation of the child's illegitimacy, and perhaps also at the request of his wife, whose brother was, though divorced, still considered to be Adam Jerzy's brother-in-law, he changed his mind. Instead, he ordered him to take up the post of minister at the court of Sardinia and leave for Italy at once, barely giving him time to brief himself on his new job and pack before going.[14]

He was forbidden to pass through Puławy, so he made his way via Międzyrzecz, where Marianna came to see him, to Vienna, where he stayed with Zofia and her husband Stanisław Zamoyski. There, he received letters from his father listing the places and the learned men he should visit in Italy, telling him not to neglect his poetic talents and to make sketches of paintings he admired in galleries. He also received instructions from the household physician Dr Goltz recommending he washed regularly and avoided contacts with women after heavy dinners or too much wine.[15]

From Vienna he made for Florence, where he met Field Marshal Suvorov, commanding the Russian troops operating against French revolutionary forces in Italy, and the sovereign to whom he had been accredited, King Victor Emmanuel I, who had fled his capital of Turin. As he had little to do, Adam Jerzy spent his time sightseeing in Florence and Pisa. Following Bonaparte's victory at Marengo, Victor Emmanuel moved to Rome, and Adam Jerzy went with him. There he indulged in some amateur excavation in the Forum, but at the beginning of 1801 he was instructed to abandon the Sardinian court and transfer his duties to that of Naples. And as the King of Naples had fled the mainland part of the kingdom and taken refuge in Sicily, Adam Jerzy was free to visit Pompei, Herculaneum and other sites.

Wherever he went, he was followed by letters from Izabela full of advice and strictures on the subject of his health, the numbers of servants he should keep, how to manage his money, and bombarding him with requests for objects of interest. She wanted fragments of famous monuments, a sarcophagus, a marble figure of a recumbent panther, images of notable figures of the past, and just about anything associated with them. She dreamed of teaming up with Marianna and joining him in Italy but was afraid of being caught up in the military operations between the French and their Austrian and Russian opponents. It would be 'paradise', she mused, if the two of them could set off, with Marianna writing up a gazette and Orłowski acting as 'scribe' to record their journey.[16]

Nothing would come of these dreams, and Izabela ended the century at Sieniawa. Adam had been spending more time there and began to think of it as his home. Izabela would spend Christmas there, as 24 December was his name day, and for that last New Year's Eve of the century Adam had hired an orchestra so they could dance.

One of the attractions of Sieniawa for Adam was that it was closer to Vienna, where he liked to spend time with his sister, who now lived there. It was also closer to his favourite spa, Bardejov in northeastern Slovakia, then in the Kingdom of Hungary, which he had discovered in 1786. It was small and dilapidated, with little in the way of amenities, so he began by camping there, then built a house and, with time, a considerable establishment. Izabela had accompanied him there in May 1799. They took their time, snaking between the country houses of friends, where they would stay for a couple of days, or putting up for the night in barns, which would be draped and carpeted for the duration. By the time they reached their destination their caravan had swelled to over a hundred carriages and carts. Once there, Adam would dress up as a Magyar and show off his Hungarian. For entertainment, he had brought over a troupe of German actors. The atmosphere was soured one night when they found themselves surrounded by Austrian troops, who had come to arrest Ignacy Potocki. He had not obtained permission to travel, and he was to languish in prison for a year before Adam's intercessions succeeded in liberating him.[17]

# The Heart of Poland

Writing to Helena Radziwiłł a couple of months after her return to the ruins of Puławy, Izabela lamented that their children would have no Motherland. 'My Darling,' she concluded, 'all that is left is friendship; it will have to make up for everything, as everything else is finished for us. Poland, it seems, will be no more.'[1] But she was already thinking of doing something about that.

She took advantage of the destruction of the rococo interiors to create a more sympathetic setting for what she meant to enact there: an idealised reincarnation of the country she had lost, a small Motherland, embodying all that was best about the Poland that had been wiped off the map. Inside the house grandeur was to be replaced by simplicity and intimacy.

The only palatial element to survive was the great golden chamber, oblong in shape with matching circular protrusions creating an immense oval at its centre, its five windows overlooking the Vistula. But even here, decorative elements and furnishings were unfussy and adaptable, as, like the rest of the house, it was to accommodate a range of functions, domestic, formal, theatrical and public. The effect was, as a French aristocrat who spent two weeks there observed, unusual. 'The Chateau was neither large, nor regular, nor even splendid,' wrote the duc de Broglie, yet 'Nowhere have I seen an abode more worthy of envy, not even in England, so renowned, and justly renowned in that as in other respects.'[2]

Izabela's and her husband's apartments were modest. They were entered not up the grand sweep of the double stairs, but through a door on the ground floor which opened onto a vaulted vestibule. To the right was Adam's apartment, to the left Izabela's. His was accessed through an antechamber occupied by his footmen and Cossacks. A second room served his valets, one French, one German. His bedroom contained only a bed, a bedside table, a few chairs and a large desk. Leading off it was a dressing and powdering room; he wore his hair in the old French style, powdered daily in the presence of his closest attendants. The only other room of note was his library, which he restocked after the sack and made available to any who would study there. Within ten years of the sack, George Burnett described it as 'one of the most extensive and valuable belonging perhaps to any individual in Europe, and one of the Duke of Bedford's sons came all the way from England to see it.'[3]

Izabela's quarters were entered through an anteroom decorated with English prints. Her sitting room, which was used by the family when there were no guests, was hung with, at various times, Rembrandt's *Landscape with the Good Samaritan*, a *Saint Martin* by Rubens, a Veronese of *Christ and the Woman of Samaria*, a Van Dyke and Leonardo da Vinci's *Lady with an Ermine*, her bedroom with portraits of her four children and a few Dutch landscapes. Her bathroom was dominated by a large faux-porphyry bathtub. One of the rooms contained a small library, from which she could step into a secluded garden. Princess Louise of Prussia, married to Helena Radziwiłł's son Antoni, thought Puławy had 'the aspect of a royal residence', yet 'the apartment of the Princess is of a picturesque elegance of a kind entirely unknown to us.'[4] There were apartments on the first floor for distinguished guests, others were lodged, along with members of the family and the household, in the wings flanking the courtyard, accessed in winter through covered wooden passages.

The surroundings of the house were also transformed, to reflect Izabela's view of how life should be led in the country. She employed professional gardeners such as McClair and Savage, and sought their advice on specifics, but the vision was hers. Although the grounds contained conventional elements such as an orangery in the Greek style and a Roman arch, these did not form part of a formal palace complex of buildings, and their relationship to the main house and each other was intentionally random; there was a 'wild walk' down to the neoclassical house which had been meant as a home for Marianna and Ludwig, known as 'Marynki', and, in the lower garden at the foot of the escarpment, a fisherman's hut, a couple of grottos housing a hermit who would entertain guests by playing the bagpipes or the theorban. There was also a chapel and a couple of bridges onto the peninsula, the Kępa, and in what may have been a reference to Powązki, Izabela built a cottage in the shade of its venerable poplars.

There was also a small farm called Zulinki at one end of the park, and another a long walk away, at Parchatka, accessed by a steep path and a wooden hanging bridge over a ravine, to which the house party would go to admire her Spanish sheep and Tyrolean cows, and take tea consisting of rye bread, wild strawberries and cream in the rustic thatched farmhouse garden.

Izabela's park embraced the surrounding countryside, as she wanted to bring nature and the inhabitants of the neighbourhood right up to the house. In her view, this should be organically integrated with the whole locality, including the town of Puławy and surrounding villages. There was no wall or barrier of any sort around it.

Just as the palatial was tamed by the intimate within the house, formality was tempered by Nature outside. The great forecourts were domesticated by a few trees planted with intended irregularity. She installed peasants and fishermen in the park with their cows and domestic animals, and 'from dawn her door was besieged by all the poor and the sick from the neighbouring villages', according to Anna Potocka. She had always displayed a fondness for such people. 'Our peasant men and women whom I love so much represent a class of my country which becomes more dear to me with every day,' she explained.[5]

Unlike some enlightened landowners, neither Adam nor Izabela saw any reason to reform the labour-rent basis of their relationship to their peasantry, and practised a benign patriarchy over them he had inherited from his father. 'If I had been born a peasant in Poland,' wrote the social activist and reformer Franciszek Salezy Jezierski, 'I would like to have been a peasant of [August Czartoryski] because he, as his peasants say, was not a master but a father to them.' Izabela's empathy was based on sentiment and personal contact; a great walker, she would go into cottages along the way and often took part in their weddings and other family festivities. With time, she came to be known among them as the *księżna kuma* (the princess godmother). Their relationship with the 30,000 or so Jews settled on their lands, the largest community being at Międzybóż, the birthplace of the founder of Hassidism Israel Baal Shem Tov, the second largest at Sieniawa, was similarly cordial.[6]

Izabela felt that as well as being wedded to the land the house should be embedded in the community, of peasants, Jews and local gentry. She paid as much attention to the town of Puławy, to the villages, to their churches and synagogues as she did to the buildings within the park. The town of Puławy was kept neat and clean, the cottages and manor farms equally tidy, and Adam built a church in honour of his mother, modelled on the Pantheon. An English colonel travelling back from India in 1817 noted that the town of Puławy had 'some very good inns, and many well-built houses of stone and brick'.[7]

The monuments Izabela placed in secluded areas of the park included a copy of the sarcophagus of Scipio Africanus, a statue of Virtue salvaged from Powązki and a sculpture representing the combat of Tancred and Clorinda from the park of Łazienki, but some were rocks or marble slabs, often in the shape of an altar, with inscriptions. One read, in verse, 'To the trees, shrubs and flowers whose husbandry has always been my beloved work! They remind me of better times and may live to see a happier future.' In her book on parks, she extolled the beauty of the wild and the natural, expressing strong opinions about trees, castigating attempts to 'torture, wound or graft' them.[8]

Hers was an open house, hospitable to all comers, its rituals informal, its hierarchy familial. As one of Elżbieta Lubomirska's grand-daughters-in-law observed, life at Puławy was in total contrast to Łańcut, which aspired to everything a grand European residence should be. Puławy breathed cordiality. 'From the first moment, the guest felt at their ease,' she noted. On arrival, guests were assigned a servant to care for their particular needs, and they would find their room stocked with books – and quill toothpicks. And while the hospitality could be on a lavish scale, it was not accompanied by displays of splendour. It did require a full complement of staff, and the accounts for 1798 list 33 female servants, 34 male, with 32 hajduks, *frotteurs*, stable staff, butchers and so on. The servants' liveries were no longer as showy as in the past; the indoor staff wore green tail-coats and white breeches, their coats and hats trimmed with silver braid, the hajduks were dressed in military-style short jackets adorned with braid and tassels, wide flowing trousers held in by a sash and tall hats with lanyards, in the Czartoryski colours of green, grey and crimson.[9]

Wealthier guests would bring their own servants when they came to stay, which did affect the picture. 'During the time of dinner, the lofty and magnificent hall is absolutely crowded with servants,' recorded Burnett. 'Every person of consequence, too, has his own footman behind his chair, in his particular livery; the whole forming a spectacle which possibly carries back the mind to the pompous periods of feudal grandeur.' He added that the effect was spoiled by the fact that 'in default of sufficient occupation, they usually amuse themselves by slily grinning, or making faces at one another across the table'.[10] While the hospitality was boundless and the setting grandiose, the fare at table consisted of simple Polish dishes, and there was no display of fine wines.

At home, Adam now wore his Austrian field marshal's blue-grey uniform with crimson facings. After the morning ceremony of powdering his hair (and, with time, his wig), he would join Izabela for breakfast, something of a formality as both had already taken coffee and neither ate anything. He would spend the rest of the morning either working in his library or chatting with guests and smoking. Unhurried, erect in his bearing, he was approachable and a good listener as well as an entertaining conversationalist, 'combining a surprising degree of erudition with a large dose of vivacity and brio, and enormous wit', according to Thomas Jefferson's friend Philip Mazzei, which made him popular with children.[11] He would often ride out before taking his lunch, usually alone. At three o'clock bells or drums would summon the household and guests for dinner, at which he ate nothing. Tea was served at eight o'clock and supper at ten, and Izabela and Adam usually retired for the night between eleven and twelve o'clock.

Izabela was perpetually busy, trimming roses and bushes, directing planting, laying out new gardens, walks or avenues, or going for long walks. She also devoted much time to her girls. When not at their lessons, they worked in the garden or indoors, sewing, knitting, mending, melting down braid to recuperate the silver or gold, and other useful handiwork. She organized games and running races. On one occasion she divided Adam's young men into two teams, one of which carried out an amphibious assault on the Kępa, which was defended by the other with water sprayers, while her girls divided up to cheer one side or the other. In the evenings there would often be dancing. Izabela now danced only the polonaise and Adam the minuet, but the younger members of the household would perform more energetic Mazurs, Cossack dances and even the fandango. There were also more rowdy games, such as blind man's buff.

On other evenings they would put on plays and pageants. 'Some of these, founded on classical fable, deserve to be ranked with the shows and pageants of Queen Elizabeth's day,' noted Burnett. 'I spent two weeks at Puławy,' reminisced Louise Radziwiłł, 'one entertainment followed another and I have never seen any that were more imaginative or more elegant, both for the costumes and the performance.' Leon Potocki pointed out that where in other grand country houses people spent their time on idle games and their money at green baize tables, 'at Puławy every entertainment had a purpose, there was a thought behind each amusement, and a reason behind every act'. For Marianna's name day in 1801, Izabela organized a tea party for thirty-two children of members of the household and neighbours, the high point of which was a lottery conducted to the sound of drums and trumpets, for which the children had spent days sewing, knitting and gluing, to make the prizes.[12]

The house always filled up on family members' name days: Izabela's on 19 November, Marianna's on 15 August, Adam and Adam Jerzy's on 24 December, Konstanty's on 11 March and Zofia's on 15 May, when the family and neighbours would be joined by friends from Lublin and Warsaw. It also attracted foreigners, either on their way to or from Russia or on their travels, ranging from Austrian archdukes, through European grandees and learned people, to a couple of American Quakers, all drawn by the renown of the place and its mistress.

Many French émigré aristocrats sought refuge in Poland, all of them in need of hospitality, including the future Louis XVIII and his sister the duchesse d'Angoulême, whom Marianna welcomed in Warsaw,

Zofia introduced clandestinely to the Queen of Prussia in the park of Łazienki and Elżbieta Lubomirska received at Łańcut, and the duc d'Enghien, who danced all night at Sieniawa, leaving Izabela a ring with a fragment of Héloïse's skull in it.

Among the frequent guests was Helena Radziwiłł, who sometimes brought her husband, whom Adam disliked and thought ridiculous; he would never leave Nieborów without his 'chicken-coop' of young girls. Others were Izabela's close friends Stanisław Jabłonowski and Kazimierz Rzewuski.

Now in her early fifties, Izabela had lost none of her verve. 'Nothing can exceed the charming condescension, the sweetness of disposition the singular amiability, which distinguish the character of this illustrious lady,' recorded Burnett. 'Her spirits have even now all the flow and vivacity of those of a girl.' A Polish guest noted that she still had wonderfully expressive, sparkling eyes and a spirited wit, and that she never commanded or reprimanded her charges, but could bring everyone to order with one look.[13]

This was essential, as the number of permanent residents had grown. Alongside Adam's boys and Izabela's girls there were young people who had been orphaned in one way or another, such as Dominik Radziwiłł, whose father had died the year he was born. An inveterate prankster, he delighted in placing things in people's beds and balancing buckets of water on half-open doors. Others had wound up at Puławy by chance. Adam had taken pity on an Irish lady, Mrs Nevill, or Neuville, who had been widowed or abandoned by her husband in Warsaw, where she became the mistress of a British diplomat who went home when Poland's political existence was extinguished in 1795, leaving her destitute. Adam enjoyed her company and provided for her and her daughter.

One member of the family who did not feature at Puławy was a pretty girl named Cecylia Beydale. By some accounts, she was born in Paris in 1787, by others in 1780, but there is no evidence for either date or place. She was presumably the daughter of Kazimierz Rzewuski; the Rzewuskis originally bore the name Beyda, and when he died in 1820 he left her his entire fortune. Who her mother was is not clear. She is thought to have been Izabela's daughter, but if so, she would hardly have been born in 1787; it is difficult to imagine a heavily pregnant Izabela travelling across Europe for her first meeting with her in-laws at Montbéliard and giving birth in Paris either just before or just after her interview with Marie-Antoinette. She might have been Marianna's, but that seems unlikely.

The first mention of her is in a letter from Izabela to Marianna, dated London 16 April 1790, in which she writes that 'Cesia's portrait hangs by my bed, next to Marysia's little pensée, everyone admires it and I love it extra, I wrote underneath it: <u>Céciliette a deux mères qui l'aiment pour quatre</u>.' The child was looked after by Marianna, who did treat her as a daughter, but so did she treat another cast-off, Maria Dzierżanowska. To Adam Jerzy in September 1798, Marianna wrote that she loved Cecylia as though she were her own daughter. 'I have taken charge of this child and have so to speak made her the chief interest and consolation of my life.' Izabela's wish not to have her at Puławy suggests she might not have felt able to behave with any distance to her own child, while given Adam's age the girl might not credibly be recognised as his.[14]

Another orphan who had turned up at Puławy in 1799 was Zosia, the daughter of a close ally of the Familia, Tadeusz Matuszewicz. Her mother had died when she was only 2 years old and Izabela embraced her as though she were her own, gradually turning her into a surrogate for her own children. She had brought them up as companions, particularly in the case of Marianna and Adam Jerzy, and she was desolate when they grew up and went their ways. Marianna would get bored in Puławy after a while, and spent more time in Warsaw, where she bought a house in 1801. Adam Jerzy was in Italy, bored and depressed, so even his letters were of little solace. Konstanty spent his time at Międzyrzecz. Zofia was away with her husband, in Vienna much of the time, as their house at Podzamcze, fifty kilometres from Puławy, had been devastated during the Battle of Maciejowice in 1794. In November 1801 her husband's elder brother died from a botched operation and he inherited a vast entail comprising ten towns and more than 190 villages as well as the fortress city of Zamość, which henceforth absorbed much of their attention.

Izabela was rarely alone, given the number of visitors and neighbours, not to mention her charges. Although she complained of migraines and loss of memory and eyesight, she kept herself busy reading and writing, in the company of her dog and parrot, going for walks, visiting the sick and needy and working in the grounds. When she was not repairing the damage caused by the severe winter of 1798, which killed many shrubs, and the flood of 1799, which carried away old trees, she was building a new bridge to the Kępa or putting up a new cottage on it.

She nevertheless felt lonely without the companionship of her children. 'There are times when I feel sick of life as I realise that I am destined to be always far from my children,' she wrote to Marianna in March 1801. A week or so later, history decreed that she would not see much of the one she missed most, Adam Jerzy, over many years.[15]

On the night of 23 March 1801 Tsar Paul I was assassinated in his bedroom at the Mikhailovsky Palace in St Petersburg, and his eldest son succeeded to the throne as Alexander I. Six days later, in Rome, Adam Jerzy received a letter from the new tsar. 'You will already have heard, my dear friend, that, by the death of my father I am now at the head of affairs,' it began. 'I will pass over the details until I speak to you in private. I am writing that you might immediately transfer all the business of your mission to whoever is most senior below you and set out for Petersburg. I do not need to tell you with what impatience I await you. May Heaven protect you along the way and bring you here safe and sound. Adieu, my dear friend, I cannot say more; I enclose a passport you may show at the frontier. Alexander.'[16]

Adam Jerzy left at once and only lingered a few days as he passed through Puławy, where an excited Izabela fought back her longing to keep him there and hurried him on his way. When he reached St Petersburg he found Alexander overwhelmed by the events of the past weeks yet determined to give substance to the dreams they had entertained together.

To help him implement these and transform the Russian Empire into a modern state, Alexander gathered around him an unofficial committee consisting of Adam Jerzy, Pavel Stroganov, Nikolai Novosiltsev and Viktor Kochubey. They began work in June 1801. Adam Jerzy put forward proposals for the abolition of serfdom on state lands and the alleviation of its conditions on private estates, reform of the Senate and the administration, and improving the status of Jews – none of which would be implemented.

Izabela's pride at her son's advancement gradually turned to desolation as it became clear she would not be seeing him for a long time. She not only wanted to have him back at Puławy, she wanted him to marry and settle down. 'I passionately desire to see little Czartoryskis,' Izabela wrote to Marianna. 'It would be a pity if such a good family were to die out. The name is for me a synonym for happiness! That name has made me a happy wife and a happy mother.' She was therefore jubilant when Konstanty fell in love with Helena Radziwiłł's daughter Aniela. The wedding, which took place at Nieborów on 20 July 1802, was a joyous affair. The two families then piled into carriages and drove to Puławy for a second round of celebrations. Izabela was beside herself when, two years later, Aniela gave birth to a boy, Adam Konstanty. 'I've quite lost my head, tears, laughter at the same time,' she wrote to Marianna. 'I rushed about the whole house, the world was not big enough for me.'[17]

And if Puławy was no longer as much of a family home as she would have liked, it was growing into something more substantial, a kind of national home. Visitors noted that there was something special about the place and the life led there. It was, in the words of one, 'a truly national and Polish house' whose old-style hospitality attracted 'people of breeding, proven virtues, cultivation and enlightenment, and above all good Poles' from all around, concluding that 'it was the Polish Epirus in which Helenus created a small Troy after the destruction of Troy', on whose shore all the flotsam that had survived the wreck of the Polish ship of state washed up.[18]

'Just as they bury the body of a deceased person in one spot and preserve the heart elsewhere, the same happened to our Motherland,' mused another who frequented Puławy. 'She was no more, the capital of our kings became a provincial town, but everyone will agree that her heart was brought to Puławy.' There, 'regardless of sex, age or class, each met with ready support, advice and consolation'. According to Kajetan Koźmian, 'the ideas, the manners, the taste and the culture of country life in the style of Puławy spread throughout Galicia', to the extent that the Austrian authorities looked askance at what was in effect a kind of national revival. It was just that, in more senses than one.[19]

When she reached Kraków on her return from Vienna following the collapse of the Insurrection, Izabela was horrified by what she saw.

The city had been briefly occupied by Prussian troops who had looted the Wawel Castle and the cathedral where Poland's crown jewels were kept. This had been inspired not so much by lust for gold as the intention of destroying the symbols of Polish statehood (the crowns and regalia of state were unpicked and melted down by the Prussians). Her instinct was to salvage whatever she could, going so far as rummaging in the ruins of a church to dig out an old altarpiece. With the assistance of the clergy she rescued captured banners that had hung in the cathedral, along with votive offerings left there by historical figures. This urge to preserve shards of Poland's past morphed into the idea of assembling objects that would testify to and commemorate her place in history. By way of inheritance and family contacts she could access an array of historical objects from which to pick out those she found significant, and the antiquary Tadeusz Czacki, who had swept through the Wawel when the Prussians left, gathering up even broken fragments, and relics from royal tombs, handed them over to Izabela when he heard of what she was doing.

She wanted to house these relics in a special building, a hall of memory which would serve the future; it was to be a spiritual base for the rebuilding of a new Polish state. As her model, she selected a half-ruined circular temple dating from the first century AD at Tivoli outside Rome. She had never been there, but one who had was the architect Piotr Aigner, a native of Puławy who had studied in Rome on a bursary from the king. He had made drawings and a scale model of the temple, and it is probably he who suggested it to Izabela as the ideal shrine.

There was more to the suggestion than aesthetics. The building was thought, erroneously, to have been dedicated to the Sibyl, allegedly the daughter of Zeus, endowed with second sight, whose shrines at Delphi and Cumae had been consulted as oracles. Thus the rotunda at Tivoli was associated with augury, which fitted Izabela's concept, encapsulated in the motto which she would inscribe over the portals of her shrine, 'The Past to the Future'; she meant to evoke all that was best and most inspiring from the past and to lay it at the service of the future. She had begun work on her temple in 1797, on the same escarpment as the house, and watched the building take shape with delight, symbolising as it did the rebuilding of the country.

It was with similar feelings that she greeted Zofia and her husband when they returned from their long voyage abroad. Taking advantage of the Peace of Amiens, they had gone to Paris, where Zofia was painted by Gérard, and, along the way, by Greuze and Isabey, and to England, where they toured the country visiting houses as far north as Castle Howard and factories, breweries and workshops. Izabela noted with satisfaction that they returned not with the silly ticks and affectations adopted by most travellers, but 'with a crowd of workmen, mechanics, and educated people, models, instruments, and a thousand useful things'. Zofia's husband Stanisław had been brought up in a spirit of frugality. He wore old clothes and drove around in an old carriage. Having inherited the enormous Zamość entail, he set about developing its agriculture and industry, founding medical and educational establishments. Although she never warmed to him, Izabela approved, even down to his dress code. 'I'm mad about shawls, particularly since my laziness has made me love not to dress,' she wrote to her husband when he sent her some in March 1803.[20]

Now in her late fifties, she complained of migraines, eye strain, fits of dizziness and other ailments, and of having to wear spectacles to play the piano, as she could no longer read the scores. But none of it dampened her spirits for long. From Puławy in February 1803 she informed Marianna that she had put on a 'masque' in which she had played a Lithuanian peasant woman; from Kraków in March she described the fun she was having at dances and dinners. From there she went to Sieniawa then back to Puławy where, in January the following year, she put on a 'masked redoute'. There were more fancy-dress parties and a pantomime involving Pan, fauns and satyrs. In the summer of 1804 she was at Wilanów, which had changed since the days when she dazzled and reigned over the festivities; the place was looking fresher and she older and uglier, as she put it to Marianna. On her name day in November there was a 'crazy' series of balls at Puławy with quantities of guests.

'My Temple is finished, and it is superb,' Izabela declared in November 1801. 'The inside will be finished in the spring.' Aigner's version is almost twice the size of the original at Tivoli, but replicates the domed rotunda ringed with Roman columns. The key that opened the heavily studded double doors, a gilt bronze replica of the staff of Hermes, entwined by two snakes and crowned by two wings topped with a pine-cone, was designed by Izabela herself. As well as being the messenger of the gods, Hermes was also a guide, and, more importantly, a link with the dead and protector of things found. The key was inscribed in Greek with the words 'I open the temple of memory', along with Izabela's initials and the date 1801.[21]

Inside, visitors found themselves in an austere space with a sacral feel. The walls were finished in marbleised stucco, decorated with panoplies dedicated to Poland's greatest military commanders, the only architectural feature being an arched niche opposite the entrance partly veiled by a curtain of crimson velvet draped from a gilded halberd. Within hung a Renaissance shield depicting the Emperor Constantine's victory battle of the Milvian Bridge in AD 312, a triumph of Christian arms, which was allegedly found behind a miraculous picture of Christ in the Wawel Cathedral and presented to King Jan III as he was setting off to do battle with the Turks besieging Vienna in 1683. It was flanked by weapons belonging to King Władysław Jagiełło and Grand Duke Witold, who had triumphed over the Teutonic Knights in 1410, and King Stephen Bathory, who had defeated the Muscovites.

The niche was surrounded by Polish banners, captured enemy standards, staffs of office and halberds. In front of it stood what was in effect the altar of the temple – the 'Royal Casket'. Made of black ebony with gold fittings, set with diamonds and lined with green velvet, it contained three removable trays with compartments for several dozen small objects, including relics retrieved from the royal tombs at the Wawel, elements of jewellery, miniatures, prayer books, crucifixes, fragments of clothing and even buttons that had belonged to kings and queens of Poland; a symbolic re-creation of the vanished crown jewels.

The rest of the collection was kept in two mahogany cabinets with glass-covered drawers. They included objects of every kind associated with historical figures. Some were works of art, others worthless pieces of metal, leather or textile, and many had emotive stories behind them; the sabre King Jan III had donated as a votive offering to the shrine of the Virgin at Loreto after his victory over the Turks had been salvaged by Polish soldiers from Bonaparte's pillage of the shrine.

The cabinets were closed and the objects hidden from view. They would be revealed to the visitor by the guide – visiting the temple was not supposed to take the form of browsing through works of art, but a didactic experience conjured by the guide, usually Izabela herself. On top of the cabinets, Izabela placed urns and miniature sarcophagi containing physical relics of kings and great men of Poland, and in front of them stood two chests containing objects of significance to Polish statehood, such as of royal charters and coins. Before these stood a table with a casket destined for visitors' offerings. These were not intended so much to help with the upkeep of the museum as to register the visitor's participation, his or her ex-voto; Izabela's spiritual microcosm of Poland was meant as a place of pilgrimage.

For many years before she started gathering specifically Polish historical objects, Izabela had been collecting affective paraphernalia connected with figures of the past, scenes of human triumph or tragedy, lost civilisations and memorable literature. Through her rudimentary education with the aid of illustrated histories and classics, she had become accustomed to live and learn through images, which fired her imagination. Her jottings show that as she read, she construed her own extrapolations of a text. When she visited places, she dreamed of what had taken place there, and when she picked up an object she connected in her imagination with the person who had made it, to whom it had belonged, or to the role it had played. Gradually, the simple desire to possess a pen used by Frederick the Great or an image of Mary Stuart had grown into an urge to probe more deeply into the past, to know its heroes and villains intimately, to experience great moments in history.

Having been collecting such things from at least the 1780s, Izabela was a couple of decades ahead of the Romantic quest for sensuous revelation through contact with ancient ruins and artefacts, and it was only later that this would develop into an urge to collect and preserve; it was after visiting the battlefield of Waterloo that Walter Scott, in writing *The Antiquary*, popularised the trend. With Izabela, it was instinctive: 'It is a real madness in me, a fever which gets ever stronger,' she admitted to a French writer.[22]

She contacted Alexandre Lenoir, who had been appointed by the National Assembly to salvage works of art confiscated from the Church, and later founded the Musée des Monuments Français. From him she obtained the relics of Abélard and Héloïse, which he had personally removed from a grave in the monastery of Le Paraclet in 1790. She also contacted the principal mover in the creation of France's national collections, Dominique Vivant Denon, who supplied her with objects connected with the kings and queens of France, their lovers and mistresses, such as a crystal hunting flask associated with Francis I, some mementos from the royal family's incarceration in the Temple prison and fragments taken from the royal necropolis at Saint-Denis while it was being destroyed in 1793. It was from him that she would receive the ashes of El Cid and Ximena, removed from a tomb in the cathedral of Burgos when it was occupied by the French in 1810.

As word spread of her interest, more and more people contributed. The destruction of Poland and Napoleonic wars had dispersed Poles all over Europe and the Americas, where they picked up a wide variety of objects. Polish soldiers serving under Bonaparte in Italy or in Saint-Domingue (Haiti) and later in Spain found rich pickings for her. One would send a sprig of myrtle from the Alhambra, another a branch of laurel from the tomb of Ines de Castro in Alcobaça, a third a black insurgent's club from Saint-Domingue. From Avignon, one sent her relics of Petrarch and Laura, from Verona another contributed a fragment from the alleged grave of Romeo and Juliet. As well as the antiquities she requested, in 1801 Adam Jerzy sent two pictures he had bought in Italy: a portrait of a young man by the famed Raphael and that of a young lady holding an ermine, supposedly the notorious mistress of Francis I of France, by Leonardo da Vinci.

She delighted in showing her treasures to guests, explaining their significance and resonance. 'I cannot express the interest and pleasure with which we listened to her as, having spent her life collecting so many rare and valuable objects, she showed them to us, linking to almost each one some fascinating story,' recorded Anna Potocka.[23] But there were only so many of them that she could show at once, and before she began work on the temple she was already planning where to display them.

She decided to house them in an intimate, supposedly gothic, cottage. It was, in fact, anything but gothic in style – baroque columns and elements of classical decoration jostled with arched windows to produce a bizarre effect. The walls were rendered and painted to imitate brickwork and broken up by windows of different shape. They were incrusted with fragments of stone taken from other buildings, metal relics and memorial tablets; with objects of Polish significance next to foreign elements; a Polish cannonball, a piece of stone from the castle of Fotheringhay, to commemorate Mary Stuart, fragments from Petrarch's house and from the castle in Moravia in which Richard the Lionheart had been imprisoned.

The inside of the building was no more consistent. Each of the six rooms was different in style and atmosphere. The oval chamber on the first floor lined with green silk was bright and airy, the downstairs rooms were plunged in gloom by the feeble light coming through stained-glass windows from the chapel of Charlemagne at Aix-la-Chapelle. The beam supporting the ceiling of the oval chamber on the ground floor was inscribed with the words: 'Tender recollection can rescue from oblivion all that fate has destroyed or time devoured'. The walls were covered with unmatched objects of every kind and widely discrepant value, which also cluttered tables and filled cabinets, showcases, chests and caskets in an exuberant chaos of allusion, in which the moss from Stonehenge and the flowers picked at Fingal's grave found their place.

The Gothic House was meant to embrace the whole of human experience. A grey marble plaque over the door bore a quotation from Virgil's *Aeneid*: *Sunt lacrimae rerum et mentem mortalia tangunt* (roughly, 'objects shed tears and the dead can touch the soul'). Her collection was meant to provoke reflection on the whole gamut of human experience, and the value of each item lay in its association with people or events. Unbeknown to her, notable people and momentous events were about to invade her world.

# Between Two Emperors

In July 1805 Izabela was taking a cure at the sulphur baths of her preferred spa, Lubień, not far from Lwów, accompanied by the 7-year-old Zosia Matuszewicz. Adam had gone with her in the summer of 1803, and, as usual with him, the trip had taken the form of an expedition, with all the servants, equipment and supplies to camp out along the way, usually on the banks of rivers, as Izabela was fond of fishing. She had returned there in 1804 and taken thirty baths for what she described as a kind of gout affecting her wrists and had experienced some relief. She had also taken a liking to the place, and enjoyed watching the bizarre collection of individuals it attracted. Having finished her cure at the end of July, she decided to make a long detour on her way back to Puławy. She went first to Lwów, where she spent an enjoyable few days, and then travelled east, into Podolia, which was now part of the Russian Empire.

The countryside reminded her of Switzerland, and the hospitality overwhelmed her, as did the patriotic spirit of her hosts. She went from one estate to another, escorted by thirty Granów Cossacks who would make camp, roast a sheep, drink mead and then sing and dance into the night. People held receptions and balls in her honour, and as she reached one of her husband's estates she was greeted by a delegation consisting of hundreds of peasants, merchants and Jews, led by their priests and rabbis, with the traditional offering of bread and salt. She was charmed by the singing of the local peasants and Jews and impressed by the good looks of the inhabitants. She inspected the estate, noted the condition of the stud and what needed to be done to improve it, did the same with regard to the cattle, checked the bridges, roads and outbuildings, and distributed money to those she deemed deserving. 'I am really intoxicated by this countryside,' she wrote to Marianna, 'it's paradise, not earth.'[1]

Her delight stemmed partly from the fact that on leaving Austrian Galicia and entering Polish lands currently under Russian rule she found a world less hidebound by irritating regulations and functionaries, partly because it was an escape from her daily cares – she even admitted in one letter that she felt 'shackled' by Puławy.[2]

One day a man from Puławy arrived with a packet of letters for her. She began asking him about his health and that of his family, but he interrupted her, saying she must read the letters as Tsar Alexander was due there in a couple of days. She could not believe this, but on opening the letters discovered it was true. She had barely recovered from her astonishment when her current host came to announce that tea was about to be served on a picturesque island on the lake, to be followed by an Italian opera, a play and a ball. She made her excuses and left immediately, travelling day and night in an open carriage, with Zosia and a maid. 'It was pouring with rain, it was cold and the wind went through us,' she recorded. She made it in three days and found Puławy surrounded by thousands of Russian troops and crammed with generals. Some said the tsar was planning to stay, others that he was not. 'I lost my head,' she recalls, when a letter from Adam Jerzy confirmed that Alexander was indeed meaning to stay.

Much had happened since she had last seen her son, who was now in charge of Russia's foreign policy. He had originally refused to take over from the ageing chancellor, Aleksandr Vorontsov, aware of the hostility and suspicion he aroused in most Russians. The nationalist Filip Filipovich Vigel saw him as 'the secret, unflinching enemy of Russia', the spawn of 'the Polish Judith' who had unmanned 'our Holofernes, Prince Nikolai Vasilievich Repnin' and brought him up to destroy Russia from within.[3] But at Alexander's insistence he had reluctantly agreed to take the job, refusing the title. Apart from not wishing to let down his friend, he hoped he might be able to give life to Alexander's wish to change the basis of Russia's foreign policy from one of continual expansion to one of peacemaker and ensure that the forthcoming war against Napoleon resulted in an equitable reconstruction of Europe.

Adam Jerzy, Novosiltsev and Alexander had decided that Prussia, which had made opportunistic deals with France in the past and was now sitting on the fence, should, if she did not join the coalition in its imminent struggle against Napoleon, be stripped of land she had acquired in the partitions of Poland, which Alexander would then reconstitute as the Kingdom of Poland with himself as king.

Against their advice, Alexander determined to lead his army in the forthcoming war. Adam Jerzy wondered whether he should accompany him to war or not and towards the end of April 1805 he had written to Izabela for advice. There was a time, she replied, 'when I would have seen your blood flow with joy', but now her 'woman's reasoning' was that he could be of little use to Alexander on the battlefield. But if he felt he had to show his gratitude by accompanying him, he must.[4] And that would bring him to Puławy, the principal ferry crossing of the Vistula south of Warsaw.

She only had three days in which to prepare for their arrival. Her husband was on his way from Sieniawa, where he had taken the cooks and most of the silver, staff, horses and carriages. Izabela despatched one galloper to him and another to Zamoyski at Podzamcze begging him to send his cooks in case hers did not arrive in time. 'I arranged the apartment upstairs myself,' she records. 'Night and day we put up portières, curtains and drapes. I moved furniture, cupboards, tables, side-tables, looking-glasses and pictures from my own rooms, and in the space of two days I arranged those rooms so beautifully that I could hardly believe the sight myself. When, by the evening of the second day, I had finished I wanted to rest, and having laid down on my bed fully dressed I was thinking over these extraordinary events, when my new young maid ran into the room to say that some unknown young gentleman was insisting on seeing me. I did not have time to answer when the door opened and I saw my son.' He told her to expect Alexander at any moment, but it turned into a long wait.[5]

The Austrian authorities had insisted on sending the tsar a carriage and guides as he entered Austrian territory, but they lost their way in a forest, where one of its wheels hit a stump and broke, leaving the party stranded in the gathering gloom. They were saved by a Jewish trader driving a cart laden with vodka. When he heard that he was in the presence of the tsar, with news of whose coming the whole neighbourhood had been buzzing, he offered to lead him on foot by the shortest route along forest paths.

Alexander reached Puławy at 2 a.m. on 28 September, led by the Jew with his broken lantern and covered in mud, to be greeted by Major Orłowski, who had been summoned by the night watchman. 'Please do not wake anyone,' Alexander said. 'All I need is a bed, for I'm tired out as I had to walk for half a mile [a Polish mile at the time was 7.146 kilometres].' He refused the offer of dinner, but having been shown to his room merely asked for his boots to be pulled off and borrowed a pair of slippers from Orłowski before wrapping himself in his cloak and falling asleep.[6]

On waking, Izabela was surprised to see sentries patrolling outside her windows. When it became known that the tsar was in residence, the whole house came to life, and Izabela began to think of his breakfast. Her theatrical sense got the better of her, as she sent it up on two gold trays, one with a rare Turkish coffee pot, a blue porcelain milk jug with a gold handle, two cups of the finest French porcelain, gem-encrusted gold spoons, English cut-glass sugar bowl and butter dish, both mounted in gold, the other tray laden with bread, husks and toast. 'The emperor drank with pleasure and conveyed his thanks, adding that he had never had such a delicious and beautifully presented breakfast.'[7]

When Izabela and her husband called on him at eleven, Alexander was in uniform, pacing up and down the room. He thanked them for their hospitality. 'For a long time I have felt I must tell you what a precious gift you made me in giving me your son, who is a sure friend and a perfect guide,' he told Izabela. She could not hold back tears as the tsar embraced Adam and kissed her, addressing her henceforth as '*Maman*' and saying how sorry that his 'dear aunt' Marianna was not there too.[8]

With the tsar in residence, Puławy was transformed by his Marshal of the Court Count Tolstoy, a 'fat buffoon' according to Izabela. Courtiers, generals and foreign diplomats took the best rooms, and over the next few days ladies of the household could be found sleeping on sofas in unlikely places. Couriers came and went, some bringing pine-apples from St Petersburg, others despatches from Vienna or Berlin. Notable Poles came from Warsaw to discuss plans for restoring a Polish kingdom.

Every morning Alexander rode out to review his troops concentrat-ing in the area, but on his return he would change into civilian dress and behave as if he were on a private visit in a country house. After lunch, he spent hours with Izabela in her apartment and bantered with other ladies of the household, making much of Zosia and the other chil-dren. Izabela took him around the gardens, and showed him the Temple, giving him a lesson in Polish history. He was so inspired by the building and its atmosphere that when she said she wanted to make the light filtering in through the glass dome more sepulchral he offered to have an amethyst-coloured dome made for her in the St Petersburg glass-works. When they visited Marynki he was horrified to see the traces of Russian musket-butts from 1794 visible on the marble fireplaces. They drove out to Parchatka and other sights, and, in the words of Adam Jerzy, 'the emperor appeared happy to find himself in a more temperate climate, surrounded by people who were sincerely devoted to him'.[9] But the idyll did not last.

Before they left St Petersburg, the plan to destroy Prussia's power was all but settled, but Alexander delayed the despatch of the ultimatum to Berlin, and instead sent one of his aides-de-camp, Prince Peter Dol-goruky, who returned with a conciliatory message from Frederick William inviting Alexander to Berlin. 'Everything is falling apart,' Izab-ela noted as the mood at Puławy descended into despondency. General Stuttenheim, Austria's representative at Alexander's side, reported back to Vienna in despair that he himself, Adam Jerzy, General Wintzin-gerode, Novosiltsev and others were 'on their knees' begging the tsar to go ahead and destroy the Prussian 'poltroons' and not let himself be seduced by Frederick William.[10]

Alexander set off in the late afternoon of 15 October. Having boasted to the ladies of the comfort of his carriage and the prowess of his coach-man, he invited Zofia Zamoyska and Konstanty's wife Aniela to join him for the first leg of the trip. At Kozienice, their first stop, there lived a renowned miracle-working rabbi whom Adam Jerzy had visited some years earlier. He went to see him again, and the old sage told him to trust neither Napoleon nor Alexander.[11] What was left of Adam Jerzy's hopes evaporated as they carried on to Warsaw. Alexander met Ponia-towski and other patriots at Wilanów but made no mention of any plans for Poland. In Berlin, he fell under the spell of the beautiful queen Louise and happily signed up to an alliance with her husband, who would, when the time came, fail to honour it, just as his father had failed to honour his treaty with Poland.

The mood at Puławy was low after what Izabela termed the two-week 'flash of happiness' of Alexander's visit, when hope had soared. But everyone still expected a victory over Napoleon. He was not popular in Poland, his early image as a liberator tarnished by his callous treatment of the Poles who had fought for him in Italy, most of whom he had sub-sequently sent to their death in Saint-Domingue. Alexander still seemed to offer the best chance for Polish aspirations.

After the tsar left Puławy, Adam headed back to Sieniawa, pausing on the way at Łańcut. It so happened that General Kutuzov was march-ing through on his way to confront Napoleon, and, hearing that there was an Austrian field marshal in residence, he paraded his troops before Adam. They joined the Austrian army at Olmutz at the end of Novem-ber. Adam Jerzy was among those who pointed out to Alexander that his presence hindered the efficient conduct of military operations and, when this advice was ignored, he joined Kutuzov in arguing strongly against giving battle. Goaded by the aristocratic young bloods on his staff, Alexander would not hear of it. In answer to Napoleon's request for a meeting, he sent Dolgoruky, who merely insulted the French emperor.

Two days later the combined Austro-Russian army was disastrously defeated at Austerlitz. Adam Jerzy, who had spent the day in the saddle at Alexander's side, lost contact with him in the ensuing chaos. The tsar fled on horseback, later transferring to a carriage, and made straight for St Petersburg, pausing only at Międzyrzecz in the middle of the night to borrow a clean shirt from Konstanty.[12]

Adam Jerzy reached St Petersburg with Novosiltsev eight days later, to face a chorus of blame as people sought scapegoats for the disaster, and he was accused of betraying Russia. Along with Novosiltsev and

Kochubey, he tendered his resignation, but it was not accepted. He wrote Alexander a long letter blaming him for changing the policy they had agreed, for allying with Prussia and for playing the soldier when a monarch's role was to rule and not expose himself to the taint of defeat. Alexander rejected his criticism, saying their views were irreconcilable, but in cordial tones, signing off 'All yours in heart and soul'.[13] It was not until June 1806 that he accepted his resignation from the post of foreign minister, and would not relinquish him from that of Councillor of State.

Izabela longed to have Adam Jerzy at Puławy. She complained of dull evenings and joyless teas. 'Yesterday I looked at those present,' she wrote to Marianna, 'two were gouty, two silent, one poor convalescent, and one asleep.' She could see little promise in the future, so she read, wrote, worked on cataloguing her collections and pasted labels on the exhibits. Although Dr Goltz's regime had cured her headaches, she was having trouble with her eyes and suffering dizzy spells, and beginning to feel old. A moment of joy came in September, when the amethyst-coloured glass dome promised by Alexander arrived from St Petersburg.

Having made peace with Austria after Austerlitz, Napoleon had returned to Paris, but Alexander was determined to carry on the war. Anticipating his support, Prussia attacked France in September 1806. Her army was thoroughly defeated in the twin battles of Jena and Auerstadt, and within weeks the Prussian state imploded. By the end of October Napoleon was in Potsdam considering his next move as Russian armies massed to the north of Warsaw.

A delegation of Poles from the provinces taken by Prussia in the partitions came and begged him help them liberate Poland. Seizing the opportunity to provide himself with local support and a card to play in his forthcoming campaign against Russia, Napoleon encouraged them, and when he reached Poznań he was received as a liberator. He went on to Warsaw where his advance guard under Murat had been greeted deliriously, and then marched north to confront the Russians. As the winter made further operations impossible, he returned to Warsaw, where he set up a provisional Polish administration. Without committing himself he encouraged the Poles to believe he would restore their country and formed up Polish regiments while stripping the country of horses and victuals to supply his troops.

At Puławy and Sieniawa, both still under Austrian rule, Izabela and her husband did not know what to wish for. In St Petersburg, Adam Jerzy was horrified. After the debacle of Austerlitz he had urged Alexander to make peace with France and use the respite to strengthen his position in Europe by doing what he should have done before, namely declaring himself king of Poland. That was the only way, he argued, to pre-empt Napoleon seducing the Poles.[14] But as Alexander had failed to take up their cause, increasing numbers were now placing their hopes in Napoleon and volunteers flocked to his standards.

In the spring of 1807 he marched out and after a brief campaign destroyed the Russian army at Friedland on 14 June. A week later Alexander agreed to meet him in person at Tilsit. The peace settlement they signed there in July resulted in the creation of a Polish state out of the Prussian share in the partitions, but it was not given the name of Poland; in order to avoid upsetting Russian sensibilities it was named the Grand Duchy of Warsaw and given a sovereign in the person of the King of Saxony. Adam Jerzy, Kochubey and Novosiltsev had discouraged Alexander from meeting Napoleon and criticised the outcome of the negotiations. Alexander sidelined the three of them.

Izabela felt let down, and although she admitted that Napoleon's appearance on the scene had made her heart beat faster, and he had put a Polish state back on the map, it was not the kind she had longed for. It was a fief of the King of Saxony and entirely subservient to France. Napoleon instructed his minister in Saxony to encourage the Poles to believe he would eventually restore a sovereign Poland, but to discourage them from anticipating anything and under no circumstances commit.[15]

He appointed Poniatowski commander-in-chief of the Polish army, but sent several of its regiments to fight in Spain. Marshal Davout was in overall command and Napoleon's minister in Warsaw, Étienne Vincent, oversaw the government. French generals received grants of land and were exempted from taxation, a class of their own with no connection to the country, and the Napoleonic administrative system transformed overnight everything from the legal system to the status of the peasants, causing economic chaos and financial hardship for all involved.

Yet Izabela could not help warming to the national revival taking place. Most of those making up the government in Warsaw were friends, relatives or close allies, such as Stanisław Małachowski, Elżbieta Lubomirska's son-in-law Stanisław Potocki, Zosia's father Tadeusz Matuszewicz and Niemcewicz, who had returned from the United States (bringing Izabela Washington's teacup, donated by the great man for the Gothic House), and Poniatowski was a friend as well as a cousin.

As both Puławy and Sieniawa lay in Austrian Galicia, she could only observe what was going on in Warsaw. Adam Jerzy was still under oath to Alexander, so while he was viewed with suspicion in Russia he was excluded from playing a role in Napoleonic Warsaw. Konstanty resigned his Russian general's rank and joined the army of the Grand Duchy. Marianna had welcomed the new state of affairs and stayed in Warsaw. Zofia and her husband had moved to Vienna, where she played host to Madame de Staël, performing her new plays with her children. But their very Polish home was in sharp contrast to Elżbieta Lubomirska's quintessentially *ancien régime* French salon, and with the creation of the Grand Duchy they too gravitated to Warsaw.

Izabela found this dispersal hard to bear and complained of 'this sad existence far from you all'. They did visit her, but she craved more of their company, and missed seeing Adam Jerzy most of all. 'My friend, consider that it is a mother who loves you that begs for a small part of your time,' she wrote to him in January 1807, 'it is a sick mother who begs you.' She did go to Warsaw in February 1808 to see her daughters and went to balls and the theatre, but she was soon back at Puławy. She was feeling old and hated being left to herself as, being physically unwell, she could no longer distract herself with activity. 'Besides, accustomed as I have been for so many years to social bustle and an active life, to varied amusements, it is harder for me to spend my days always alone,' she wrote.[16]

As well as longing to see him, she was worried about Adam Jerzy. He had not been happy in St Petersburg from the moment he returned from Italy. Alexander's new position ruled out their camaraderie of old, and his wife Elizabeth had found another lover, so he had nobody to confide in. He was therefore delighted when Piattoli had turned up in St Petersburg in 1803. He had been imprisoned by the Austrians following the Insurrection. General Bonaparte had tried to obtain his release in 1797, and Adam Jerzy persuaded Alexander to do the same three years later. On being freed, Piattoli was employed by the immensely wealthy Duchess of Courland at her palace of Löbichau in Saxony, where she lived with her current lovers, Count Aleksander Batowski and Baron Gustav von Armfeldt – who was also having an affair with the eldest of her daughters, Wilhelmina, Duchess of Sagan. Piattoli had come to St Petersburg to press the duchess's claim for compensation following Russia's annexation of Courland, but he was also involved in unofficial diplomatic efforts around the creation of the coalition against France. Adam Jerzy had taken him into his lodgings and obtained a pension for him from Alexander. (Piattoli would provide Tolstoy with the figure of Abbé Morio in *War and Peace*.)

While he was employed as secretary to the duchess, Piattoli also acted as tutor to her youngest daughter, Dorothée. Though only 10 years old, the strong-willed, free-spirited and intelligent Dorothée developed a profound admiration for him, encouraged by her governess, Mademoiselle Hoffmann, who had been close to him when they had both been in the employ of the Potockis.

Piattoli remained in contact with Dorothée when he went to St Petersburg and, having decided that the solitary Adam Jerzy would be an excellent match for her, a view shared by Mademoiselle Hoffmann, his letters conveyed an image of him which intrigued her intellectually as well as emotionally. He sent her a portrait of him which she found handsome, and they began corresponding directly. 'At the end of a few months I had come to desire this marriage as eagerly as those who had imagined it', she recorded.[17]

To avoid the military operations, in 1805 the Duchess of Courland moved to Berlin and, after Napoleon's victory over the Prussians at Jena the following year to her erstwhile capital, Mittau (Jelgava), none too pleased to find the future Louis XVIII installed in her palace. Adam Jerzy passed through on his way from St Petersburg to join Alexander at headquarters in Prussia in April 1807, and spent nearly three weeks there, seeing Dorothée almost daily, studying her closely but saying little, and before he left he declared himself and asked her to pass through Warsaw on her way back to Berlin so she could meet Izabela.

There is no trace of such a plan in the sparse correspondence between Izabela and her son. On her side it consists largely of regret at his absence – 'in the past eleven or twelve years I have only seen you for a few months, and that in passing,' she complained in January 1807. 'My health is poor. Night and day I long to see you again.' At least one of her letters is smudged with her tears.[18] She also complained that he never wrote, but many of their letters went astray in what was still a war zone (and some of those that did not had clearly been opened). He meant to go to Puławy to inform Izabela of his plans, but could not obtain leave from Alexander until the spring of 1808 and his departure kept being delayed, so by the time he did, in August, she was no longer there; on 18 June she had set off for Töplitz in Bohemia, not just for a cure in its hot springs.

Whether he had mentioned his marriage plans to her is unclear, but sometime in May or June Izabela had received from Piattoli a memorandum setting out the merits of the match, with a request she pass it on to her husband and Marianna. On 16 June, as she was about to set off for Töplitz, she wrote to Adam Jerzy in vague terms that she would respect his wishes.[19]

She had set off from Puławy in four coaches, accompanied by Zosia Matuszewicz, Konstancja Dembowska and her son Leon, her new physician Doctor Karol Khittel, two chambermaids and an unspecified 'kitchen' and 'pantry'. She visited Marianna at Gruszczyn, an estate Adam had recently bought for her, and then she made for Warsaw, where Poniatowski held a military parade for her. From there she travelled to Nieborów to see Helena Radziwiłł. Marshal Davout, who had been given an estate not far distant, drove over to make her acquaintance. From there she made for Töplitz via Kalisz, Breslau and Dresden. The roads in Silesia were worse than she had imagined, and the horses provided at the posting stations of poor quality, often tired after spending the day pulling a plough, and the postillions lazy. It was lucky she had taken her 'kitchen', 'pantry' and bedding, as the inns were filthy.[20]

Not one to be put out by such things, Izabela eagerly drank in the landscape and the people as she walked alongside her carriage with her new dog Szczurek (Ratty). 'I did not allow a single humble pedestrian to pass without engaging them in conversation,' she wrote to Marianna from Breslau. 'Nobody escaped me and I know all the gossip of Greater Poland and Silesia.' She did likewise at every inn they stopped at, and at Kalisz she discovered that the manager of the hotel had once been in the service of Ludwig. 'We congratulated each other, him for no longer having him as a master, me for no longer having him as a son-in-law.' At Oels (Oleśnica), when everyone had gone to bed, she sat for over an hour at her open window which gave onto the moonlit square, reflecting on the past to the sound of someone in the sleeping town playing the flute.[21]

Ever on the lookout for objects to enrich her collections, she paused at Hundsfeld (Psie Pole) where the King of Poland had won a victory over the Germans in 1109 but was unable to find anything worthy of the Temple. Breslau, which she reached at the beginning of July, had suffered in the previous year's siege by the French, but she did manage to buy some incunabula for the Gothic House.

At Töplitz, Izabela found comfortable lodgings and was warmly received by the lord of the place, Prince Clary. The town was full of acquaintances, including Archduke Ferdinand and the prince de Ligne, who greeted her at her lodgings in a false beard and fancy dress pretending to be a fortune teller, accompanied by the Clary children dressed as 'Chinese singers'. Helena Radziwiłł also turned up with two daughters. Stanisław Potocki passed through on his way back from Bayonne and entertained the company with his account of the antics of the Spanish Bourbons who had been summoned there by Napoleon.

Izabela went on an outing to Eger, from where she wrote that on Marianna's name day as she could not give her a present she distributed money to the servants and made an old peasant woman happy with a substantial sum. In order to amuse Zosia, she arranged a fireworks display. She did not take part in an excursion to her Waldstein ancestors' castle at Dux but inspected a collection of 'old things' and met Goethe, whom she found 'extra polite', adding that 'I would like to get him to Puławy for my husband'. She also met Ludwig's elder brother Wilhelm, who told her that Marianna's son Adam was the best-looking man of his age, with a good heart, but spoilt and arrogant.[22]

In early August Izabela left Töplitz for Karlsbad (Karlovy Vary), from where she went for a longer cure at Franzenbrunn (Frantskovy

Izabela in London in 1791, by Richard Cosway.

The house at Puławy from the front, watercolour by Józef Richter.

The view of the house from the Kępa, with the Temple
visible on the right, watercolour by Józef Richter.

Adam painted in Vienna in 1795 when he had lost all his property, by Élisabeth Louise Vigée-Lebrun.

The house at Sieniawa, where Adam felt most at home, watercolour by Juliusz Kossak, *c.* 1880s.

Izabela by Kazimierz Wojniakowski, painted early in 1796, a few months after her return to the ruins of Puławy, showing her increasingly homely style of dressing.

The hermit's hut at Puławy.

The Temple of the Sybil, built by Izabela to house her collection of historical memorabilia, by Jean-Pierre Norblin de la Gourdaine.

Izabela's lifelong friend and equally enthusiastic builder and collector, Helena Radziwiłł, painted by Ernst Gebauer in 1816 with some of her acquisitions.

The Gothic House, where Izabela created a world of sensuous remembrance, by Jean-Pierre Norblin de la Gourdaine

Adam Jerzy, aquatint by A. Geiger after a lost portrait by Josef Abel. This was painted as he passed through Vienna in 1799 on his expulsion from Russia, following the Tsar's discovery of his affair with the Grand Duchess Elizabeth.

Adam Jerzy's future wife Anna Sapieha, miniature by an unknown artist.

Zofia at the time of her marriage to
Stanisław Zamoyski, copy of a lost
portrait by Giuseppe Grassi.

Konstanty in 1811,
by Jean-Baptiste Augustin.

Konstanty's future wife Maria Dzierżanowska
with the already depressive Cecylia Beydale.

Marianna as romantic authoress,
copy of a lost portrait by Heinrich Füger.

Lazne) and Eger, from where, passing through Töplitz once more, she went for a short stay at Dorothenau, one of the Duchess of Courland's residences.

What Izabela thought of Dorothée as a bride for her son is not known, but she had for some time decided that her beloved 11-year-old Zosia would make the ideal one. Adam Jerzy himself was irresolute; on 7 August he wrote to his mother saying that he agreed with Piattoli, but left it entirely up to her. Dorothée's mother might have been expected to be against the match, given the number of grand, and even royal, suitors in the wings, but it seems that she was for it. Presumably so as not to compromise either party, their meeting and its outcome were not mentioned by either side, and when Izabela met Piattoli in Dresden on her way back to Poland she was positive but careful not to commit. Dorothée herself felt that she was as good as engaged.[23]

Izabela was by then distracted by the death on 16 September 1808 of Konstanty's wife Aniela. She had always been frail and never fully recovered from giving birth. Konstanty had inherited some of his father's character and philandered among Izabela's young ladies, but was inconsolable when Aniela died, and Izabela was concerned. Adam Jerzy had joined him in Vienna and she urged him to take his brother on a tour of Italy in the spring of 1809, arguing that it would do them both good. In the event, Konstanty went to Paris, where he met Napoleon and fell under his spell. And the decision as to Adam Jerzy's marital plans would soon be taken out of Izabela's hands.

On 16 October 1808 Tsar Alexander turned up at Löbichau on his way back from meeting Napoleon at Erfurt. At dinner, he turned to Dorothée who was seated next to him and, pointing to a young officer further down the table, asked her if she did not think he resembled Adam Jerzy. The officer in question was Talleyrand's nephew Edmond de Talleyrand-Périgord.

The childless Talleyrand wanted to set him up financially and had asked Alexander, who owed him a favour for spying on Napoleon, to arrange the match. Alexander duly informed Dorothée's mother that the girl was to marry Périgord. She bridled, but he said that he had given Talleyrand his word and insisted, referring to Izabela as 'a trouble-maker and a dangerous old Polish woman'. He broke down the mother's resistance by blackmailing her financially, which the daughter called 'a revolting abuse of his position'. Dorothée stood firm in the face of arguments and threats, and it was only when, having been perfidiously misled by Batowski, Piattoli wrote saying he had heard Adam Jerzy was to marry Zosia Matuszewicz, that she gave in. When she met her husband to be it was with tears in her eyes, saying she felt nothing for him, only to hear that he felt the same. They married in April 1809 but separated within three years. She would outlive him and make a life for herself throughout Europe under his title as the Duchess of Dino.[24]

Izabela was soon back at Puławy, arranging her collection in the Gothic House and was delighted with the way it was turning out. 'It's a real jewel,' she wrote to Adam Jerzy on 12 December.[25] She wished she could join her husband for his name day on Christmas Eve but could not face the journey; the weather was awful and she had a bad back, which would have made the jolting of the coach agony. 'My darling,' she wrote to him on 20 December, 'I wish I could pour my soul into this letter.'[26] He came to join her at Puławy in the spring, when Izabela's hopes for her country were allowed to soar again.

## 15

## War

I n April 1809, while Napoleon was pursuing the British army of Sir
John Moore in Spain, Austria invaded France's ally Bavaria and sent
30,000 men under Archduke Ferdinand into the Grand Duchy of
Warsaw. As he passed through Puławy on 13 April, he bade Adam do his
duty as an Austrian field marshal by calling out the nobility of Galicia
to fight for Austria. Adam pleaded illness and pointed out that nobody
would answer the call anyway. The archduke pressed on to Warsaw,
pushing back Poniatowski, who had tried to bar his way with the 14,000
men at his disposal. An Austrian colonel who had made camp nearby
invited himself to lunch, during which he told Izabela that they would
soon deal with Poniatowski and his 'canaille'. Izabela was delighted
when his daughter, who had gobbled her lunch, was sick on the stairs as
she left.[1] Whatever her misgivings about Napoleon, there could be no
doubt which side she was on.

While the Austrians occupied Warsaw, Poniatowski outflanked
them, forcing them to fall back in the autumn. Izabela noted with satisfaction that this time the archduke bypassed Puławy and, as she
informed Adam Jerzy, she had not felt so well for years, even if the
future looked more uncertain than ever.[2]

A Polish force pursuing the retreating Austrians reached Puławy,
and its commander, General Sokolnicki, held a torchlight parade in
front of the house. He read out a poem in honour of Adam and the
troops cheered him and Izabela, who held a ball for the officers afterwards. A few days later Poniatowski followed with the main body of his

army and made camp nearby. The next morning he set off with a body of troops to salute Izabela and her husband. He had already sent an officer to Puławy to take Adam's surrender as a prisoner of war, choosing for the task Major Józef Szumlański, who had been captured by the Austrians on his way back from Egypt, where he had served under Bonaparte, and been freed at Adam's intercession.

Not to be outdone in theatricals, Izabela set off to meet Poniatowski, accompanied by her husband in Austrian field marshal's uniform, Szumlański riding at his side bearing the sword he had accepted as a mark of surrender. They were preceded by twelve boys in the armour of the seventeenth-century Polish winged hussars mounted on fine horses, and others in traditional Polish dress brandishing the swords and batons of command of past military heroes, along with standards captured from Swedes, Russians and Turks. Behind these came a dozen maidens bearing royal relics. Izabela herself clutched the key to the Temple, and after the troops had paraded before her, she took the officers around it, firing up their patriotic ardour with her tales of Poland's glorious past. She then got down to the more practical matter of feeding the troops and setting up a field hospital for the wounded in one of the outbuildings, and tending to them herself.

Poniatowski pursued the archduke into Galicia, which rose up against the Austrians. Konstanty raised an infantry regiment at his own cost. Zofia's husband, who had left Vienna and seized the fortress of Zamość from the Austrians, did likewise, fitting out 4,000 men. Having liberated Galicia, Poniatowski nominated him provisional governor of the province.

Following his victory at Wagram, Napoleon imposed a peace on Austria in October 1809 which stripped her of possessions in favour of France, Bavaria and even Russia, but only allowed the Poles to keep a fraction of the territory they had liberated. This increased the size of the Grand Duchy by over 50 per cent and its population from two and a half to just over four million. But although Puławy and Kraków were now in Polish hands, the area around Sieniawa and the city of Lwów were handed back to Austria, which meant that Izabela and her husband were separated by a frontier.

As she struggled with the difficulties of managing Puławy in wartime conditions, she was cheered by the arrival of Zofia, who had been hounded out of Vienna following her husband's rebellion against Austria. He had been given the position of *Geheimrat*, or privy councillor, and she that of *dame du palais*, so his defection was viewed as particularly insulting. Zamość and their main estate were now in the Grand Duchy, so their life in Vienna was over. Zofia was followed by four of her children, who had travelled back from Paris, where they had been at school, packed tightly into a carriage up to their necks in hay against the cold.

Marianna also had to change her habits, having been used to spending her winters in Vienna, which was no longer an option given the hostility of Viennese society. Konstanty, who had also enjoyed spending time in Vienna, now divided his time between Warsaw, his estate at Międzyrzecz and Marianna's Gruszczyn, drawn there by Cecylia Beydale, who had grown into a beautiful girl, a good pianist and a dashing horsewoman, and the flirtatious Maria Dzierżanowska.

Adam Jerzy was in an awkward position, given that he was still a Russian subject in the tsar's service living at Puławy, now in the Grand Duchy, an outpost of Napoleon's empire. Russia and France were allies, but he was aware that Alexander was preparing for a decisive confrontation with Napoleon in which he hoped to involve the Poles, the Prussians and most of Germany, and repeatedly asked Adam Jerzy to investigate how to engage the Poles on his side. Adam Jerzy told him that he had missed his chance; what freedom the Poles were enjoying they had received from Napoleon and they would not turn against him on vague prospects no more solid than those Alexander had dangled before them in 1805. Alexander nevertheless continued massing a large army on the eastern border of the Grand Duchy in preparation.[3]

Izabela complained she was passing sleepless nights worrying about Adam's predicament, fearing he might find himself in the position of being seen by his countrymen as an agent of a foreign power. He kept begging Alexander to release him from his service, arguing that he wanted to settle down at Puławy and marry, a desire Izabela approved of. 'But the difficulty lies in finding that wife for you and daughter-in-law for me,' she wrote disingenuously in August 1809; she had long ago found one in her beloved Zosia.[4]

Izabela was growing despotic with age, not hesitating to impose her views. When someone suggested a husband for Cecylia, she dismissed the suggestion as absurd. She chided Stanisław Zamoyski for sending his sons to Paris for their education, maintaining that it would produce polite people but poor Poles, and dismissed his argument that if left in Poland they would be flattered and spoilt. At one dinner early in 1810, she ticked off some young officers for their bad manners. In a letter to Adam Jerzy, she boasted that when at a lunch in Warsaw attended by a number of foreigners she heard one Pole make deprecating remarks about the Polish language, 'as a good citizen I ranted so loud I almost ran out of breath'.[5]

She kept herself busy, making trips to Kraków and Warsaw, where she spent the first three months of 1810 with Konstanty and Zofia, who gave birth to her eighth child on 23 January. She liked to be present when her children or friends were giving birth, and even when this was not possible she was solicitous and prolix with advice and instructions on diet and exercise while breast-feeding – in this case advising Zofia against riding a horse.

Konstanty's widowhood, good looks and gallantry during the war with Austria won many hearts, and on 9 March Izabela proudly reported to Marianna that he was greatly in demand Warsaw's drawing rooms for his singing voice. This is intriguing as family history has him running off with Marianna's protégée Maria Dzierżanowska to Vienna where, according to all genealogies, they were secretly married on 20 March. He is then said to have kept away from Izabela for the next couple of years to avoid her disapproval by travelling abroad.[6]

This is improbable: an Austrian subject who had raised a regiment to fight against his sovereign would not have been comfortable in Vienna a mere five months after the conclusion of peace, even if he had managed to obtain a passport to travel there. It is also not possible: from Izabela's correspondence it is clear that he was in Warsaw, where at the end of March he and Zofia were joined by Marianna and her two charges, Cecylia Beydale and Maria Dzierżanowska, and in a letter dated 3 April from Puławy, where she had returned, Izabela asks Marianna to thank Konstanty for his charming letter.[7] What *is* true is that in early May Konstanty made Maria Dzierżanowska pregnant with a child who would be born on 7 February 1811.

Izabela was aware of her younger son's flirtatious nature but would not have seen him in the company of Maria Dzierżanowska, as Marianna did not bring her to Puławy, so there is no reason to suppose that she knew anything of these goings-on. Her attitude to Konstanty was not affected in any way or noticeable in their letters. Nor did he keep away from her or travel abroad during this period.

The King of Saxony, who was also Grand Duke of Warsaw, was making progress through the territory recovered from Austria, and Izabela was not best pleased on being informed he intended to stay at Puławy on his way to Warsaw. Although she could not resist the compulsion to plan new walks, build a bridge to the Kępa and plant more trees on it, she was beset by material worries. The repeated passage of troops in the previous year had denuded the countryside of victuals and, what was worse, livestock and seed. Exceptional taxes were being levied to pay for the war, and in a letter to Adam Jerzy on 28 April 1810 she complained that 'money is beginning to run out'. 'Things have never been so thin,' she added, asking him whether he could find his way to borrowing some.[8]

She did not even know how she should dress to receive the king – she asked Marianna to consult Helena Radziwiłł, adding that she did not like the idea of dressing up for a German. She had plenty of other things on her mind, and she had cut her finger while pruning young trees in the park. But they could not refuse to receive him and she asked Konstanty to come and support her. 'As he was making a detour in order to give us this mark of particular favour, I wished to show my gratitude by the care I took in receiving him,' she explained. She picked out the best pieces of furniture for the queen's bedroom. As she knew her to be pious, she included a prie-dieu and 'a superb painting of the Virgin', and filled the room with flowers. But when the queen's ladies-in-waiting arrived they moved it all out – furniture, pictures and flowers – replacing them with an austere steel bed, '*chaises de commodité* and all the things necessary for the functions of nature'.[9]

Frederick Augustus greeted Izabela warmly and embraced her husband. As one of his diplomats observed, his Saxon subjects disapproved of his 'instinctive predilection' for the Poles, and resented the fact that he had sent Stanisław Zamoyski rather than one of them to Paris to represent him at Napoleon's wedding to Marie-Louise (Napoleon greeted him with particular warmth, to annoy the Austrians present, who regarded him as a traitor for his behaviour the previous year).[10]

The king insisted on dining alone with Adam, the queen dined with Izabela, and the remainder of their court, some sixty people, sat down with the rest of the household. Izabela did her best to entertain the king, giving him a tour of the gardens and the Temple, but both she and her husband were put off by the stiff Saxon etiquette and felt that when staying in a private house he should have dined with all the guests. They compared him unfavourably with Alexander and disliked having to settle on this man as their sovereign by the grace of Napoleon. The king nevertheless seemed content with his stay and when it was time to leave he handed out presents to the staff before boarding the elaborately festooned ferry to cross the river. One of the courtiers then asked how much they owed per head for the food and wine. 'These Germans are not like us Poles,' Izabela reflected.[11]

She and her husband followed the royal party to Warsaw, where, according to the Saxon minister Count Senfft von Pilsach, 'the presence of the princess was like a celebration in which society eagerly paid the homage due to the outstanding grace of her mind and the superiority of her personality'.[12] But her mind was occupied by more than just shining in society. She helped Zofia, who was collecting money for the poor, which was particularly difficult as the country was suffering from a dearth of specie. And as she had always been interested in the education of young women, Izabela joined Marianna and other ladies in drawing up a curriculum for girls' schools and inspecting those in Warsaw. Izabela took an interest in Marianna's literary ventures; she was about to start work on a novel and held a literary salon on Saturdays.

After the king's return to Dresden, Izabela went back to Puławy, where she would spend the summer alone, her husband having gone to Sieniawa. 'I feel as though I were breathing in happiness and health here,' she wrote to Marianna on 13 June. 'God is very, very, very good to grant me such happiness.' This would not last. At the beginning of August there was a heatwave, so she only went out at dawn or at night. 'I find myself in a vast solitude, with many memories and few hopes,' she wrote to Marianna. In another letter she reflected that she was not suited to such solitude. 'I feel that at my age, with my heart, on leaving my room I need to meet someone I love. This isolation gives me a kind of anxiety concerning all those who are not here.' That, she explains, is why she was so desperate to receive even the shortest of letters. Konstanty suggested she write a novel, presumably hoping that would occupy her, and she did begin planning one, based on an old soldier going on a sentimental journey through Poland, in the manner of Laurence Sterne.[13]

She was in fact never quite alone, and her day, as she described it to Marianna, was hardly monastic. It began with her taking coffee in her garden, then she would set off to the town on some errand and to Zulinki to inspect the farm, going back to the house to give Zosia a lesson, then she might while away an hour or so playing old dance tunes from memory on her clavichord, catalogue her collections, and have dinner, followed by another lesson with Zosia, then a long walk, tea, then supper, after which she would enjoy the moonlight out in her buggy or on a boat. She visited her husband at Sieniawa and Marianna at Gruszczyn, where they were joined by Konstanty and Zofia, and she went to Warsaw for the carnival early in 1811, which was far from brilliant, as everyone was suffering from the financial crisis, and even the Queen of Saxony wore an old dress which had seen better days judging by the stains on it.[14]

Back at Puławy that summer Izabela once again gave vent to feelings of loneliness and frustration, which, now that she was in her mid-sixties, probably had more to do with anxieties over the future of her country and her family, and a general sense of impermanence. 'I confess that the thought which recurs most often in these daydreams is about Master Adam and the ardent wish I have that God would inspire him to marry during my lifetime and that of my husband,' she wrote to Marianna, explaining that she believed an unmarried person would always live without a purpose. And that was not the only consideration. 'It is a bitter thought that I shall take to my grave that the name under which I have been so happy in so many ways, the name of a family whose unblemished reputation is universally known, that this name I have borne will die out with us.' Both she and her husband worried that Konstanty's son Adam was too frail to carry on the line.[15]

She joined him at Sieniawa before Christmas and was worried at the numbers of people who had announced they would come to celebrate his name day on 24 December, as there was little money. Adam Jerzy had come to stay and they ushered in the year 1812 with a New Year's Eve party enlivened by *tableaux vivants* in the drawing room decorated with greenery, followed by a tour of neighbours' houses. In the spring she returned to Puławy, which was looking glorious as the trees had come into leaf and the fruit trees were bearing blossom. But the previous two harvests had been poor and the peasants were looking skeletal. They could not afford seeds for planting, so Izabela persuaded Adam Jerzy to buy some for them and distributed money to the worst affected. She gave them the wheat she had bought for sowing her own land so they could bake bread.[16] Things would only get worse.

Exasperated by Alexander's failure to act in the spirit of the Treaties of Tilsit, Napoleon resolved to intimidate him into compliance by a show of force. In the early months of 1812 a huge army, drawn from every corner of his empire, began to assemble in Prussia and the Grand Duchy, and Puławy was soon crawling with Saxon troops looting the local peasants, getting drunk and molesting their women. Their commander, General Reynier, restored order and posted guards to protect the house. But Izabela begged her husband to obtain a passport for her and send 'a male being' to escort her and her girls, and on 27 April she set off with them for Sieniawa.[17]

Warsaw was full of Westphalian troops under the command of their king, Napoleon's younger brother Jérôme. He was married to Ludwig's niece, Trinette, whom Izabela had befriended at Montbéliard, so on arriving in Warsaw he called on Marianna and Zofia. Ever hopeful and unaware that Napoleon considered Jérôme an idiot, Izabela urged them to persuade him of the necessity of restoring the Kingdom of Poland. She was exasperated by the fact that her health did not allow her to play an active role herself and resigned herself to 'hope for something good in the end, because God is just and must reward us'.[18]

At the end of May, Napoleon met Tadeusz Matuszewicz in Poznań and told him the Poles should rise up and raise an army to fight alongside him against Russia and reclaim their former lands. He suggested they should elect Izabela's husband to lead them. At Puławy, Izabela was making preparations as she had been warned that Napoleon might be passing through. 'I even sent to Lublin for a dress, as I cannot very well show myself in tatters,' she wrote to Adam Jerzy.[19]

Napoleon did not come to Puławy. He even avoided Warsaw. But the hopes he aroused were enough to galvanise many Poles, and at over 90,000 men they made up the largest non-French contingent of the army he would lead to its doom. 'Everyone is agreed that [the war] will not last long,' Izabela wrote to Adam Jerzy. 'God grant it ends happily.'[20]

Adam was persuaded to stand for the Sejm and arrived in Warsaw with Izabela for the election in mid-June. The Blue Palace, which had been bought by Stanisław Zamoyski the previous year, throbbed with life once more, but money was so scarce that the fare was simple. At the receptions for as many as 200 supporters, Izabela served only tea, barley water and some pastries. Dinners were no more sumptuous, yet Izabela complained she would soon run out of money altogether, and that year had to let go twenty-six of her staff. But she was happy to see Adam fêted and cheered, and the pleasure it gave him. 'Every day of my life I have been happy to belong to you and my heart is full of you,' she wrote to him. Napoleon's foreign minister, the duc de Bassano, went out of his way to cultivate her, and having heard of her collecting gave her a gold watch which Henri IV had given to Gabrielle d'Estrées.[21]

Warsaw had come to life and the French Resident Baron Édouard Bignon pronounced the social life as elegant as that of the Faubourg Saint-Germain. 'Renowned in her day for her charms and her wit, the princess Czartoryska had preserved all the attractions of her mind, and I was very sorry that she only made a short stay in Warsaw,' he wrote, and would later visit her at Puławy, which he described 'le Versailles de la Pologne.'[22]

Adam Jerzy's position was more difficult than ever, and he repeatedly wrote to the tsar begging to be relieved of his duties. His father wanted him to come and join the national movement, but Izabela understood that he could not do so without betraying Alexander. Anticipating that a call would soon be made for all good Poles to come forward and his failure to do so would place him in a bad light in the eyes of his coun-trymen, she urged him to disappear from public view while she did her best to justify him in the eyes of the French diplomats in Warsaw.

The Sejm convened on 26 June, and Izabela's husband was elected marshal, as he had been fifty years earlier. At a banquet following the first session, a despatch from Napoleon was read out, in which he announced that on 24 June he had crossed the River Niemen and invaded the Russian Empire. 'My heart beats for Poland and for Konstanty,' Izabela wrote to Adam Jerzy in a paroxysm of excitement. The Sejm assembled in the same chamber with herself and her daughters in the same gallery as in 1788, showering the deputies with ribbons in the national colours of azure and amaranth to wear on their sleeves. Helena Radziwiłł felt they were overdoing it a little.[23]

On 28 June the Sejm transformed itself into the General Confederation of the Kingdom of Poland. 'The word has been uttered and Poland exists!' Izabela wrote to Adam Jerzy. 'My God, my God, You have given us back our Motherland, and my ears have heard those words which are forever graven on my heart, Poland lives, Poland exists!' Her husband's impromptu speech reduced the deputies to tears, the streets around the castle rang to shouts of 'Poland lives again! Poland has risen up!' 'Forty years of misfortune wiped out, and a future left to our future generations,' Izabela wrote, but she had her doubts.[24]

'The Princess had lived too long, she had experienced too many extraordinary events to share with complete confidence the illusions to which younger imaginations were abandoning themselves,' observed Bignon. Another Frenchman, Achille de Broglie, observed that although 'the old princess Czartoryska and her two daughters, the princess of Württemberg and countess Zamoyska, renowned in France and England for her beauty, acted as the hostesses of the Diet, with much grace and amiability', they were not convinced things would work out well.[25]

Adam's role was largely titular, and the work devolved on the council constituted by the confederated Sejm, headed by Matuszewicz, in which Stanisław Potocki, Zamoyski and other Czartoryski associates also sat. He soon retired to Sieniawa, from where he continued to fulfil the formalities. Izabela remained in Warsaw, hosting balls and dinners with her two daughters and did not go home to Puławy until 8 August. A week later, she was celebrating Marianna's name day with ball games, blind man's buff, skittles and dancing.

Three weeks later she announced to Adam Jerzy that Konstanty had been wounded at the capture of Smolensk. 'I cannot describe every-thing, as I am trembling all over,' she wrote. 'My son has paid his debt to the Motherland, the blood flowing in his veins inspired the courage of a real Pole.' His wound was not grave, and Napoleon himself had decorated him with the Legion of Honour.[26]

There was bad news as well; while Napoleon was marching on Moscow, further south marauding detachments of Cossacks were ravaging estates belonging to various members of the family, and the Austrian contingent in the Grande Armée, commanded by Prince Schwarzenberg, was requisitioning men, horses, carts and victuals. But such worries could not dent Izabela's natural optimism.

On 25 September she noted down that she had never felt happier. The weather was fine and Puławy was at its best, showing the first tinges of autumn. She spent the day walking around the gardens and inspecting new planting, her heart filled with joy at the thought that Poland was to be reborn.[27] That same day in Moscow, Napoleon, too, was enjoying the unseasonably fine weather and shrugging off warnings of the perils that would accompany the approach of winter. He lingered too long, and when he did begin his march back to Poland nearly a month later, it quickly turned into a disastrous retreat in which he lost his army. Its remnants trudged back across the Niemen in the first week of December.

As Russian troops approached the border of the Grand Duchy on their heels, Adam Jerzy wrote to Alexander urging him to implement his old plan of declaring himself king of Poland.[28] Alexander issued a proclamation to the Poles promising to rebuild their kingdom and tried to persuade Poniatowski to bring the remains of the Polish army over to his side. But his appeal came too late. As the Russians advanced and all other elements of the Grande Armée continued to retreat, Poniatowski and the government fell back on Kraków.

Zofia had moved there from Warsaw in January 1813, to be joined by Izabela and Marianna, who had left Puławy in a cart drawn by oxen since the various armies had requisitioned every available horse. Other members of the family and household also congregated in Kraków. When Konstanty turned up the servants refused to let him in; he was unrecognizable in the remains of his uniform, a peasant's sheepskin cap and a woman's pelisse, his feet wrapped in rags.[29] He had recovered from his wound at Smolensk but at Borodino his horse took a cannon-ball full in the chest and he suffered severe concussion. The rigours of the retreat had also told on him and he looked like a ghost.

Izabela waited in Kraków with Marianna, Cecylia, Zofia and Konstanty, unsure what to do next. The situation was chaotic and dangerous; there were troops on the move, provisioning themselves at will and sowing chaos, as well as deserters and stragglers looting wherever they could. Reports circulated of estates belonging to those who had taken part in the invasion of Russia being confiscated. Creditors were circling. The Austrian authorities were levying draconian taxes to pay for a huge increase in their army and sequestering estates of those who could not pay. 'They begin by taking the grains, then the horses and the cattle, and eventually the furniture and anything else they come across,' Izabela wrote to Adam Jerzy in March.[30] They communicated by letters bristling with code and nicknames, often entrusted to passing friends rather than the post. Those that were sent by regular channels showed signs of uninhibited opening.

Izabela's fears for the future of Poland overshadowed anxieties about shortage of cash and the possibility of losing her property. The Grand Duchy was unlikely to survive, but the whole of it was now in the hands of Alexander, who had so often expressed the wish to restore Poland. He had summoned Adam Jerzy to Warsaw, instructing him to help the military governor General Lanskoy restore order and together with Novosiltsev set up a provisional administration. He had written that his feelings for him and his country had not changed, that he could think of nothing he wanted more than to stay with the family at Puławy when the war was over, and that he was still his 'in heart and soul'.[31]

Adam Jerzy knew the tsar too well not to anticipate many a change of mind ahead and feared the influence of Alexander's entourage. His own relationship with Novosiltsev had soured, while not all Poles could be counted on to fall in with his views. At Sieniawa, where she had joined her husband, Izabela read the letter, which he had forwarded, over and again. She admired the tsar's magnanimity, yet no longer dared believe in its promise. 'No, hope has died in my heart,' she wrote back on 23 February 1813. 'Thirty years of misfortunes of all kinds. Every moment in which one could see some kind of ray of happiness, always dashed. Besides which, only ruins, misfortunes, loss, always struggling against a kind of hatred on the part of the Germans, always threatened, always misunderstood. Oh, my dear friend, I repeat that I do not hope for anything. I can see that the Emperor wishes us well, but so many people are ill-disposed to this Poland, to this Motherland which, as you know, is for me the most important thing. [. . .] It is as though the Heavens and Destiny were against us.' She had wept over the passage in Alexander's letter in which he wrote that he would dearly love to be with them at Puławy, but lamented that they could not possibly receive him in their present bereft and miserable state.[32] She could not even go there herself, as fresh levies were on the march from Russia to join the allied forces in Germany and alarming tales of their behaviour reached Sieniawa.

She found solace sitting out in the garden in what was turning into a beautiful early spring. On 5 April she organized a party for her husband's birthday in the course of which 'the ladies, grown and small, acted out a little play'. On 17 April a Cossack rode up with the message that Alexander's sister, the strong-minded Grand Duchess Catherine, widow of the Duke of Oldenburg, was due at Łańcut, and since Elżbieta Lubomirska was in Vienna, Izabela must receive her there. She was nervous as she hurried over but her apprehensions were dispelled at once when the Grand Duchess declared herself delighted to meet the mother of Adam Jerzy, and they 'chatted really like old friends'.[33]

She was back at Sieniawa for Easter. Not long after, Marianna turned up from Kraków. Zofia was ill and longed to come, too, but the Austrians refused her request for a passport and when she tried to leave she was stopped at the city gate and turned back. She received notification from Vienna that as a traitor to the Habsburg monarchy she would not be allowed to set foot on Austrian soil as long as she lived. Her husband was in Prague while four of her children were travelling back from Paris through areas swarming with troops of all nationalities. Surprisingly, Konstanty did obtain permission to visit his parents at Sieniawa in May. He was recovering from his wounds and hoped to follow Poniatowski, who had marched his army westwards to join Napoleon in Saxony.

In mid-May the first confused reports of Napoleon's victory at Lützen reached Sieniawa. He had mustered new forces and marched back into

Saxony, determined to reimpose his hegemony over Central Europe. After a second victory over the Russians and Prussians at Bautzen, it looked as though French garrisons which were still holding out, as at nearby Zamość, would be relieved and the Grand Duchy or some other Napoleonic Poland might be restored.

Izabela found the uncertainties draining. 'My head is splitting,' she wrote to Adam Jerzy, complaining that nobody knew what was happening. Reports of property being sequestered or confiscated kept reaching her, and she was determined to go home to Puławy, fearing it might be for the last time: 'As only God knows whom it will belong to!'[34]

# 16

~⌐〇 〇⌐~

## *The Tsar's Promise*

Izabela was back home in July 1813. 'Never has Puławy been as beautiful as this year,' she wrote to Adam Jerzy. Heavy rains had produced
'supernatural' vegetation. 'The good, the excellent Savage', who had not
been paid for lack of funds, had used his own money to tend the gardens. Unfortunately, in an excess of zeal he had planted a 'cacophony' of
roses, poppies, lilies and other plants together. Although the effect was
ghastly she had not the heart to say anything.[1]

Her delight at being back at home was short-lived, and the peace she
craved would elude her over the next two years. She was soon complaining of having 'all the nations of Asia' trudging past as columns of
troops drawn from every corner of the Russian Empire passed through
on their way to reinforce the army fighting Napoleon in Germany. This
prompted requests from her husband to find out more about the
Bashkirs and Kalmuks, whose literature and culture interested him. She
promised to question a Bashkir if she could catch one but informed
him the Kalmuks were not interested in literature, only in their horses,
so she acquired one and sent that to Sieniawa. But her playfulness did
not reflect the reality.[2]

Alexander had ordered the Russian commander General Bennigsen
to safeguard Puławy and Podzamcze, but the surrounding countryside
was devastated. Not only did the troops requisition victuals, they took
cattle, depriving the inhabitants of oxen to pull their ploughs and of the
cows which fed them with milk, butter and cheese, and forced them to
work on a bridge they were building, leaving nobody to bring in the

harvest, and commandeered all the carts, which meant the harvest could not be brought in when they could get around to it. And as the troops were billeted on the peasants, up to six in their small cottages, they spread the typhus which was sweeping through from the east. Izabela did what she could to alleviate the suffering, but her means were limited, as the authorities ordered the collection of the next four years' taxes in advance. This entailed further reductions in staff levels, and another seventeen were taken off the payroll – which did little to help, as the budget was weighed down by swelling numbers of pensioners. The accounts for 1814 show the staff reduced to fifty-one, less than half that in 1808, but list no fewer than fifty-seven pensioners, including widows, children and handicapped former servants. In 1815 the seventeen pensioners in the Sieniawa accounts included children of *frotteurs*, a blind man, several poor Jews, a beggar and a number of 'cripples' in hospital.[3]

Although calculations of its value differ, Adam's estate was still huge when, in 1812, he divided it up among his four children, keeping only Sieniawa for himself. It was also heavily loaded with debt, of over half its value according to some sources. And it was lumbered with obligations of one sort or another, as both Adam and Izabela had insisted on granting pensions to retiring staff and making endowments. These and the interest on the debt ate into the income, already reduced by poor harvests and wartime depredation.

Izabela managed to keep her spirits up. The herbal baths prescribed by Dr Khittel made her feel better despite the sweltering heat of that August. As soon as that subsided she resumed her routine of long walks followed by writing, schooling Zosia and having dinner and supper in a different spot outside. She remained at Puławy partly to mitigate the damage caused by the passing troops and partly because she felt so well there. Adam Jerzy came down and joined her in managing the estate for six weeks, allowing her to devote more time to the curriculum of her school in the village of Włostowice and setting up a choir with the help of Lessel. She instituted prizes for the inhabitants of the villages on the estate and the town of Puławy; a cow for the tidiest yard, a heifer for planting the most trees in clumps on hillocks, and so on. She may have been motivated by aesthetics, but she believed such things enhanced the environment, and was keen to help people by every means. When she heard complaints that the inhabitants of a nearby village were being unfairly taxed by an overzealous official, she insisted her son do something about it 'You know that in my heart I am always on the side of the peasants,' she wrote.[4]

She was by now desperate to see him married, and had convinced herself that Zosia, from whom she could not bear to be parted, would make the perfect wife. Now 15 years old, she was pretty, charming, vivacious and much admired – the tsar often picked her as a dancing partner at balls. Adam Jerzy found her attractive but feared that, surrounded by love and admiration from her childhood and spoilt for attention, she might not be the best companion for him.

He was still in love with the Empress Elizabeth, whose relationship with Alexander had disintegrated. As soon as the retreat of Napoleon's armies made it possible, she went to stay with her family in Baden, contemplating the possibility of a separation. She was in contact with Adam Jerzy and although her letters have not survived, their contents gave him hope.

In mid-October Izabela left Puławy in his care and went to join her husband at Sieniawa. She was happy to be with him again and delighted when Konstanty came to stay and Marianna came over from her nearby estate at Wysock. But only two weeks later they heard news of Poniatowski's death at the Battle of Leipzig. For days Izabela and her husband clung to the hope it might prove untrue, but when it was confirmed she gave way to despair. 'I have fits of hatred which I never experienced before,' she wrote to Adam Jerzy and her mood was not improved when she heard that Dominik Radziwiłł, who had been an aide-de-camp to Napoleon, had died of typhus after the Battle of Hanau, aged 26.[5]

Adam Jerzy was debating whether to join the tsar at the allies' headquarters in Germany, fearing he might be manipulated by others in his absence, yet aware that his presence might be counterproductive. Izabela begged him not to go. Although she believed in Alexander, she had grown fatalistic about his ability to achieve anything for her country and feared for her son's mental health as well as the typhus.

As a distraction from gloomy thoughts, she applied herself to broadening her mind; 'over the past few months I have read an entire library and written volumes,' she informed Adam Jerzy. Her 'most faithful companion' Papuzia the parrot perched on her writing table and chattered at her while Szczur, now too old to accompany her on walks, lay at her feet. She compiled textbooks for her village schools: a catechism for children, a collection of fairy tales and a set of health tips, cures and warnings for their parents. She was by no means fluent in German, but 'by the sweat of her brow' she managed to translate books by the Swiss educational reformer Johann Heinrich Pestalozzi and produce a version of Goethe's *Leonhard und Dorothea* adapted for children. At Adam Jerzy's suggestion she also worked on 'a very concise reduction of the history of Poland'.[6]

As she pondered how to construct this, she fell back on the idea she had previously entertained of writing an old soldier's sentimental journey through Poland. The soldier had now become a pilgrim, who, passing through a village, has to pause there because the wounds he received in battle have opened up. To pay for his keep he gathers the children together every evening and tells the country's history, chapter by chapter. 'Each evening story is short,' she explained. 'The following day's begins with questions and answers about the previous evening's. I have some idea that I may be able to mix in some songs, but I am not sure [she had been collecting folk songs]. I think this genre will work, as it is amusing.' In order to capture the attention of the children and excite their imagination, she inserted an element of 'the marvellous' into the early chapters.[7]

Christmas festivities at Sieniawa were muted that year, as a result of penury as much as political uncertainly. None of her children were there, only Zosia and her friend, Mrs Nevill's daughter Lila. 'In the evening my husband plays billiards and we vegetate on the sofa,' Izabela wrote to Adam Jerzy. In January 1814 she went to Kraków to see Zofia who was still stuck there with her children. She found her in poor health and her children charming but 'poorly managed'. 'They need a sensible and firm mentor,' she decided, as Zofia could not be expected to handle eight children, and 'loses her head', and she was relieved to hear that Stanisław had engaged a Swiss pastor.[8]

She took advantage of her stay in Kraków to collect some antiques and new publications, to visit the botanical gardens, a cabinet of natural history and to attend lectures at the academy. But she was reminded of harsh realities by news that there was a possibility of their lands in the Grand Duchy being sequestered for non-payment of taxes, and wrote to Adam Jerzy begging him to at least ensure the house and park at Puławy were exempted if the worst came to happen. 'If they ruin that I shall spend the rest of my life in tears,' she pleaded.[9]

Disregarding her entreaties, Adam Jerzy had decided to join Alexander at the headquarters of the allied forces, where the Austrian Chancellor Metternich, his Prussian counterpart Baron Hardenberg and the British foreign secretary Lord Castlereagh were deciding the future of Europe. As she could not stop him, Izabela pleaded with him to take precautions against the typhus, by eating oranges and drinking vodka and wine, and taking along plenty of vinegar and salt to purify the air in the rooms of inns he would be staying at by sprinkling them on a hot brick. She recommended pharmacies in Warsaw that stocked the best emetics to take when he felt the slightest symptoms, begging him not to mock her 'old woman's' fears and advice. 'You can have no idea of what my heart feels for you, you are unique in your way, there is nobody on earth like you.'[10]

'I spend my days in my room, forever anxious lest the next day bring some fresh misfortune,' she wrote. Their estates were seemingly safe, but the Austrians were recruiting so many men that there were none left to work the fields. She did not particularly enjoy being at Sieniawa – 'not a happy place, sandy, the house uncomfortable, the outbuildings poor, the rooms cold, the furniture broken, the fireplaces smoky' – but she had made her little room comfortable and there was a small enclosure outside her window with cows, chickens, rabbits and pigeons. Her husband was well, considering his seventy-nine years, but he was frustrated by no longer being able to read and had lost his habitual gaiety, which alarmed her, as she could not imagine life without him; her longing for his companionship pervades every letter she wrote when they were apart.[11]

Some of the uncertainty was lifted by news of Napoleon's abdication on 6 April 1814. Two weeks later he set off for the Island of Elba which he had been given to rule. The victorious allies signed a treaty with France and before going home agreed to reconvene at Vienna in the autumn to reorder Europe. This revived Izabela's hopes that 'the wonderful deputy of the Gods on earth' would restore her country and with it her happiness. But the odds were against him; Alexander was determined to recreate a Polish state, but he could only make that palatable to his own people if it remained a Russian satellite, with himself as king. Britain, France and Austria could accept an independent Poland but saw Alexander's proposal as an unacceptable westward extension of Russian power. And Prussia would only give up her pretensions to Polish territory if compensated elsewhere.

The end of hostilities meant that Izabela could go back to Puławy, where she was joined by her daughters and Konstanty, as well as Cecylia, and it seemed as though they could recover some of the pleasures of old times. They went for long walks and picked wild strawberries. On 4 July Zosia recorded in her diary that they had gone to have tea in a peasant's cottage at Włostowice and while they were there an old beggar had turned up with a hurdy-gurdy which he started playing in the yard. 'The country girls began to dance, we joined in, and no ball has ever given me so much fun.' Yet the peace Izabela longed for was disturbed by the stream of Russian troops now returning from France, whose generals insisted on staying at the house.[12]

At the beginning of September she heard that Alexander would be passing through on his way to Vienna. The house had been denuded and supplies eaten up by the passage of troops and she was short of funds, but she set to work with her two daughters and Zosia preparing for his stay, a task made no easier as, hearing of Alexander's impending arrival, Antoni and Helena Radziwiłł, Tadeusz Matuszewicz and many others began arriving and needed to be put up. Her husband had considered it politic to remain in Sieniawa.

Alexander arrived at Międzyrzecz on 19 September and dispelled Konstanty's apprehensions. 'We have been in opposite camps but we have never been enemies,' he said as he embraced him. 'I have always liked and esteemed you, but I esteem you all the more since you have fought for your Motherland. I regard that as the most sacred of duties.' He asked Konstanty to become an aide-de-camp without duties, 'not as a monarch, but as a brother, as a friend'. They were joined by Novosiltsev and Field Marshal Barclay de Tolly, and the next day drove to Puławy.[13]

'I am glad to be back at Puławy,' he declared on arrival, kissing

Izabela's hand, 'I feel as if I were *en famille*.' He embraced Marianna and Zofia, and, seeing her husband, who had also been on Napoleon's side, greeted him warmly. Addressing Izabela as '*Maman*', he assured her that he admired the Poles for having fought for their cause in 1812 and would do everything in his power on their behalf. 'Now my principal aim is to re-establish Poland,' he said, adding that it would not be easy.[14]

Between conferences with Adam Jerzy, Novosiltsev and Barclay de Tolly, he chatted with the ladies and joined the company at lunch and dinner, telling everyone to sit where they chose as they were all at home. To Marianna, whom he always addressed as '*Ma tante*', he unburdened himself on the subject of his love for his mistress, admitting that he felt 'the opposite of attraction' for his wife, and inviting sympathy for the guilt that tortured him. He spent the next morning with Izabela, dressed simply in a brown coat, walking around the grounds and her collections, and had lunch in her apartment, later joining the rest of the company. He announced that he would leave at two o'clock in the morning and bidding them goodnight at eleven said his farewells, begging them not to stay up to see him off. But when he came down at two o'clock, he was annoyed on finding nobody there. 'What!' he exclaimed, 'Nobody here, not even Prince Adam or Prince Konstanty?' He drove down to the ferry, where he was gratified to find the entire household gathered on the jetty. On parting, he gave each of the ladies a feather from his hat.[15]

His behaviour filled Izabela with hope, but her son was more doubtful. He attended the tsar throughout the Congress of Vienna, aware that his presence was inconvenient to all, and depressed by the role he had to play and by Alexander's inconsistency. He was also repelled by the immorality of the proceedings, both ideological and physical, and disgusted by the intrigues and bad behaviour of almost every participant, and found solace at the house of his aunt Elżbieta Lubomirska.

He does not record what he felt on meeting Dorothée, now Talleyrand's mistress (her sister, Wilhelmina, was being fought over by Alexander and Metternich). But there is plenty in his diary on his feelings for Elizabeth, which astonished him by their strength considering the passage of time and the fading of her physical charms since they had last seen each other. He pressed her to divorce Alexander, and tackled him on the subject. The tsar was not amenable, but before Elizabeth left Vienna in March 1815 she and Adam Jerzy made vows of some kind.

Izabela knew nothing of this, as he only confided in Marianna, and in Sieniawa where she spent the autumn of 1814 she prayed for her son's and Alexander's efforts on behalf of Poland. For the winter she moved to Warsaw, where she joined her daughters in their charitable work. Distressed by the sight of maimed soldiers and starving peasants who had congregated in the capital, filling the streets and begging for food, Zofia had expanded this. Along with Marianna, Cecylia, her husband's sister Anna Sapieha and other friends she founded a Benevolent Society. She converted an abandoned convent into a hospital and in addition to street-by-street collections, she began putting on amateur theatricals with herself, her children and other members of the family at the Blue Palace to raise funds, and soon the whole of Warsaw society and even the Russian generals stationed there joined in the charitable activities. 'You can have no idea how fashionable charity and devotion have become here,' Helena Radziwiłł wrote to her daughter-in-law. 'Madame Zamoyska and Princess Württemberg can only be seen prostrate in churches, ignoring society and the pleasures of this world.'[16]

Izabela was pleased to be back in town, noting that 'half of Warsaw' called as soon as news of her arrival was known, including all the senior Russian officers in town, from Barclay de Tolly down. Two days later as she sat in her knitted dressing gown, her hair in a mess, having a last cup of tea before going to bed, Grand Duke Constantine was announced and unceremoniously joined her in a cup.

The tsar's younger brother was a complicated character, explosively violent yet capable of feeling and occasionally of behaving honourably. Alexander had made him commander of the Polish army, against the advice of everyone who knew him; he was a martinet who held frequent parades which were balletic expressions of his sense of power aimed at humiliating the troops. He took a jaundiced view of Zofia's Benevolent Society, resenting any organization beyond state control, and forbade his officers from attending her fundraising events. This upset Izabela, who had rejoiced at the numbers of Russian officers who had been attending these and her own soirées, noting with satisfaction that 'the two nations are amalgamating'. But when he called on her that evening he stayed two hours drinking tea and was as charming as she could have wished, friendly yet respectful.[17]

On 5 April, he received a letter from Alexander announcing that the Great Powers at the Congress of Vienna had agreed to the restoration of a Kingdom of Poland with himself as king. This provoked jubilation, with people embracing in the street, even the Russians joining in. Izabela was exultant but remained anxious: a couple of weeks earlier, on 18 March, news of Napoleon's escape from Elba had reached Warsaw, which raised the possibility of a resumption of hostilities. Troops were once again marching westward through Poland and while Puławy was 'looking like a bouquet' when she returned there at the beginning of May, they had taken all the grain. The peasants were starving and there was no seed to sow.[18]

Another source of concern was that her husband wanted to go to Vienna to stay with his sister, and Izabela was worried the journey would kill him. 'My darling, you are everything to me, absolutely everything,' she wrote. 'Happiness, hopes, memories, joy, pleasure, health, all of it comes from you.' His physician Dr Goltz was against it too, but he was determined, and Izabela knew how much his sister meant to him. She sent detailed instructions as to diet and insisted he have someone with him at all times to prevent him falling.[19]

In September she went to Sieniawa to greet him on his return from Vienna. Zosia, without whom she never went anywhere, noted that Izabela was in a sour mood, making sarcastic and barbed comments even to her. The atmosphere only cleared with his arrival, when Izabela became serene and happy.

The reason for her ill-temper was probably that sometime that spring or summer Konstanty's liaison with Maria Dzierżanowska had come to light. She had borne him a son in 1811 but this had been kept quiet. The truth came out when, in 1815, Konstanty decided to move to Vienna, taking with him Dzierżanowska and his two sons. This came as a double shock, as Izabela and her husband had hoped the only one they knew about, Aniela Radziwiłł's, would be brought up in Poland under their eye. In a letter to Adam Jerzy probably late that summer, Izabela wrote that Dzierżanowska 'was created to embitter the last years of my life'.

'If at least she had a proper soul and heart. But' – the rest of the sentence is heavily inked over. At a later date, she explained that she could never forget what she had done at Sieniawa, without giving any clue as to what it was or when she did it.[20]

At the end of October 1815 Izabela was in Warsaw, which was full of people eager like her to greet Alexander on his return from Paris. 'Every heart went out to him who having pacified Europe was coming to wipe away our tears,' she wrote, and the news that he was due on 12 November prompted 'universal joy, bordering on delirium'. He rode into the city on a grey horse, dressed in Polish uniform, the crowds on either side cheering him as their new king, the houses decorated with carpets and flowers, schools and city corporations drawn up in bodies. Izabela was on a balcony on the Nowy Świat with her daughters and as he rode by he spotted them and raised his hat.[21]

The following evening, Alexander unexpectedly called on her as she was getting ready for bed, with Zofia and Marianna. They were unprepared and embarrassed, but he embraced each of them 'like a son and a brother'. He told Izabela that the previous day had been the most wonderful of his entire life, as he had at last been able to right some of the wrongs done to Poland by Russia. 'My dear friends, I regard you as my dearest friends and my family,' he went on as he sat down for a chat lasting an hour and a half. 'It would be difficult to find a more beautiful soul,' Izabela reflected afterwards.[22]

The next day, she opened the dancing with him at a ball given by General Lanskoy. At the ball given by the city of Warsaw, which Izabela had been delegated to host, Alexander led her in as the 1,500 guests hailed him as King of Poland. He responded by praising the Poles for having fought so valiantly for their country even against Russia. Izabela wept with joy as she opened the ball by dancing the polonaise with him. 'So I have a Motherland,' she said to herself, 'and I will leave one to my children.' Helena Radziwiłł could not repress an amusingly catty description of Izabela's attire on the occasion, which she saw as an attempt to cast herself as the heir to the Jagiellon dynasty. It consisted of a crimson velvet dress with hanging double sleeves in the Sarmatian style, with plenty of gold gauze and embroidery, and a sort of turban adorned with heron feathers, bejewelled with chains and brooches which, according to Helena, had been pillaged from the Temple. She admitted that the sight was striking, but felt it was inappropriate given Izabela's age.[23]

There were more balls, as well as dinners and other receptions. At Marianna's, Alexander danced until four in the morning. When it came to her turn, Izabela gave a children's ball, for which they were told to dress in allegorical costumes. She could hardly have done better, as Alexander loved playing with children, and he danced with a succession of juvenile spirits of glory, love, friendship, the various arts and so on late into the night.

He practically lived with what he liked to call his family. On 19 November he gave an intimate dinner for Izabela on her name day and stayed on, chatting for hours afterwards. He often came for an informal supper at the Blue Palace, which now belonged to Zofia's husband. When he presented their children to the tsar, he said: 'I have to warn Your Imperial Majesty that they were warm supporters of Napoleon,' to which Alexander replied: 'And who wasn't? I myself belonged to that number once.'[24]

Helena Radziwiłł felt that Izabela was again giving way to exaltation and overplaying the part of 'Mother of the Motherland'. But it is hard to blame her: she had placed her hopes in Alexander from the moment in 1797 when Adam Jerzy had told her of his friend's wishes to right the wrong of the partitions, and despite subsequent disappointments and Adam Jerzy's warnings about Alexander's weakness, she had held firm to her faith in him. He had vindicated her by re-creating a Kingdom of Poland with a liberal constitution written by her son, and had more than once said he would add to it the formerly Polish lands which had been incorporated into the Russian Empire. She could also not be blamed for feeling a profound satisfaction that Adam Jerzy's dedication had at last borne fruit and he would reap the reward he so richly deserved. Yet in this respect, she would be mortified by her idol.

17

# A Brave Face

Alexander had placed his brother Constantine in command of the Polish army and appointed Novosiltsev as his commissioner, but he had not yet named the person who was to be his lieutenant in the kingdom. Everyone assumed this paramount post would go to Adam Jerzy, with whom he had a long conference on his last evening in Warsaw. It was only after he left that it became known he had appointed not Adam Jerzy but General Józef Zajączek.

The news caused astonishment. Zajączek was a one-time Jacobin who had served under Napoleon from his Egyptian campaign in 1798 to the invasion of Russia in 1812, where he lost a leg defending the Berezina crossings. He tried to refuse, citing his age, wounds, deafness and lack of experience, but Alexander insisted. He had explained to Adam Jerzy he could not make him his lieutenant because it would lead to conflict with Grand Duke Constantine, and because it would be unacceptable to public opinion in Russia, which was opposed to the creation of the Kingdom of Poland and would view a Czartoryski in that post as a prelude to its independence.

Zajączek's nomination was well received in the army and democratic circles. Ironically, some identified Adam Jerzy with Russian policy and Zajączek with the more heroic patriotic tradition linked with Napoleon. Others were just pleased to see the Czartoryski family snubbed; according to Helena Radziwiłł, someone left a pile of manure at Izabela's door with a placard reading: 'The mother of the Motherland has miscarried'. Wiser heads realised Alexander's choice had been dictated by the need to have a more malleable lieutenant and a wish to free himself from promises he had made to Adam Jerzy.[1]

Writing to his father, Adam Jerzy admitted that this was one of the hardest to bear of the many breaches of faith he had experienced at the hands of Alexander, but he suppressed his feelings of bitterness and made the best of things. He had been given the post of minister without portfolio in the government and busied himself with administrative matters. He had also been appointed curator of Polish educational establishments now in western Russia, including the prestigious University of Wilno (Vilnius).

Izabela also put a brave face on it, explaining to her husband that 'the poor Emperor is in a very slippery position. The whole of Russia is against us. This hatred they bear for us is a hydra which shows itself in every quarter.' She did her utmost to cheer her husband by describing the ceremony at which the Senate swore allegiance to the constitution on 24 December, after Adam Jerzy's presentation; it was splendid, with all the senators, generals and dignitaries in uniform and the gallery filled with beautifully dressed ladies. 'My son is in a splendid mood,' she added, 'he is walking on air.' Everyone was cheering and complimenting him, she added. Nothing was perfect, she admitted, 'but at last we are breathing the air of hope, and God will take care of the rest.'[2]

After the ceremony, Izabela attended Christmas Eve dinner at the Blue Palace with Zofia and her husband and their children. She had hoped to go to Sieniawa, but the state of the roads made that impossible; she was now 70 years old and had spent the last three decades on a rollercoaster rising to bright hopes for Poland and plunging into depths of despair, which had taken its toll emotionally and physically. Instead, she sent him books, lavender water and a Gloucester cheese.

In January 1816 she went home to Puławy. She busied herself with arranging the Gothic House, for which donated objects kept arriving, and was pleased to see that ever greater numbers were coming to visit the Temple, including school parties, and was delighted to see the children were making notes. She visited her schools, which were doing well; all the children could read, write and count. And there was now a proper choir in church, thanks to Lessel's singing lessons. She was also putting the finishing touches to her history, which she entitled *The*

*Pilgrim at Dobromil,* in the company of her grey parrot, which also reigned at tea, occasionally biting a guest but much admired by all, and the ageing Szczurek, sometimes *le chevalier Szczur* or *Szczurino,* who was now allowed to sleep in her dressing room.

Izabela's husband had agreed to come over from Sieniawa in May to the great excitement of all at Puławy, 'I burst into tears, laughing at the same time. And what shouts of joy from the children,' she wrote. 'We hugged each other, we congratulated each other! My daughter's eight children ran about as though they had gone mad at the news.' Zofia's children loved him for his practical jokes, which had not matured with age, and were desolate when he left for Vienna in June.[3]

At the end of the month, Izabela left for Warmbrunn (Cieplice) in Silesia, hoping its hot spring would bring relief to aches in her leg (they had got so bad she had recently taken to being carried about in a sedan chair). Before she left she had said goodbye to Marianna, who was off on a tour of Italy, and could not rid herself of the fear she might never see her again. The journey distracted her as she chatted with everyone she met along the way, writing down her impressions on every place and monument she visited. She never missed a church, and always paused after inspecting it to say a prayer or two.

At Warmbrunn, she decided on full immersion in the communal bath. 'One has to be really convinced of the efficacity of the baths to take them in this manner,' she recorded. 'It is a circular chamber built over the spring of the water which, to be fair, keeps flowing and renewing itself ceaselessly, but into which one immerses oneself up to the neck, higgledy-piggledy with around forty women, all of them more or less sick, as they come here to take the baths. There are young ones, there are old ones, there are pretty ones, there are very ugly ones. There are red ones, white ones, yellow ones, pale ones. Every now and then one sees the door open and a person draped in a long white gown immerses herself in the water like some apparition and loses herself in the crowd. I cannot conceal that I felt a kind of disgust when I saw this fine medley.' Getting out was the worst part, as she had to take off the wet gown and put on a flannel one and slippers which would not stay on. But in less than a week she had come to enjoy the experience and fairly took over, chatting with the other women, who came from all classes and walks of life, telling them stories, making them laugh, listening to theirs and singing with them. She even stage-managed a ball and had them waltzing in the bath. She moved effortlessly from this to balls and dinners with the Schaffgotsch family who owned the place and other grandees of the locality.[4]

Back at Puławy in the beginning of September she found a despondent Adam Jerzy. As Alexander had expressed the wish to see his father, he had fetched him from Sieniawa and brought him to Międzyrzecz to meet the tsar as he passed through on his way to Warsaw to open the Sejm. He was saddened by his father's senility, and although Alexander was friendly, Adam Jerzy sensed he no longer trusted him and suspected him of hidden ambitions to seize power in Poland.[5]

His mood was not improved by Izabela, who was pressing him to marry Zosia; not only had she made up her mind as to the benefits to him of the match, she also saw it as a way of keeping her beloved child companion at her side for ever. He doubted whether at his age he was up to marrying at all and considered remaining single, possibly setting up house with Marianna. And he could not tear his thoughts away from Elizabeth, with whom he corresponded and whose every move he watched, still hoping she might separate from Alexander.[6] Soon after Izabela's return to Puławy, Zofia turned up with another proposition – that he marry Princess Anna Sapieha, the daughter of her husband's sister. Adam Jerzy was persuaded; since he was unlikely to fall in love with anyone, he might as well make a dynastic marriage.

Izabela was furious. There were violent scenes in which she accused him, Zofia and Marianna, who approved of the match, of turning against her, saying that it was the cruellest blow she had ever received, and that it was monstrous Zosia should be made to feel her marrying Adam Jerzy would demean him, and declared she would go abroad so as to avoid being present at his wedding. 'Sorrow, pallor, failing strength, lack of sleep, the effort of not showing her sadness, all of this assailed my poor mother so that it was over her health one had to worry most,' noted Adam Jerzy. Her anger was understandable, as, probably under pressure from her, Adam Jerzy had given Zosia to understand that he loved her, and even made some kind of proposal.[7]

The arguments continued as they went up to Warsaw for the opening of the Sejm. Izabela was gratified when Alexander called on her and talked at length of his plans for Poland as well as gracing her ball. Although she was feeling the strain and hated being jostled in the crowds in Warsaw, being back at the centre of things improved her mood. She was delighted to see how the city had recovered, with new factories and shops opening and new buildings going up on streets that were clean and well lit. She visited the new mint, went to the theatre and saw much of Helena Radziwiłł, who had also come to town.

Adam Jerzy did not share her enthusiasm, as he could see that Alexander was gradually abandoning his liberal beliefs and meant to subject Poland to Russia. This made him feel that he had wasted his best years, and he was not in a good frame of mind as he contemplated his forthcoming marriage. To make things worse, General Ludwik Pac, a dashing Napoleonic officer who had set his cap at Princess Anna, challenged him to a duel. To Izabela's relief, Adam Jerzy emerged unscathed and inflicted a minor wound on his opponent. 'Master Adam behaved like a gallant gentleman, Pac like a madman,' she reported to her husband, but could not help adding: 'The mother like a vulgar gossip, and the daughter like a coquette with little sense.' Pac refused to accept the result and, goaded by brother officers and possibly even Grand Duke Constantine, declared he would go on challenging him until he killed him. A second duel was to take place in Silesia in September according to the London *Times*, but Pac seems to have been arrested on his way there.[8]

The next couple of months were not happy ones at Puławy, which had split into rival camps, one supporting Anna, the other Zosia. 'Everyone is trying to compose themselves for the sake of others, nobody dares say what they think, people avoid each other and meet only to utter reproaches or accusations,' Zosia noted. She had taken things better than Izabela, who was so upset that she could not bring herself to write to her son's future mother-in-law and, of all the insensitive things to do, asked Zosia to compose the letter for her.[9]

The wedding took place at Radzyń on 25 September 1817. Adam was ill and did not attend. 'The wedding ceremony in itself is always emotional,' recorded Zosia, 'and on this occasion Anna was so beautiful, looked so very young, her mother was so moved, [Izabela] so pained, and everything was so inexpressibly sad, that the whole room was drowned in tears.'[10]

When she went to Puławy with Adam Jerzy, Anna was silent and shy; only 17, she had not been out in the world much. But she quickly gained the affection and respect of her father-in-law, and Izabela admitted that she was 'pleasant' and seemed to have 'a gentle and good nature'.[11]

But she was more than usually glad to be able to go and stay with her husband at Sieniawa, where she recovered her spirits. On her name day, 19 November, there was a large house party and a merry ball. The jollities went on through that winter, with dances, amateur dramatics and trips around the surrounding country. But she was profoundly wounded by the episode. She poured out her misery to Marianna on 14 January 1818, saying she had been let down by Adam Jerzy and cast aside by other members of the family and sensed she was losing her authority – even Konstanty had not written for months. She had worked herself up so much she was suffering from insomnia and felt so 'stupefied' by it all that she could only release her feelings with fits of laughter.[12]

By April, she was back at Puławy, but she had left Sieniawa with regret. 'Because, my dear friend, I no longer desire or like people. I am prone to a mass of contradictions, of anxieties.' She felt that only the presence of her children could make the world bearable and was looking forward to going to Warsaw, where Zofia was so pregnant with her ninth child that she could barely walk.[13] But that was not the end of it.

After the wedding, Pac published an open letter accusing Adam Jerzy of stealing his fiancée, which placed him in the position of having to challenge Pac. Hearing of the affair, the tsar forbade the duel, but it did take place outside Warsaw on 12 March 1818, with Adam Jerzy suffering a slight wound to the thigh. He convalesced at the Blue Palace, where Alexander sent his own physician and visited him.

The tsar was there to open the Sejm and fulfilled the function with his usual grace and cordiality. Izabela's belief in his good intentions blinded her, as she watched the apparent harmony of its closing session, to the fact that he was already infringing the constitution. At the end of April Alexander was at Puławy on his way back to Russia and could not have been more amiable with the whole family. Izabela's spirits rose as she felt that some of the things she had fought for lived on.

Her mantle had been taken up by her daughters, who dominated the social and cultural life of Warsaw. According to one contemporary, the Blue Palace, where Zofia Zamoyska and her sister-in-law Anna Sapieha held court, was 'the paragon of good taste, national aspirations and the strict observance of social dignity'. 'These hospitable doors were, for the purpose of bringing together people of learning with those of society, open to all who distinguished themselves in literature and the fine arts, recognised for their higher talents even if they lacked the polish which high society normally expects.' At their balls it was 'difficult to tell which of the guests were more important' to the hostess. They carried on with their fundraising events, and on 24 February organized a recital by an 8-year-old prodigy by the name of Fryderyk Chopin who had never been heard in public before.[14]

Marianna's salon dominated the literary scene. She had written a romantic novel, *Malwina*, which was published in 1816, and subsequently in French and Russian. On returning from her Italian tour, she wrote a sentimental journey in the style of Sterne. She would go on to write other works, which were not published in her lifetime, but she encouraged her mother to publish hers.

Izabela had been writing on and off, principally reflective jottings on various subjects which reveal a remarkably open mind and a vivid imagination, whether they record a chance encounter on one of her walks with a peasant, a Jewish girl or a soldier, whose stories led her to speculate on human emotions and life in general, or dwell on specific subjects. She thought of writing the story of her own life, but did not like to write without a practical purpose.

The only thing she had written for publication was *Various Thoughts on the Manner of Laying Out Gardens*, begun in 1801 and published in 1805, with a second edition in 1808, and it was only when she became involved with education that she found good reasons to write *The Pilgrim*. This was published in 1818, and its success led her to take a greater interest in writing. In Warsaw that summer she attended a course of lectures on Polish literature by the poet and translator Ludwik Osiński. She wrote some poems herself, as well as prayers, three of which, *Prayer for the Motherland*, *A Rural Litany* and *A Mother's Prayer for her Child*, became popular. She had written a collection of *Country Tales* in 1819, and in 1821 published a second volume of *The Pilgrim*, which dealt with the countryside and rural life, propounding a constructive morality of hard work and honesty. It met with wide acclaim, and not only in Poland. On 28 November 1821 the *National Gazette* of Philadelphia carried a notice, reprinted from the London *Literary Gazette*, which ran: 'The Princess Izabella [sic] Czartoryska has published *The Pilgrim at Dobromil; or, Rural Instruction* [. . .] The style is simple and adapted to the comprehension of that class of people [the peasantry] for whom it is designed. A second volume is in the press, which is to inculcate the principles of morality in the same pleasing dress.' The book would see several editions in the course of the nineteenth century.

Izabela would not have seen that notice, or a piece in *The Times* of 4 January 1822 from its Paris Correspondent reporting on the publication of 'a singular book' which was causing a 'great sensation' – the memoirs of the 'Don Juan', duc de Lauzun. Various people, including Talleyrand, had tried to prevent publication, as it exposed 'the frailties' of some of the most 'illustrious' ladies of France and even England. The greater part of the book, however, described his affair with Izabela.

She loved being back with her dogs and her parrot at Puławy, but even there she was prone to anxieties which she could not pin down. 'I sometimes have moments of sadness and melancholy which I cannot overcome,' she wrote in August. 'I work, I write, I translate, I arrange my coins and my medals. I try to occupy myself, but that does not always help.' But she always sought refuge in hope, which she described as 'an opulent and generous Capitalist, who lends to present misfortune on the security of future happiness, so nobly, with such grace, that one believes, in spite of oneself, the loan to be secure.'[15]

She ended the year with her husband at Sieniawa where, on 26 December, Alexander stopped on his way back from the Congress of Aix-la-Chapelle. He greeted Izabela with his usual warmth and had a long conversation with her husband. When he was about to climb into his carriage, the old man said the only thing he could give him in return for everything he had tried to do for Poland was an old man's blessing. The tsar bowed his head while Adam made the sign of the Cross on his forehead, then, raising it, he embraced him.[16]

Izabela saw in the New Year of 1819 at Sieniawa, but was in Warsaw by mid-January for the wedding of her beloved Zosia who had fallen in love with a good-looking soldier, Lieutenant Colonel Ludwik Kicki. As her father was ill, she was led to the altar by two of Izabela's grandsons: Zofia's son August Zamoyski and Marianna's Adam Württemberg. Following the death of his father in 1817, he had moved to Poland and joined the army, and Izabela felt proud seeing him in his Polish uniform. 'Marynia is very happy with her son,' she wrote. 'A far as I can judge, I believe that he has much good in his character.'[17] Seeing Zosia happy helped Izabela get over her disappointment at Adam Jerzy's behaviour and made up for the loss of her company. She was also delighted by the fact that 'the *Pilgrim* is all the rage' and selling well. She enjoyed the trade fair which had brought merchants and manufacturers to Warsaw from all over Europe, and particularly the various sideshows which accompanied it; a Panorama of Paris and a 'delightful' performance by 'a genuine Indian', whose 'bronzed' body, carpets and musical accompaniment 'transported' her to India.[18]

One of the attractions of being in Warsaw was that she could spend time with Helena Radziwiłł. 'My God! What would I not give for Puławy to be nearer to Nieborów,' she wrote to her. 'I would give thousands, no, I don't know what I would give – with nobody else do I look the same, see the same, feel the same, enjoy the same, as with you.' Although she knew how to keep herself busy at Puławy, she missed seeing those she loved and moved about the country to visit them at what must have been a punishing rate, given her age.[19]

She made a long stay with her husband at Sieniawa, but soon after getting back in September she was already missing him. 'You are the only goal in my life', she wrote, telling him to look after his health and not bother about praying too much as she felt sure that he was 'in good odour up there'. Her letters were full of admonitions, prescriptions and pleas to follow Dr Goltz's advice in everything. 'The sight of your handwriting, my darling, is like a talisman that brings me joy, health and happiness,' she wrote in June 1818, saying that even his ink spots were precious to her.[20]

She went up to Warsaw that autumn, feeling she should be present at the opening of the Sejm for the sake of Alexander, as Adam Jerzy had decided not to take part in that year's session. He was angry at the way the constitution he had written was being violated by the tsar and distressed by his increasingly reactionary behaviour. To avoid a possible confrontation, he took his wife on a trip abroad. When Alexander stopped at Puławy on his way back to Russia he found only Izabela there. He was 'charming and polite as usual' but, as she wrote to Adam Jerzy, he was not pleased that she was the only Czartoryski at this session of the Sejm.[21]

It was to be their last meeting. When he came to open the Sejm in 1820, it was Zofia who greeted him. Izabela was then 75, her husband a progressively senile 86, and although they both commanded enormous respect, they were venerated as relics of another age. Many of those now prominent in Polish public life had been brought up by them to a greater or lesser degree, in the Cadet Corps, as pupils at Puławy or by the example of constructive patriotism they had set there. And their children had taken over their legacy.

Konstanty, now settled in Vienna, played no part in goings on in Poland, but Adam Jerzy applied himself to the preservation of Polish culture at Wilno University and other educational establishments in the former Polish provinces of the Russian Empire. Marianna was playing a notable role in the literary life of Warsaw. Zofia carried on her charitable activities, but also had to play hostess to Alexander, as her husband was politically active and became president of the Senate in 1822. He had brought the valuable library of the former Academy of Zamość to Warsaw and opened it to the public in an annexe of the Blue Palace, which he had rebuilt in a severe neoclassical style.

Izabela concentrated on the schools she had founded and the Temple, rearranging the exhibits to provide a coherent narrative of Polish history. And she never stopped tending the gardens at Puławy, and laying out new areas, planting prodigious numbers of trees and shrubs. But there were days when she felt so despondent that even Puławy lost its charm. 'Oh my Marynia, the end of my life is nothing like old times. But I throw myself into the arms of Providence,' she wrote to Marianna. Her spirits only lifted when her husband arrived.[22]

A visitor to Puławy who had not seen Izabela for twenty years did not immediately recognize her as one of two old ladies bent over their needlework in a corner of the drawing room. Izabela was dressed in an old well-worn dress, but her eyes retained the old sparkle. As she could no longer walk long distances, she would drive out in the afternoon in a wickerwork trap drawn by four ponies. Before getting into it, she was handed her hat, coat, an umbrella and a paper roll of coins, which she would hand out to beggars she met along the way. She would chat with each one and listen to their woes. When asked by her companion whether she was sure they were all genuinely in distress, she answered: 'I prefer to be deceived a hundred times rather than refuse to give to one who is genuinely needy'. The parlous state of the Puławy finances never interfered with her wish to help any more than bouts of ill-health and backache.[23]

She arranged marriages for her girls, and went to stay with Zosia at her new home the other side of Siedlce to help when she became pregnant. She was devastated when, after giving birth prematurely and not recovering her health, Zosia died, in November 1822, aged only 26.

A happier event was the birth three months earlier of Adam Jerzy's son, Witold. Izabela was overjoyed that he had produced a boy to carry on the name. But moments of joy were soon dispelled by bouts of illness or simply exhaustion, which prevented her from avoiding gloomy thoughts through activity, and this would lead to periods of sad reflection and even depression. A major cause of sadness and anxiety was her husband's increasing frailty. She visited him at Sieniawa whenever she could, and with Marianna's help she ensured the carnival of 1822 in Sieniawa would be one to remember. The main chamber was decorated in the gothic style, its walls draped in white and adorned by panoplies of arms surrounded by garlands of flowers, each with a romantic chivalric motto. At either end there was a kind of altar, one representing a lady, the other a knight. As they arrived, guests were met by pages in fifteenth-century dress who offered them wreaths and bouquets, and a choice of motto, which they were to enact during the evening. They danced till late, and took home their mottos as mementos.

Adam no longer moved from Sieniawa. She wrote frequently to entertain him with news and gossip but many of her letters were no more than expressions of her love for him and sound like a desperate need to keep up a running contact with him. His letters were also brief, but she rejoiced when they arrived.

As he grew frail, Marianna moved to Sieniawa from her own house at nearby Wysock to be near him. She read to him and played the piano, which brought him to life. He was often confused, occasionally forgetting which of the many languages he knew he was currently speaking, and carry on in another, leaving listeners baffled as he switched from Polish to French, Latin, German, Greek, Russian, Spanish, English, Italian, Hebrew, Turkish, Persian, Arabic or Hungarian. He died on 19 March 1823.

His body was to be laid to rest in the family crypt beneath the Church of the Holy Cross in Warsaw. The Austrian authorities escorted the coffin with the solemnity due to a field marshal, and it was met at the border by a guard of honour which escorted it all the way to Warsaw.

It was greeted at the city limits by Grand Duke Constantine, who then walked the considerable distance to the church behind the coffin, flanked by Izabela's grandsons Władysław Zamoyski and Adam Württemberg. The latter had not wanted to attend but had been summoned by Constantine and given a severe dressing down. When the cortège reached the church, noticing that Württemberg avoided the pew reserved for the family, Constantine ostentatiously joined them himself. Afterwards, he berated the young man for his apparent contempt for the Czartoryski family. 'As for me, who am but a grand duke and brother of the emperor of Russia, I consider it an honour to be related to them,' he declared.[24]

## 18

## *Defiant to the Last*

'There are many surprising things happening, some of them upsetting, but one cannot entrust them to the post,' Izabela wrote to Adam Jerzy on 15 August 1824. 'Poor Poland, unfortunate country.' Alexander's liberalism had been worn down by the realities of governing Russia and dissipated after 1815 by fear of revolution. He was displeased by the views expressed in the Polish Sejm and within a couple of years began violating the constitution he had granted. His brother Constantine drilled the army to the point of torture and humiliated its officers, while Novosiltsev clamped down on behaviour he deemed subversive. Adam Jerzy had given up his political functions in 1819 and now resigned his curatorship of the University of Wilno and the Polish schools in the Russian Empire. Izabela was distressed but understood that his position had become untenable. One of the surprising things, which amused rather more than it upset her, was that in March 1824 Novosiltsev, who had taken over from him, banned her *Pilgrim* from schools and libraries.[1]

What saddened her even more than the upsetting things going on in the country was that in the summer Adam Jerzy set off on a long trip with his wife to Germany, Switzerland and Italy, and Izabela hated the prospect of not seeing him for a whole year, and possibly never again if her health should fail.

At times, she enjoyed the solitude. 'I live in the past, I sometimes weep,' she wrote to him on 4 August. The gardens and collections were drawing crowds – 204 signed the visitors' book in the Temple on a single day. As it was so hot, she only went out at night, sometimes dining outside by moonlight and then, 'when all Puławy sleeps', driving down to the Vistula in her little trap or walking to the Kępa, where she would let her thoughts dwell on the past, on God, and on Providence. As she found it difficult to walk to the church at Włostowice for mass every day, she converted a room next to her bedroom into a chapel in which she could have it celebrated for her. She was increasingly finding that God was her only refuge in moments of sadness.[2]

In October she set off for Wysock to stay with Marianna, and, fearing the 'sweet and cruel' memories the sight of it might stir, she gave Sieniawa a wide berth. But she found people of every condition assembled by the roadside, and bodies of peasants and Jews escorted her part of the way. 'I owe this to the memory of the unforgettable being whom we still mourn,' she wrote to her son, adding that it was thanks to Zofia's merits that as she drove through the Zamoyski heartlands she had been treated 'like the Queen Mother'.[3]

Back at Puławy in November she prepared for the anniversary of Teresa's birth, which would remind her of 'the angelic being whom I can never cease to regret'. Her letters record frequent changes of mood, probably because with the death of her husband and the dispersal of her children she had lost the mainstays of her life. 'I do not know what is happening inside me,' she wrote to Adam Jerzy. 'I am not ill, yet I cannot say that I am feeling well. I cannot efface the past, and I fear the future. What worries me most is that occupations no longer inspire me as they once did. But perhaps that will pass.'[4]

Much as she loved being at Puławy and her gardening, it was no longer the same place. The whole point of what she had created there was that it should be full of life, with her family at its core and people coming and going, a living theatre with dances and pageants. Like Powązki, Puławy was a set on which she organized performance, both in the plays and pageants she staged, and in the way of life she created and involved others in. Her preferred means of expression had always been through performance. She used it to educate her children and to inculcate civic virtue and patriotism, but with time she also conjured spectacle to express a thought, a feeling or a wish, an event, moving, comic or tragic, usually in the form of a masque in which players performed symbolic roles to the sound of music. Even the arrangement of her collections, in the Temple and the Gothic House, was theatrical; it was only when a guide, initially Izabela herself, brought out or pointed to the objects, describing their origins and associations, that they acquired a role and came to life. Yet with her family dispersed and the household depleted, she no longer had a cast to direct.

She made up for the absence of her children with a stream of letters, some only a day or two apart, many saying nothing more than how much she loved them, but all of them either insistently or implicitly begging them to come. Such was her longing to have them at her side that those to Adam Jerzy in particular are sometimes heartbreaking to read and must have made painful reading to their recipients. But, as she put it in one of them, he and Marianna were 'the two strongest and sweetest bonds which attach me to life'.[5]

At the same time, she could not accept the loss of control over her family. There had been tension between her and Konstanty from the moment he had decided to take himself and Dzierżanowska to Vienna. She suffered from not being able to see him, but he would not come to Puławy unless she recognized Dzierżanowska as one of the family by allowing him to marry her. He had in fact done so, secretly, in Paris in 1821, but he wanted his mother's sanction. On 21 December 1824 Izabela wrote to Adam Jerzy stating that she bowed to the pressure of all three of his siblings and would accept Konstanty marrying her on condition she never had to see her. Yet when, a year later, Konstanty wrote asking whether he could bring his son by Dzierżanowska to Puławy, Izabela melted. 'My God, can I refuse such a thing?' she wrote to Adam Jerzy. 'Let him come, let me see him, let me embrace my little Kostuś, let my last years be enlivened by his presence.' He did come, in July 1826.[6]

Izabela was in fact rarely alone, as various members of the Puławy circle, such as the Dembowskis, Ciesielskis and others who had settled in the vicinity, were in constant touch. Others, such as the Nevills, cannot have been far away, as they recur in the news she gives in her letters. And travellers of all nations rarely missed the chance of meeting the renowned chatelaine as they passed Puławy. She also moved about, going to stay with Marianna and Zofia and her ten children, and further afield, to the theatre in Lublin, to Niemcewicz's house at Ursynów out-side Warsaw and to Wilanów.

At the beginning of November 1826, hardly recovered from an ill-ness, Izabela insisted on going to supervise planting on the Kępa and caught a cold. For a time it looked as though she might die, and prayers were said for her in the parish church and the synagogue. 'God was already summoning me, but the prayers and tears of His good children stayed His voice,' she told one visitor. Her recovery might also have had something to do with her new physician, Dr Rheinberger. Either way, there was a merry house party for her name day a couple of weeks later.[7]

The death in February 1827 of another adopted 'daughter', Konstancja Dembowska, who had become one of her closest confidantes, affected her deeply. 'O my Master Adam, when I feel too dark, I say to myself, my son will come back,' she wrote to Adam Jerzy. Yet only a few days later she threw herself into the merriment at a Mardi Gras organized for her, at which the company danced until five o'clock in the morning, and she only retired, in pain, at two.[8]

A few months later, at Pentecost, she had a full house; 'all the rooms have been booked,' she wrote to her grandson Władysław Zamoyski, saying that as she no longer had to organize things she would be able to enjoy the proceedings as an onlooker and garner the praise for her work on the Kępa, where she had built more cottages. While she felt proud watching people coming to visit the Temple, she got even more pleasure when she went 'to look at the Kępa, which is a joy to me'. She created a new set of 'English steps' in the park and erected monuments to Kościuszko and Poniatowski. In January 1827 she wrote to Adam Jerzy, then in Rome with his wife and child, to chase up an order she had placed with Thorwaldsen for a bas-relief for the park.[9]

Adam Jerzy returned from his travels in 1828 and in July his wife Anna gave birth to a second son, Władysław; by naming his sons Witold, after the last independent Grand Duke of Lithuania, and Władysław, after the king who founded the Jagiellon dynasty in Poland, he was laying founda-tions for the future, whatever it might bring. Izabela had wanted the boy to bear her father's name, but she was delighted that, as she put it, she had acquired a grandson and Poland a Czartoryski. She could not resist show-ering Anna with advice on breast-feeding and other useful tips.

Zofia found her 'very merry' when she came to stay that year. She was busy all day around the gardens, particularly as a flood in June had swept away much of her work on the Kępa. She was writing the third volume of her *Pilgrim*, and, at the instigation of Stanisław Zamoyski, jotting down memories of Puławy. She often had to ask others to take dictation, as her eyesight was so poor she could not always see what she was writing; she was too weak to hold a lorgnette while writing and spectacles slipped down her nose. But she could see enough to indulge her new passion in the evenings – playing whist with whomever she could corral.

She did not stop adding to her collections. As soon as she heard of Kościuszko's death, in Switzerland in 1817, she despatched the Puławy librarian, Karol Sienkiewicz, to get hold of as many relics as possible. Independently, Marianna acquired for the Temple a lock of Kościuszko's hair, his nightcap and a ring when his effects were sold off. In 1828, George Washington's grand-daughter sent Izabela a manuscript, a piece of the shroud in which he was laid to rest and a sprig of the cedar planted over his grave.[10] That same year saw the catalogue of the Temple published in Warsaw. This was a straightforward register, as the people and events the exhibits evoked were familiar to anyone with an elementary grasp of Polish history.

As she could no longer take visitors around herself, she began working on a catalogue of a different kind for the Gothic House; there, the significance of each object had to be explained, its spirit invoked in such a way as to inspire the imagination, otherwise its worth as she saw it would be lost. It therefore needed to be more descriptive, which gave Izabela the chance to unleash her imagination, and every object evoked associations which connected with others in a sometimes quite extended flight of fancy, intriguing and moving, in line with Virgil's words.

Robbed of the means of performance, she was transferring her theatrical instincts to paper in order to perpetuate the life of her collections, which she saw as her most important legacy. She devoted huge effort and loving care to the task despite failing eyesight, rheumatic pains in her right hand, backache, migraines, 'dazzlements and dizziness', anxieties, and the lingering sadness of the losses, human and material, she had suffered, little realizing that this, too, would be lost.

She had been saddened by news of Alexander's death in November 1825. Even if he had betrayed the promise of his youth and her trust, he had at least left behind a Kingdom of Poland. His brother Nicholas had never had any liberal instincts and disliked the Poles. The succession had not gone smoothly; on hearing of Alexander's death a group of officers in St Petersburg had led their men out in revolt hoping to put Constantine on the throne as a constitutional monarch. The mutiny was crushed and they were ruthlessly dealt with, and Nicholas ordered the investigation of like-minded elements in Poland.

This placed members of the family in a difficult position. Adam Jerzy still had a seat in the Senate, Zofia's husband was its president and chaired a commission tasked with investigating connections between Polish subversives and the Russian mutineers, and his son Władysław was aide-de-camp to Grand Duke Constantine. Yet the instincts of all three, like those of the rest of the family, were at odds with the new regime.

It was not until May 1829 that Nicholas came to Warsaw for his coronation as King of Poland. He was greeted at the Castle by Constantine's wife, the Princess of Łowicz, and Zofia Zamoyska. He was gracious to all and made a good impression. But when he crossed the Vistula at Puławy on his way back to Russia on 27 June he made his feelings towards the family clear. On stepping off the ferry, furnished by Izabela with carpets and chairs, orange trees and flowers, he greeted her courteously but refused to be lured into the house for refreshments, and made a cryptic comment from which she understood that Constantine had told him to have nothing to do with any member of the Czartoryski family.[11]

Everything she had worked for and brought up her children to strive for was viewed with hostility in Russia. She continued working on a third volume of *The Pilgrim*, playing whist in the evenings, feeling sometimes a little better, sometimes worse, but maintained in reasonable health by Dr Rheinberger, and the beginning of 1830 found her in good spirits. There was a merry carnival at Puławy, ending with a ball at which she stayed until ten, the children till eleven and the guests till nine in the morning. She also held a ball for the children for which she had the room decorated with chivalric themes. Each boy was given a shield and a lance, one was elected king of the evening, and he chose Izabela as his queen.

She celebrated Marianna's name day in August with Adam Jerzy and Zofia, their spouses and children, and many friends from Warsaw and Lublin as well as the neighbourhood. Adam Jerzy had brought the latest news about the revolution that had overthrown the Bourbon monarchy in Paris less than three weeks earlier. 'Every face was bright and merry, as if they were expecting something good for the independence of Poland to come from these upheavals in Europe,' noted one. 'The old princess was in a particularly good mood.' After dinner, the company took tea outside to the accompaniment of a brass band, which thrilled them by playing the banned 'Dąbrowski Mazurka' (now the national anthem).[12]

But the revolution in Paris only served to heighten the vigilance of the forces of repression. In Warsaw, the police were on the trail of subversives among the young intelligentsia and subalterns in the army, and it was a matter of time before they would be tracked down.

Adam Jerzy was at Puławy for Izabela's name day on 19 November when he was alerted by Niemcewicz that a plot was afoot to assassinate the Grand Duke, so he hurried off to Warsaw. Izabela was distressed and wrote in tears, begging him to come back soon. Marianna and Zofia were with her, but she complained that Puławy was not the same without him.

Realizing they were about to be arrested, on the night of 29 November the conspirators tried to assassinate Constantine and sparked off a revolution in Warsaw. Constantine made his escape and took refuge among Russian troops outside the city, while the Polish authorities and senior officers tried to restore order. Zofia's son Władysław rode between the two camps trying to negotiate an agreement. But the intransigence on both sides forced him to make his choice, and he resigned his post at the side of the Grand Duke to rejoin his regiment in the Polish army. One who jumped the other way was Marianna's son Adam Württemberg, resigning his commission in the Polish army and taking a command in the Russian. Ignoring her entreaties, Zofia's husband went to St Petersburg with other senators to try to placate the tsar.

On 2 December, Adam Jerzy was elected president of a provisional government, which sent a delegation to St Petersburg to negotiate a way out of the impasse and avoid open conflict. But Nicholas demanded complete submission before any talks could take place, which only encouraged the more radical elements in Warsaw, and the Napoleonic veteran General Józef Chłopicki was named Dictator.

Withdrawing from Warsaw, Constantine crossed the Vistula at Puławy on 6 December and invited himself for the night. According to one source, Izabela took the opportunity to tell him that he had brought the trouble on himself by his intemperate behaviour and lack of regard for people.[13] Despite her poor health, she was in exalted mood and determined to remain at Puławy, confident that this time Polish arms would succeed in defending the country. While most sensible people feared the worst, a mood of exhilaration spread through the country at the news that the hated Constantine, Novosiltsev and their spies had been sent packing, and Izabela was not one to hold back. People were full of hope, she informed Adam Jerzy on 13 December. 'God is good, and Poland has already paid enough for her errors, for her sins. She will be happy,' she wrote. Ten days later she wrote wishing she could go to Warsaw to be at the baptism of his newborn daughter, who would also be named Izabela, and sending her wishes for his name day. 'Oh God, may my son be happy, may his mother's blessing, my tears and my prayers obtain happiness for him and for Poland,' she wrote, the tears clearly visible on the paper. She wrote again on 2 January, saying how proud she was of him and what he was doing, urging him to send Anna and the children to Puławy, and declared that she was not going to move out.[14]

The more realistic Sienkiewicz had begun packing up the most valuable books and manuscripts in sturdy cases which he prepared to immure in blind areas of the cellars. Izabela soon followed suit, ordering her collections to be either immured or sent for safekeeping to a nearby monastery.

The house had filled up with people seeking refuge there, believing the Russians would not attack it. 'We are in good spirits,' she wrote to Adam Jerzy. 'The Lord God is with us. Do not worry about us, we risk nothing.' He had sent his two sons down to Puławy and, realizing the danger, in February told her to send them on to Kraków.[15]

In view of the tsar's intransigence, on 25 January 1831 the Sejm and Senate voted to dethrone Nicholas as King of Poland. Adam Jerzy took over foreign relations and began renewing his contacts among the Great Powers in the hope of inducing Austria and Britain to mediate a settlement which might place an Austrian archduke or one of the British royal dukes on the Polish throne.

'We are just women here,' Zofia wrote to one of her daughters on 10 February. 'We are trying to keep up each other's spirits. My mother is calm, almost merry. We weep, pray and sew shirts for the regiment' – Izabela and Adam Jerzy had provided funds for a regiment of light cavalry. Before going to St Petersburg, Zofia's husband had fitted out a regiment of lancers to fight the Russians, and three of her sons took their place in its ranks.[16]

On 13 February a Russian force under General von Kreutz crossed the Vistula at Puławy, making for Warsaw. Possibly at Izabela's behest, someone crossed before them and alerted Polish forces on the left bank, and they drove the Russians back across the river with substantial losses. Suspecting Izabela's involvement, Kreutz detailed Adam Württemberg, who had joined his corps after leaving the Polish army, on a punitive expedition with a regiment of dragoons and four guns to sack the town of Puławy, which he did. For good measure, he then shelled the house, in which his grandmother, mother and two aunts were giving shelter to local ladies and old men, as well as peasant women with their children. 'Cannonballs were raining into our rooms,' Zofia wrote to her husband.[17]

Württemberg had been given orders to pack up the archives and library for removal to Russia, in order to secure the most politically sensitive papers. While he set about this, a body of Polish cavalry under General Dwernicki arrived and, after a lively battle fought in the immediate surroundings and even the outbuildings of the house, he put the Russians to flight. Sienkiewicz gathered up the fifty-seven cases of papers collected by Württemberg and took them to Warsaw under military escort.

Dwernicki was astonished when he entered the house to find so many ladies assembled. 'Following the princess's example, they showed not the slightest trace of fear, even though cannonballs and grapeshot had been raining down in the court but an hour before,' he recalled. He was even more astonished to find the bedrooms full of peasant women and their children.[18]

Izabela was determined to stay on, but at the insistence of Adam Jerzy she agreed to leave, at night on 5 March, on foot, accompanied by Zofia, Marianna and Cecylia, Dr Rheinberger and a few servants, crossing the Vistula under cover of darkness. At the first stop, Góra, she wrote to her son protesting at having been dragged away from Puławy, leaving nobody to look after it. 'I cannot bring myself to be afraid,' she insisted. Soon after they left, the Russians returned and began looting the house, beating up the staff and raping the maids. They also packed up more papers and some of the objects remaining in the Temple and Gothic House.[19]

From Góra, Zofia went up to Warsaw while the rest of the party made for the safety of Austrian territory, travelling south to Zawichost, where they recrossed the Vistula into Galicia. On 20 March, after a difficult journey, which Izabela claimed nearly killed her but during which she was the only one to show no fear, they reached Wysock. She was moved by the hospitality they met with along the way, and the sympathy of the governor of Galicia, Prince Lobkowitz. News of their arrival brought neighbours out to help; as Marianna had spent the last years either at Warsaw or Sieniawa, the house at Wysock was unprepared, so they brought victuals, furniture and bedding. Izabela was touched by their kindness but leaving behind Puławy and the Kingdom of Poland weighed on her. 'Our only consolation is trust in God and the valour of the Poles,' she wrote to Adam Jerzy, complaining that the worst privation was lack of news. She was overjoyed to receive his wishes for her eighty-sixth birthday, on 31 March, but her spirits were flagging. 'Oh God, do not abandon us,' she prayed. She occupied herself as best she could, going for walks, tearing linen into strips for bandages and being read to in the evenings.[20]

She soon fell ill again and was bedridden for most of April with Dr Rheinberger watching over her night and day as she hovered between life and death. 'I thought with despair that my life would end and that I would not see you again,' she wrote to Adam Jerzy. Although she was out of danger by then, her legs and back were so weak she could not walk without being supported by two people; 'they carry or they drag me,' she quipped. As soon as she could, she started going for short walks and drives, and even doing some gardening.[21]

Her scribbled notes to Adam Jerzy are barely legible as she could hardly hold a pen. 'I write to you again because it is the only thing left to me. My soul is overwhelmed, my heart is full of courage as I no longer value life. I only ask God to be allowed to live long enough to see you again,' she wrote.[22]

In May, Marianna had had a small teahouse built for her so that she could sit outside. There was a constant stream of callers, neighbours concerned about her health or refugees passing through. At one point there were so many homeless that the great drawing room had to be divided up with curtains and drapery to provide sleeping quarters for them.

Izabela was tormented by what she saw as the end of her dreams. She was appalled at the behaviour of Zofia's husband, which she saw as unpatriotic, and by that of Konstanty, who had not moved from Vienna and shown no interest in joining the Insurrection. The only one true to her cause was Adam Jerzy, and she had no news of him. 'When will I see you again, when will I press you to my heart,' she scrawled in one. 'O my Master Adam, how many tears I have shed, how many sleepless nights, how many cruel days.'[23]

In June she recovered enough to write two chapters of the third volume of *The Pilgrim*, but there were moments when she was too weak to speak. She longed to go back to Puławy, anxious that there was nobody looking after it, unaware that events had moved on. According to Natalia Kicka, who went there a couple of months later, the house had been sacked, Izabela's bedroom had been vandalized and used as a kitchen by Russian troops, who had also made a bonfire in the golden chamber, leaving a burned patch in the parquet.[24]

By the end of September, Izabela was growing desperate, as she heard only rumours as to her son's whereabouts and wished she had the strength to go and look for him, on foot if necessary. The situation had indeed become critical. In his efforts to get the Great Powers to mediate in some kind of solution, Adam Jerzy had despatched one of Zofia's sons on a clandestine mission to Vienna, where he hid in Konstanty's house, only emerging to attend secret nocturnal meetings with Metternich, who was cordial but would not accept that the events in Warsaw had not been part of the worldwide conspiracy to bring down European civilization, and told him that the only thing for the Poles to do was to submit to the tsar. Adam Jerzy also despatched Konstanty's son, Adam, who had been wounded and invalided out of the army, to Prussia; his late mother Aniela Radziwiłł's brother was married to Princess Louise, daughter of Izabela's friend Prince Ferdinand.[25]

The military situation was hopeless. While the army was in good shape and eager to fight, the commanders, who had been distinguished Napoleonic officers, lacked self-assurance and the qualities of leadership required. Nor was there strong political leadership either. By mid-August left-wing elements in the Sejm were in the ascendant and the populace of Warsaw grew more radical, blaming lack of success on 'traitors' and 'spies'. Adam Jerzy was at one stage confronted by a baying mob and even shot at in the street. On 17 August he set off to join the army in the field. But it was not long before the various Polish corps, no longer under unified command, were forced to avoid surrendering to the Russians by crossing the border into Prussia or Austria, where they were disarmed. Warsaw was stormed by the Russians in early September and the rising petered out with the fall of Zamość on 21 October 1831.

Adam Jerzy had reached Kraków, which was a Free City, on 26 September. He called on a notary to try and transfer his estate to members of his family. But as Russian troops entered the city, he had to flee across the Vistula into Austrian territory, followed later by his wife and three children, the youngest, Izabela, only eight months old. Metternich issued him with a passport, urging him to leave Habsburg territory as soon as possible, with only a single attendant. He reached London on 22 December 1831 with one travel bag.

Izabela remained at Wysock with Marianna and Cecylia. They were joined by Zofia, who had escaped from Warsaw and come through Kraków with her two youngest children, aged 12 and 14. After a few months, on hearing that her husband, imprisoned by Nicholas for refusing to denounce the act dethroning him, had been freed, she left to join him in Italy.

Life at Wysock was made no easier by Cecilia having fallen into depression. Marianna, on whose shoulders all rested, had broken her hip and could only move about on crutches. The Russians awarded her house in Warsaw and country estate to her son, while the debts and liabilities remained with her. Her one support was her chaplain, Father Dziewulski, a white Marian priest.

Izabela longed for Adam Jerzy, but there was no way he could come to her, as the Austrians would never give him a passport. He had hoped to settle in England, intending to continue agitating on behalf of Poland through his contacts there, but his reduced means would not support him. All he had left in the way of property was Sieniawa, whose negligible income was needed to keep Izabela.

His mother-in-law, Anna Sapieha, had managed to hold onto her property. She had also gone into action at Puławy as soon as it became clear the estate was to be confiscated, salvaging everything she could, down to the copper cooking pots, and moving whatever sheep and cattle were left to the estates of friends. By 1834, she and her daughter had joined Adam Jerzy in Paris, bringing their three children. King Louis-Philippe was friendly and France was sympathetic to the Polish cause.

Izabela kept three portraits of Adam Jerzy by her bed, one of which would accompany her to the dining room so that they could dine together. She kept begging him to write, and whenever she did get letters from him she would press them to her heart, assuring him they provided the only joy in her life. She was sinking fast. Writing to him on 25 January 1834 she admitted that her speech was becoming muddled, but asked him to drink champagne on 31 March, when she would begin her ninetieth year.[26]

She wrote how proud she was of the praise of him she heard from all quarters, but his fine behaviour would come at a cost. Constantine had repeatedly warned his brother against Adam Jerzy and shortly after the outbreak of the Insurrection, on 29 December, he wrote to Nicholas saying that he had been perfidiously planning the revolution since 1815. Puławy and all his property in the Kingdom was confiscated and, after repeated summons to return to stand trial, in September 1834 he was condemned to death by beheading. Every day, Izabela begged God to let her see him just once more. 'I could forget about all the disaster, misery and losses,' she wrote, if only she could see him once more before she died and his hand could wipe away her tears. It would never happen.[27]

In March 1835 a visiting neighbour found Izabela 'with a weakened mind'. Marianna was carried in in a chair and read to her, but Izabela seemed not to take very much in. She livened up when a letter was read from Władysław Zamoyski from Algiers, where he had been checking on Poles who had joined the French Foreign Legion, but soon slumped back into a stupor.[28]

During Izabela's last days, she was surrounded by Marianna, Cecylia, Zofia's daughter Celina, Dr Rheinberger and Father Dziewulski reciting prayers. She only suffered for a few days before the end came, on 17 June 1835.

In a letter to Adam Jerzy, Marianna described Izabela's death as 'truly inspiring, as sweet as could be'. 'Life was extinguished gradually and reached its term quietly. She was entirely conscious to the end, but could not speak on account of her weakness. She had asked for the Last Sacrament herself, laying all her cares, anxieties, torments and pain at the feet of her God, and, having made her peace with Him, full of submission and comfort, she lived on only to love and bless, without fear, without impatience, good, sweet, calm, loving all those who were with her to her last breath. She gave up her soul to God, and a moment after her death such a look of serenity came over her dear face that she looked as though she were sleeping sweetly.'[29]

Marianna washed and dressed her mother and laid her out on a bed surrounded by flowers and herbs and erected a small altar flanked by two orange trees. They said mass at the altar every day until she was embalmed and removed to the chapel Marianna had built at the nearby convent in Moszczany. Her body would be moved to the crypt of the church at Sieniawa in 1860.

# Postscript

Marianna left Wysock the following year, having sold the estate to her nephew, Zofia's son Zdzisław. Accompanied by Cecylia and her chaplain Father Dziewulski, she went to join Zofia, who had rented the Villa Medici at Careggi outside Florence. Zofia was worn out and not expected to live long. She died on 27 February 1837, surrounded by her sons Władysław and August, Marianna, Cecylia and Adam Jerzy who had come from Paris. Her husband, who had settled in Vienna, was too ill to travel. She was laid to rest in the church of Santa Croce, in a striking monument designed by Lorenzo Bartolini.

After Zofia's death, Marianna went to Paris and settled in with Adam Jerzy's family on the Faubourg du Roule, bringing with her Cecylia, by now incapable of looking after herself. Adam Jerzy had created a political agency supported by the more conservative among the emigration, which operated offices in places as diverse as London and Istanbul to monitor the political situation and act on any circumstance that might be exploited to promote the cause of restoring an independent Polish state.

He left the family finances and material establishment to his wife and mother-in-law, who took advantage of the opportunities offered by the Paris of the 1830s to provide the necessary funds. They rented apartments and then an *hôtel particulier*, but by the beginning of the 1840s they felt the need for something permanent and large enough to accommodate the family and its retinue, as well as Adam Jerzy's political secretariat, and to provide space for large gatherings.

The ideal place was found in 1843 by Chopin's friend, the painter Eugène Delacroix, who came across a derelict building on the Île Saint-Louis about to be sold at auction. It was an *hôtel particulier* built in 1642 for Nicolas Lambert de Thorigny by the architect Louis Le Vau in collaboration with the painters Charles Le Brun and Eustache Le Sueur. Determined to save these works of art, he alerted the Czartoryskis, who outbid the City of Paris, which planned to pull it down. The Hôtel Lambert became the family home and Adam Jerzy's political headquarters, the seat of what was in effect a government in exile, its name synonymous with a political party.

It also became the social and cultural centre of Polish life in Paris, where the country's principal writers and artists had turned up following the debacle of 1831. It attracted the cream of French society and artistic elite; Lamartine, George Sand, Balzac, Berlioz and Liszt were among those who frequented Anna Czartoryska's soirées, along with Chopin and Poland's foremost poets, Adam Mickiewicz, Juliusz Słowacki, Zygmunt Krasiński and Cyprian Kamil Norwid. For many, the Hôtel Lambert symbolized Polishness itself, having quite naturally taken on much of what Puławy had stood for since the 1780s. Parisian society came to regard Adam Jerzy as the uncrowned King of Poland, and without his knowledge one group of émigrés actually proclaimed him Adam I of Poland and struck a medal to that effect.

Sheltering in the shadows of the Hôtel Lambert were a number of émigré institutions. Acting in the spirit of Izabela, in 1845 Adam Jerzy's wife opened a Polish Young Ladies' Institute, whose forty-five pupils, drawn from émigrés scattered in London, Paris, Odessa and Stockholm as well as the Polish lands in Russia, Germany and Austria, were brought up in the values of Izabela's Puławy. She remained actively involved up to her death, at Montpellier in 1864. Her mother, who predeceased her in 1859, had also looked after émigré Poles and nursed Chopin, the child prodigy she had introduced to the Warsaw public, through his last illness. There was also a school for young men, a Polish library, the Polish Literary and Historical Society, and even a newspaper. The spirit of Izabela's Puławy lived on, and when, in December 1981, many Solidarity activists and dissidents who had been stranded abroad by General Jaruzelski's imposition of a State of War in Poland were given a disused building in the Paris banlieue, it was promptly dubbed the Motel Lambert.

Konstanty did not escape the wrath of Nicholas even though he had taken no part in public life for two decades. When he moved to Vienna, in 1816, he turned his estate at Klewań into a college, to which he donated his extensive library, a physics laboratory and mineralogical collection, which he endowed with scholarships. In 1831 the Russians confiscated the estate, closed down the college and removed the library and laboratory to a Russian one.

In the 1840s his residence at Weinhaus outside Vienna hosted a notable musical salon, much admired by Berlioz when he visited the city. His daughter-in-law Marcelina was one of Chopin's best pupils and one of the leading lights of the Hôtel Lambert. He did not leave Vienna, where he died in 1866. Marianna visited him and in 1839 briefly moved in to be near her son, who had also taken up residence there; she had never given up hope she might one day manage to win his affection. She had written out for him all that she would have wished to impart if she had been able to bring him up: a reasoned gloss on the Ten Commandments, advice and injunctions on how to lead a good life. She remained in contact with him until his death in 1847.[1]

Back in Paris, she looked after the by now manic-depressive Cecylia, and continued to play a part in the social and charitable life of the Hôtel Lambert. She sat out the revolution of 1848 there and, having nursed Cecylia through a lingering final illness and buried her in 1851, died in the cholera epidemic of 1854.

Adam Jerzy's political agency was active in the Polish cause in the 1840s and he went to Poznań in 1846 when it looked as though the Prussian-ruled provinces of Poland might regain their freedom. The Hôtel Lambert was active throughout the revolutions of 1848, in Poland, Germany, Italy and Hungary, where Zofia's son Władysław organized units of Polish volunteers and fought at their head, and again during the Crimean War, in which Władysław commanded a division with the rank of general in the Turkish and British service. The last political involvement of the Hôtel Lambert was in the Polish Insurrection of January 1863. Adam Jerzy had died in 1861 and his sons could see no useful purpose in carrying on after the failure of that.

The elder, Witold, died without issue, but Władysław kept the family's royal pretensions alive by marrying the daughter of Queen Cristina of Spain and, after her death, Marguerite d'Orléans, daughter of the duc de Nemours, son of King Louis-Philippe, and Victoria of Saxe-Coburg, first cousin to Queen Victoria. While he did not continue his father's political activities, he emulated his grandmother by creating a notable collection of antiquities, medieval and Renaissance art, and seventeenth- and eighteenth-century Old Masters. When the political situation permitted, he moved that, along with the remainder of Izabela's collections and the family archives, to Kraków where he opened the Czartoryski Museum in 1876. His sister, Izabela, made a dynastic marriage with a scion of the notable patriotic family of western Poland, the Działyński, and created a world-class collection of art, particularly of Greek, Etruscan and Roman antiquities, which she opened to the public in in 1883 in her castle at Gołuchów, which was looted and dispersed by the Germans in the 1940s.

Among the 6,000 or so of Izabela's descendants born to date, there was one cardinal, a handful of bishops and dozens of religious, at least two of whom have been beatified; many generals, ambassadors and other notable public figures in various countries, three prime ministers of the Habsburg Empire, at least one artist of note, a couple of Olympic skiers and a champion kickboxer, along with a colourful array of writers, actors, musicians, travellers and mountaineers. They took part in revolutions and uprisings, in all the major wars, on both sides in the Great War, and on land, sea and in the air, alongside each of the Allies in the Second World War. They were exiled, imprisoned, sent to Siberia, to the Gulag, to German concentration camps and murdered, in the forest of Katyń and elsewhere. In the process they lost all their property in Poland. A number married into royal families such as the Bourbons, Habsburgs, Orléans, Württembergs, Saxe-Coburgs and Bonapartes; today they include a pretender to the throne of the Two Sicilies, the Prince Napoleon, pretender to that of France, and the Queen of the Belgians.

The three known fathers of Izabela's children died during her lifetime: Stanisław Augustus in St Petersburg in 1798, Repnin in a state of religious exaltation in 1801 (as he left no legitimate male issue, the son of his sister, who had married a Prince Volkonsky, was entitled to carry on the name as Repnin-Volkonsky).

Lauzun was elected to the French National Assembly in 1789 and, as General Biron, fought in the Army of the North, then in the Army of the Rhine, in the Var, where he captured Nice from the Piedmontese, and against the royalists in the Vendée. Arrested in 1793, he spent five months in the prison of Sainte-Pélagie. When offered the chance to escape, he said he could not be bothered, and when interrogated by the arch-inquisitor of the Terror, Fouquier-Tinville, he made flippant replies. 'You're being impertinent!' fumed the inquisitor. 'And you're a bunch of chatter-boxes,' retorted Biron. 'Get on with it and guillotine me!' When the gaoler came to fetch him he was eating oysters and drinking white wine. Biron poured him a glass, saying: 'There, have a drink! You must get thirsty doing your job.' He died under the guillotine on the cold, grey morning of 9 January 1794.[2]

*

Izabela's cultural legacy is difficult to disentangle from that of the Familia as a whole. Yet she was its leading light and most energetic actor in inspiring and promoting literature, music, drama, education, taste and manners, and deeply influenced Polish culture during her lifetime and beyond. Her artistic patronage lived on in such figures as the boy she plucked from the inn at Siedlce, Aleksander Orłowski, who made a brilliant career in Russia, and through the descendants of Norblin. One of his sons followed him as a mediocre painter, but another, Ludwik, was a cellist who played with Chopin and prominent musicians of the Romantic era. One great-grandson was a notable industrialist, another, Stefan, a portrait painter, illustrator and interior designer who produced some of his finest work in Indian palaces, notably Jodhpur's Umaid Bhawan, before committing suicide, having lost his sight, in San Francisco in 1952.

*

No trace of the house at Wołczyn survives, the site of Powązki is now the main Warsaw cemetery, Puławy was extensively rebuilt as a girls' school under the Russians, Sieniawa was devastated during the Second

World War and has been insensitively restored as a hotel, Wysock was gutted in 1916 and again in 1945, and now houses an old people's home. The Blue Palace was bombed and reduced to rubble in September 1939 and only its exterior was rebuilt. Marynki has survived, along with the Temple and the Gothic House, but these are empty shells.

*

It was Prussian troops that destroyed Powązki, the Russians Puławy, Sieniawa and Wysock, and the Germans who looted the collections in the Second World War. Izabela's very body, laid to rest in the crypt of the church at Sieniawa, was twice turfed out of its coffin by Russian soldiers in search of jewellery, once in 1916 and again in 1944. Yet it is from her own people, to whom she devoted most of her life, that she might have expected better. Most biographers have treated her with either fulsome piety or coy indulgence, others have appropriated her in sentimental fantasies of their own, while sensation seekers and one female novelist have represented her as a mindless nymphomaniac and her private life as pornography.

More serious, successive ministers, art historians, museum directors and curators have failed to recongnise the importance of Izabela's greatest legacy: her collections.

Their significance was fully understood by contemporaries, and by the Russian occupiers. Hidden in haste during the Insurrection by servants, gardeners, local peasants, priests, a village doctor and a family of Jewish traders, the objects were gradually moved, at night, on peasant carts, covered with hay or straw, and smuggled out of Russian Poland into Galicia, dodging Cossack patrols at the border. They were secreted mainly on the Zamoyski estates of Podzamcze, Kozłówka and Klemensów and the Sapieha castle of Krasiczyn. The Russian police tracked their movements as if they were dangerous subversives, and persons found in possession could expect unpleasant consequences. Part of the archives had to be burned as the police were on their trail, and some historical mementos from the Temple hidden by a local parish priest were discovered and confiscated. In 1834, the Russian authorities imprisoned those suspected of having played a part in salvaging the collections. The tsar's lieutenant, General Paskievich, ordered them to be prosecuted, but local officials obstructed the execution with delays, and most of them were able to escape to Sieniawa.

As a result of this and further acts of courageous devotion by members of the family and their staff during the Second World War, sometimes at the risk of their lives, a large proportion of the objects has survived, as have Izabela's catalogues. Yet due to the limited mindset of the local museum establishment the point of her unique work of intellectual and artistic expression has been entirely lost. Some of the objects are exhibited, devoid of meaning, jumbled up with others collected by Izabela's grandchildren and family possessions confiscated by the communist regime after 1945; others lie in storage, robbed of their sensuous significance and their mission to teach and inspire.

*

Izabela's work is at least appreciated in one quarter. Although the inside of the church at Sieniawa has been defaced with kitsch murals and disfigured by a hideously inappropriate floor, the crypt underneath tells a different story. When I first visited it in 1968, and every time I went there while I was restoring it in the 1980s and 1990s, I found laid on Izabela's coffin flowers and badges of primary schools from all over Poland; by unspoilt minds she is at least venerated for her pioneering work in the field of popular education.

# Notes

*In the case of digitized manuscripts from the Czartoryski Library in Kraków, I give the page numbers on the screen, not on the actual pages, since only alternate ones are numbered, and these often bear more than one number.*

**Abbreviations:**

AGAD – Archiwum Główne Akt Dawnych, Warsaw
BC – Biblioteka Czartoryskich, Kraków
Berlin – Geheimes Staatsarchiv: Preussischer Kulturbesitz
Kórnik – Biblioteka Kórnicka, Kórnik
Lublin - Biblioteka im. H. Łopacińskiego, Lublin
MNW – Muzeum Narodowe, Warsaw
KMSK – Księgi Metrykalne Kościoła pw Śwįego Krzyża w Warszawie
PAK – Landesarchiv Berlin
Stuttgart – Landesarchiv Baden-Württemberg, Haupstaatsarchiv Stuttgart
Vienna – Oesterreichische Staatsarchiv, Vienna

**Chapter 1**

1. BC 6067 IV t.1, p. 7; Frączyk, 120, 119; Matuszewicz, II/175.
2. Stanisław Augustus, 225–6; see also: Czartoryski, A. J. 1887, I/3; BC 6029, 183 and Kicka, 82.
3. Matuszewicz, II/175; Frączyk, 120, Aftanazy IIa, 188–9.
4. Frączyk, 120–6; Wyrwicz.
5. Aftanazy, IIa, 187; Czartoryski, A. J. 1887, I/2.
6. Matuszewicz, II/174.
7. Stanisław Augustus, 226; Zamoyska, 39.
8. BC 6067 IV, t. 2, 16–24; another version in BC 6070 – 002 III, 234ff.

9. BC 6067 IV, t. 2, 40; Moszczeński, 60; Stanisław Augustus, 310; Zawadzki 1965, II/62–3; Radziwiłł, pcesse Antoni, 190; Wyrwicz, 3.
10. Lauzun, 124.

## Chapter 2
1. Stanisław Augustus, 55.
2. Bernardin de Saint-Pierre, 15.
3. Cieszkowski, 57; Kicińska, 66.
4. Zaleski M., 20; Dębicki I/14.
5. Kitowicz, 1882, I/16.
6. Poniatowski, 44; Voltaire, 186.
7. Wraxall, II/10.
8. Ochocki, I/91.
9. Malmesbury, I/26.
10. Wybicki, I/31; Matuszewicz, II/72.
11. Matuszewicz, I/471, II/105; Kitowicz 1970, 25.
12. BC 6070 – 002 III, 284.
13. BC 6067 IV, t. 2, 18.
14. Dębicki, I/18.
15. Przeździecki, II/428–9.
16. Nieć, 198.

## Chapter 3
1. There is some disagreement as to the date of this trip. Izabela records it as taking place in 1762, and this has been accepted by Dernałowicz, Putkowska and Pauszer-Klonowska, but according to Frączyk, Adam's first visit to Paris was in 1768. Izabela complicates matters by placing the anecdote about her being taken for the young King of Denmark in 1762, while Christian VII only ascended the throne in 1766. But she must have been in Paris in 1762, since Rousseau left Montmorency in July 1762.
2. BC 6067 IV, t. 2, 178.
3. Weston, 47.
4. BC 6067 IV, t. 2, 180.
5. BC 6067 IV, t. 2, 180.
6. BC, 6067 IV, t. 2, 69/74.
7. BC 6067 IV, t. 2, 47–52.
8. Catherine, 237.

9. BC 6029, 183.
10. Stanisław Augustus, 3.
11. Matuszewicz, II/542–3, 546.

## Chapter 4
1. Malmesbury, I/10.
2. Zawadzki 1965, I/62, II/482.
3. Frączyk, 237–9; BC 6077, t. 1, 1–6.
4. BC 6079, t.4.
5. Zawadzki 1965, II/149, I/424; Karpiński 83.
6. Wraxall, II/116, 108.
7. Bernardin de Saint-Pierre, 15; see also Zawadzki 1965, II/509.
8. Lauzun, 124.
9. Pauszer-Klonowska, 23.
10. The French death certificate quoted by Strzałkowa gives Adam Klewański's date of birth as 1763, but according to the entry in *Polski Słownik Biograficzny*, vol. XI, 1967, it took place in 1767, which is more likely to be correct as it is based on his admission to the Cadet Corps.
11. Stanisław Augustus, 316–17.
12. Ibid., 318; Lauzun, 124.
13. Zamoyski, Adam, 119.
14. Malmesbury, I/19.
15. Rhulière, II/220.
16. Moszczeński, 84–5, 91; Frączyk, 244.
17. Lauzun, 124, 136–7.
18. Malmesbury, I/29.
19. BC 6079, t. 2, 1; Frączyk, 270–1.
20. BC 6067 IV, t. 2, 178–80.
21. *Listes des seigneurs, etc.*, 1768, no. 7 (Frączyk, 273, gives the date 25 June).
22. Frączyk, 274.
23. BC 6020 III, 17ff.
24. Coke, II/361; Delaney, I/151, 155, 157, 161, 192; *Caledonian Mercury*, 21 September 1768.
25. BC 6067 IV, t. 2, 49–54. This episode is usually placed during her first trip to Paris, which seems unlikely, since she was only 17 years old and inclined to say nothing in company for fear of compromising herself. There is also no mention of Zabiełło being of their

party on the earlier trip, while he was certainly on this one.

## Chapter 5

1. *Bumagi* 1870, 152–6; Lublin, 2110, 46.
2. Lauzun, 124; *Bumagi* 1870, 153.
3. KMSK, 117 U-1765-72, 148; *Bumagi* 1891, 402; Moszczeński, 86; Frączyk, 289.
4. Burnett, 325.
5. BC 6033, 129.
6. Putkowska, 26; BC 1894 II.
7. Coxe, II/157–8; Zawadzki 1965, I/425.
8. AGAD, Archiwum Radziwiłłów z Nieborowa, Seria I, zespół 355, 95 cz IV, 1 & 3; BC 6067 IV, t, 2, 9, 160; Radziwiłł M. P., xiii–xiv. Radziwiłł, pcess Antoni, 170–1, maintains that the two ladies were rivals and that Izabela's friendship was false, but this belies the evidence, as do her later comments about Konstanty's marriage to her daughter.
9. KMSK, 117 U-1765-72, 216.
10. Craven, 88.
11. *Bumagi* 1870,163–7; Lauzun, 137.
12. Lauzun, 124–5.
13. Lauzun, 42.
14. Lauzun, 107.
15. Lublin 2110, 138.
16. BC 6067 IV, t. 2, 60
17. BC 6067 IV, t. 2, 60; see also Lipowski, 363; Walpole, XXXII, 96.
18. BC 6020, III, 24ff.
19. BC 6030, III, 7–8, wrongly dated as 1772.
20. Walpole, XXXII/108–10.
21. BC 6030, III, 11.
22. BC 6030, III, 12; Lauzun, 116–17.
23. BC 6030, III, 13.
24. BC 6027, t. 4, 3; BC 6028, IV; BC 6030 III, 12–14, wrongly dated.
25. Lauzun, 118–19.

## Chapter 6

1. Lauzun, 121.
2. Stanisław Augustus, 424.
3. Lauzun, 122; Maugras 1893, 398–9.
4. Lauzun, 123, 125, 126, 129.
5. Lauzun, 131–2, 136–8; Fiszerowa, 176.
6. BC 6137, 390.
7. *Bath Chronicle*, 14 October 1773; *Leicester and Nottingham Journal*, 16 October 1773.
8. Lauzun, 140–1.
9. BC 6077 IV, t. 1, 3. The date 1771 has been added to some of these bills in a different hand, and she was not in Paris in February 1771.
10. Maugras 1893, 423.
11. Lauzun, 143–4.
12. Lauzun, 144–5; KMSK, 100 Ch – 1774–88, 025.
13. Lauzun, 145–150.
14. Michalski.
15. Michalski; see also Maugras 1909, 15–57; also Waszczuk, 203–18.
16. Lauzun, 154–7.
17. BC 6070 – 002 III, 358.
18. Lauzun, 161–2; Zawadzki 1965, II/31 ; Ligne, 201.
19. Czartoryski, A. J. 1887, I/80029.

## Chapter 7

1. Wraxall, II/11.
2. Mably, 8–9.
3. Cieszkowski, 67.
4. Stanisław Augustus, 575.
5. Czartoryski, A. J. 1887, I/4.
6. Stanisław Augustus, 424, 528–9, 567.
7. Lauzun, 122; KMSK, 100 Ch – 1774–88, 210.
8. BC 6070 – 002 III.
9. Zawadzki 1965, II/62-3; Fiszerowa, 177–8.
10. Cieszkowski, 12ff.
11. Pauszer-Klonowska, 72; BC 6027, t. 1, 1, 103.
12. Bieliński, 28; BC 6067 IV, t. 2, 40.
13. BC 6067 IV, t. 2, 203.
14. BC 6110, 13, 9; Ostrowski, 133; Czartoryski, A. J. 1887, I/5.
15. Fiszerowa, 77.
16. Czartoryski, A. J. 1887, I/10; Karpiński, 77, 88.

17. Czartoryski, A. J. 1887, I/10–12; Ligne, 201.
18. BC 6070 – 002 III, 248, 272.
19. Karpiński, 74–5.
20. Karpiński, 83.
21. ibid., 79.
22. Pauszer-Klonowska, 68. According to other sources, Elżbieta Lubomirska received 45 million złoty.
23. BC 6027, t. 1, 42.
24. Ostrowski, 133, 146; BC 6008 IV, nos 4 & 5; BC 6034, 43ff.
25. Żychliński, VIII/80–1; Koźmian, K., I/79–80; Czartoryski, A. J. 1887, I/19–22.
26. BC 6067 IV t. 2, 46–9.

**Chapter 8**
1. Bieliński, 33.
2. Dębicki, IV/274–5.
3. Kórnik, 07784.
4. Fiszerowa, 248.
5. Koźmian, K., I/227.
6. BC 6137, 14.
7. BC 6137, 35.
8. BC 6137,103.
9. Stuttgart, G.247, 5.
10. Stuttgart, G.252, 321, 365, 366.
11. Stuttgart, G.246, 25–31.
12. Oberkirch, II/139; The letter in BC 6137, p. 67 dated 23 March from Izabela to Marianna which refers to 'votre sort décidé par mes soins les plus tendres', is not evidence, since the year '1784' was added later, and it should almost certainly be 1785; BC 6136 II, 20.
13. BC 1998 III, 117.
14. BC 6149 III, 168.
15. BC 6149 III, 170.
16. BC 6111, 25.
17. Lehndorff 1920, 241–2.
18. BC 6034, IV, 307.
19. BC 6034, 71.
20. Sekrecka 134; see also BC 6030 III, 39, 41; Dębicki, I/229
21. Oberkirch, II/141 (the Grand Duchess's letter of December 1784

and the soupy account of the reconciliation are either wrongly reproduced or did not take place until the spring of 1786); Lehndorff 1920, 242, 263; Stuttgart G. 252, 366, 367; Dębicki, I/230; Stuttgart, G. 247, 9; Stuttgart, G.246, 36–9.
22. BC 6137, 134.
23. Lehndorff 1925, 22; BC 6137, 598.
24. Berlin, Rep 47, 1078, 1; Lehndorff 1920, 286–7; Lehndorff 1925, 1–5.
25. BC 6067 IV, t. 2, 66.
26. Lehndorff 1925, 5–6; Radziwiłł, pcesse Antoni, 19.
27. Radziwiłł, pcesse Antoni, 19; BC 6067 IV, t. 2, 92.
28. Lehndorff 1925, 59.
29. Lehndorff 1925, 5–6, 11, 12; Fiszerowa, 176, 177–8; Lehndorff 1925, 19, 64.
30. Duchińska, 30.
31. BC 21940, 161–2.
32. Lehndorff 1925, 20.
33. Lehndorff 1925, 24–5.
34. Lehndorff 1925, 12, 17, 20, 22.
35. BC 6137, 189.
36. BC 6067 IV, t. 2, 64.
37. BC 6137, 172.

**Chapter 9**
1. Berry, III/ 462–3, writes that it was in 1786, but Izabela's movements in that year exclude that, and according to Zamoyska, 297, Izabela carved her name in the bark of a beech at Castle Howard with the date 1785.
2. BC 6137, 212, 216.
3. BC 6149 III, 149.
4. BC 6137, 224; BC6149 III, 178.
5. *Autographen*, 389–90; Dębicki, I/236–7; Oberkirch, II/143.
6. BC 6137, 200–18.
7. BC 6137, 193–9.
8. Czartoryska 1891, 4, 6, 14.
9. Ostrowski, 133, 256; Soroka, 174.
10. BC 6137, 208.
11. BC 6137, 236–8; Aleksandrowicz 2011, 23, 33–4, 36–7.

12. Kórnik 01327, 84–5; Lublin 2110, 292.
13. BC 6136, 41.
14. Czartoryski, A. J. 1887, I/301–2.
15. BC 6103, 12ff.
16. BC 6067 IV, t. 2, 100.
17. BC 6067 IV, t. 2, 56, 100.
18. BC 6067 IV, t. 2, 100.
19. Dębicki, I/251; BC 6137, 352.
20. BC 6137, 258.
21. BC 6107, no. 6; BC 6137, 386.
22. BC 6067 IV, t. 2, 56.
23. Czartoryska 1891, 20; Garlick, 142.
24. BC 6149, 240–1; BC6103 III, 12.
25. BC 6137, 580, 390; BC 6107, no. 15; BC 6137, 577; BC 6103 III, 39, 14.
26. Czartoryska 1891, 25–6, 30, 16.
27. BC 6107, no. 7.
28. Radziwiłł, pcesse Antoni, 49–50.
29. BC 6149, 192–5.
30. Aleksandrowska 1992, 216.
31. Koźmian, A. E. 1867, I/409.
32. BC 6027, t. 1, 9ff.; see also Dębicki, I/167.
33. BC 6070 – 002 III, 19.
34. Koźmian, K. 1867, I/131–2.
35. Koźmian, K. 1867, I/132; Koźmian, A. E., 28; Żychliński 83.
36. Tarnowska, 8–9; BC 1988 III, 333; Aleksandrowicz 2011, 45.
37. BC 6137, 290; Aleksandrowska 1992, 216, 219.
38. BC 6137, 366.
39. BC 6137, 372.
40. BC 6107, no. 8; Prek, 185.
41. BC 6107, no 8; Sekrecka, 82, 85, 87.
42. Sekrecka, 99.
43. BC 6137, 394; BC 6017, no. 8; Aleksandrowicz 1998,160.
44. BC 6137, 398.
45. BC 6107, no. 21.

**Chapter 10**
1. Whelan, 260; BC 6107, no. 10.
2. Czartoryska 1891, 83–4.
3. BC 6066, 1.
4. BC 6137, 348; Czartoryski, A. J. 2016, 328.; BC 6137, 406.

5. BC 6107, no. 11; Czartoryski, A. J. 1887, I/194.
6. BC 6137, 410.
7. BC 6137, 349.
8. BC 6107, no. 11.
9. BC 6107, no. 11; BC 6137, 330.
10. BC 6137, 330; BC 6107, no. 11.
11. Sekrecka, 122.
12. BC 6107, no. 12.
13. *Bath Chronicle*, 1 July 1790.
14. BC 6107, no. 15.
15. BC 21940, 55; *Derby Mercury* 11 August 1790; *Jackson's Oxford Journal*, 6 August 1790; Whelan 292.
16. BC 6137, 324.
17. BC 6137, 326.
18. BC 6137, 326.
19. BC 6066 II, 29.
20. BC 6137, 464.
21. BC 6066 II, 64–5.
22. BC 21943, 113; BC 6137, 314.
23. BC 6137, 418.
24. BC 6030 III, 31.
25. Sekrecka, 124–5; BC 6030 III, 33; BC 6107, no. 12.
26. BC 6107, no. 16.
27. Kórnik, 01367, 208.
28. BC 6137, 302, 306.
29. BC 6103 III, 31.
30. BC 6107, no. 20; BC 6137, 312.
31. BC 6030 III, 34.

**Chapter 11**
1. Zamoyski, Adam, 335.
2. BC 6067 IV, t. 2, 82; Frączyk, 452.
3. Zaleski, M., 202; *The Times*, 16 April 1792, p. 3.
4. von der Recke, 101–2, 109–10.
5. Ochocki, II/107–9; Kórnik 07784, 22; Dębicki, IV/293.
6. Zamoyski, Adam, 347.
7. BC 6137, 588; Kórnik, 07784, 23.
8. Aleksandrowicz 2011, 92; Stuttgart G.246, 67, 71–5.
9. Zamoyski, Adam, 380–1; Koneczny, 243.

10. BC 6070 – 002 III, 301; BC 6107, 22,
    23; see also Lucchesini, 243;
    Rymszyna and Zahorski, 25.
11. Lublin 2110, 521.
12. Kórnik, 07734, 24.
13. Kórnik 07734, 24; Szymanowski, 56–7.
14. Skowronek1994, 29.
15. AGAD, Archiwum Radziwiłłów z
    Nieborowa, 355, Seria I, teka 2,
    149, 4.
16. Sekrecka, 132–3.
17. BC 6079, 1793.
18. Kórnik, 07734, 27; Rymszyna and
    Zahorski, 124, 183.
19. Rymszyna and Zahorski, 183.
20. BC 6067 IV, t. 2, 87.
21. Buccholtz, 103, 145, 166–7; Dębicki,
    I/390; Danilczyk, 76; Czartoryski,
    A. J. 1887, I/39, 74; BC 6067 IV,
    t. 2, 92.
22. Engelhardt, 111.
23. Dębicki I/395; BC 6034, 167; *Bumagi*
    1875, 85, 44.
24. BC 6067 IV, t. 2, 92, 268; Skowronek
    1994, 32.
25. Skowronek 1994, 8.
26. *Bumagi* 1875, 113.
27. Tarnowska, 93, 102, 107–8; *Bumagi*
    1875, 327.
28. *Bumagi* 1875, 143, 159.
29. Czartoryski, A. J. 1887, I/39, 55;
    *Bumagi* 1891, 402.
30. Czartoryski, A. J. 1887, I/67–8.
31. *Bumagi* 1875, 283, 296.
32. Czartoryski, A. J. 1887, I/96;
    Skowronek 1994, 49.
33. Czartoryski, A. J. 1887, I/98, 150, 159.
34. BC 6103, 3.
35. Vienna PHSt331. 1797, *passim.*; BC
    6070, 311.

**Chapter 12**
1. BC 6067 IV, t. 2, 96; see also BC
   6131, 149–52
2. Czartoryski, A. J. 1887, I/161;
   Burnett, 259.
3. BC 6067 IV, t. 2, 96.
4. Sekrecka, 135, 37–8.

5. AGAD, Archiwum Radziwiłłów z
   Nieborowa, Zespół 355, Seria I, teka
   2, 149, 18.
6. BC 6138, 34.
7. BC 6137, 721–30.
8. Stuttgart, G.247, 15–35, 216, 190,
   28–30, 25–7; BC 6138, 146, 177, 327.
9. AGAD, Archiwum Radziwiłłów z
   Nieborowa, Zespół 355, Seria I, teka
   2, 149, 34; BC 6138, 5.
10. BC 6138, 71–3, 77, 165, 664–6.
11. Czartoryski, A. J. 1887, I/159–60.
12. Golovin, 109–15, 166, 216–17;
    Czartoryski, A. J. 1887, I/159–60; BC
    6107, no. 29.
13. Radziwiłł, M. P., 96–7.
14. Golovin, 221-4; Skowronek 1994, 52.
15. Skowronek 1994, 54.
16. BC 6137, 689, 737; BC 006288 – 002
    III, 78.
17. Dembowski, I/28-30; Vienna
    PHSt134.1800.

**Chapter 13**
1. AGAD, Archiwum Radziwiłłów z
   Nieborowa, 355, Seria I, teka 2, 18.
2. Broglie, I/189.
3. Burnett, 304.
4. Radziwiłł, pcesse Antoni, 190.
5. Potocka-Wąsowiczowa, 45; BC
   6107, nr. 19.
6. Żychliński, VIII/76; Klimowicz, 325;
   see also 006288 – 002, III, 51
7. Johnson, 348.
8. Potocki, 129; Czartoryska 1808;
   Aleksandrowicz in Goliński &
   Kostkiewiczowa 1996, 618.
9. BC 6028 IV; BC 6027 t. 2, 53;
   Potocka-Wąsowiczowa, 43.
10. Burnett, 223-4.
11. Garlick, 143.
12. Burnett, 255–6; Radziwiłł, pcesse
    Antoni, 190; Potocki, 113.
13. Grzegorzewska, 8.
14. The first reliable mention of her
    presence at Puławy I came across
    was in Zosia Matuszewicz's diary in
    July 1815. Her near-contemporary

Dembowski, who spent six years of his teens at Puławy, maintains [I/44] that she was part of their group, but he is not always reliable. Łętowski, 46–7, claims she was Izabela's child.

15. BC 006288 – 002 III, 14.
16. Czartoryski, W., 3.
17. BC 6062, 47; BC 6138, 68; BC 006288 – 002 III, 86. Louise of Prussia-Radziwiłł's view of the marriage and the relationship between the two families conflicts with the documentary evidence; she makes out that Izabela did not like Helena, whom she saw as a rival, and that Helena was taken in by her supposedly feigned marks of affection. She writes that Aniela's father was against the projected marriage and that Izabela was against it, too.
18. Koźmian, K, II/54; Czacki, 30–1; Koźmian, K, I/283.
19. Potocki, 113; Koźmian, K., I/284.
20. BC 006288 – 002 III, 39.
21. BC 006288 – 002 III, 78.
22. Pougens.
23. Potocka-Wąsowiczowa, 47.

**Chapter 14**
1. BC 6030 III, 22, 25, 27.
2. BC 6138, 222.
3. Vigel, 100.
4. BC 006288 – 002, III, 101: letter wrongly dated 1806.
5. BC 6067 IV, t. 2, 103–10.
6. ibid. 111; other sources give the date of his arrival as 30 September; Tarnowska, 110.
7. 6067 IV, t. 2, 112.
8. Koźmian, K., II/55; Tarnowska, 111.
9. Kicka, 422; Czartoryski, A. J. 1887, I/399.
10. BC 6067 IV, 110; BC 2000 IV, 929ff.
11. Hertz.
12. Kozmian K, II/60.
13. Vigel, 193; Czartoryski, W., 6–62.
14. Czartoryski, A. J. 1887, I/148.

15. BC6067 IV, t. 2, 9; Bourgoing, 55.
16. BC 006288 – 002 III, 117, 111, 137.
17. Dino, 163, 202.
18. BC 002688 – 002 III, 111, 117.
19. BC 6103, 5; BC 006288 – 002 III, 141.
20. Dembowski, I/360–5.
21. BC 6138, 361.
22. Dembowski, I/375–6; BC 6138, 365–73.
23. BC 6093 III, 33–6; Dembowski, I/380–2; her letter of 6 April 1809 in BC 6342, t. 2 betrays a deep sympathy; BC 006288 – 002 III, 144; Dino, 224.
24. Dino, 226–45.
25. BC 006288 – 002 III, 151.
26. BC 6030 III, 71.

**Chapter 15**
1. Dębicki, II/130–3; BC6067 IV, t. 2, 87.
2. BC 006288 – 002 III, 153.
3. Czartoryski, W., 69–74, 77–8, 92–102, 130, 127–57.
4. BC 006288 – 2 III, 193, 157.
5. BC 6138, 243; BC 006288 – 002 III, 167; BC 6138, 403; Czartoryska 1891, 4.
6. BC 6138, 429 (letter wrongly dated – no Friday 9 March in 1809).
7. BC 6138, 433 (3 April 1810), 431 (6 April 1810).
8. BC 006288 – 002 III, 167.
9. BC 6138, 414, 431–2; BC 6067, IV t. 2, 84.
10. Senfft, 110–12.
11. Niemcewicz 1871, I/217; BC 6138, 414; Koźmian, K., II/53; BC 6067 IV, t. 2, 84.
12. Senfft, 116.
13. BC 6138, 415–16, 459, 470 (I believe this note has been wrongly placed in 1811 and belongs to August 1810); BC 6030 III, 97.
14. Niemcewicz 1871, 280.
15. BC 6138, 454–6.
16. BC 6138, 482; BC 006288 – 002 III, 204.

17. BC 6140 IV, 11; BC 006288 – 002 III, 203–9.
18. BC 6140 IV, 16–18.
19. BC 006288 – 002 III, 282, 215, 217.
20. BC 006288 – 002 III, 220.
21. BC 006288 – 002 III, 221–3; BC 60630 III, 35–6; BC 006288 – 002 III, 228.
22. Bignon, 132, 139–40, 135.
23. Niemcewicz 1871, I/227; Skarbek 135–6.
24. BC 006288 – 002 III, 233; Koźmian, A. E., 125; Skarbek 137.
25. Bignon, 139; Broglie, I/187–8.
26. BC 006288 – 002 III, 243.
27. BC 6067 IV, t. 2, 128.
28. Czartoryski, W., 197.
29. Sapieha, 13.
30. BC 006288 – 002 III, 316.
31. Czartoryski, W., 210–11.
32. BC 006288 – 002 III, 307–8.
33. Ibid., 317; BC 6067 IV, t.2, 140–1.
34. BC 006288 – 002 III, 346.

**Chapter 16**
1. BC 006288 – 002 III, 352.
2. BC 6031, 19; BC 6030, 110.
3. BC 006288 – 002 III, 353–5; BC 6027 t. 1, 17, 34, 41–2, 61, 64.
4. BC 006288 – 002 III, 417.
5. BC 006288 – 002 III, 381–3.
6. BC 006288 – 002 III, 346, 396.
7. ibid., 416.
8. ibid., 453, 428, 442.
9. ibid., 430.
10. ibid., 301, 402.
11. ibid., 402, 415, 447; BC 6030 III, 109–15.
12. Wodzicka, 31.
13. BC 6067 IV, t.2, 94, 159; BC 6030, 316.
14. BC 6067 IV t. 2, 154, 155; Koźmian, K., II/350.
15. BC 6067 IV, t.2, 154–9; Wodzicka, 32–5.
16. Radziwiłł, pcesse Antoni, 300.
17. BC 6030 III, 148–60.
18. Ibid., 170–3.
19. BC 6030 III, 227.

20. BC 006288 – 002 III, 495.
21. BC 6030 III, 279; BC 6067 IV, t. 2, 164.
22. BC 6030 III, 279.
23. Radziwiłł pcesse Antoni, 256–7.
24. Koźmian, A. E., 139; BC 6030 III, 286; Zamoyski, W., I/69.

**Chapter 17**
1. Radziwiłł, pcesse Antoni, 247; Koźmian, A. E., 141; Skarbek, 148–9; Koźmian, K., II/129.
2. BC 6030 III 307, 314; Niemcewicz 1871, I/259–60.
3. BC 6030 III, 342.
4. BC 6067 IV, t. 2, 182–201.
5. Czartoryski, A. J. 2016, 413–17.
6. Czartoryski 2016, 404–36; BC 6164, 64; Wodzicka 38–41.
7. Czartoryski 2016, 427.
8. BC 6030 III 380.
9. Wodzicka, 79.
10. Wodzicka, 83.
11. BC 6030 III, 383.
12. BC 6141, 1.
13. BC 6141, 3–11.
14. Skarbek, 210.
15. BC 6158 t. 2, 73; BC 6070 – 002 III, 274.
16. Wodzicka, 110.
17. BC 6030 III, 455, 465.
18. BC 6030 III, 494.
19. Radziwiłł, M. P., 291.
20. BC 6030 - 003 III, t. 3, 43, 21.
21. Skowronek 1994, 233.
22. BC 6141, 58.
23. Grzegorzewska, 23–6, 29–30.
24. Sapieha, 199.

**Chapter 18**
1. BC 6290, 41.
2. BC 6290, 30; BC6141, 78; BC 6290, 92, 107, 295.
3. BC 6290, 82.
4. BC 6290, 97.
5. BC 6290, 167.
6. Archives Nationales, 340 AP (Archives Poniatowski), I, 6, no.

19/20 is a page torn out of the parish registry of the Church of Saint-Roch in Paris dated 5 February 1821, which reads: 'Mariage de Constantin Adam Alexandre Thadée Czartoryski avec Mlle Thérèse Marie Dzierzanowski, née à Varsovie le 18 octobre 1794, fille du Colonel Jean Dzierzanowski et Elisabeth Dobian.' He gave his address as 7 rue Richepanse, she as 11 rue Royale. The witnesses were, on his side: Nicolas Bernard and Frédéric Boudin 'négociants du quartier', hers: Pierre Viant, 'notaire', and Michel Bienkowski (rue Richepanse).; BC 6290, 120–3, 217.

7. Prek, 104.
8. BC 6290, 337, 338.
9. Zamoyski, W. I/196–7 ; BC 6290, 302, 311–12.
10. BC 6290, 418.
11. BC 6290, 555
12. Koźmian, K., II/180; Dembowski, II/15; 6290, 582.
13. Prek, 430.
14. BC 6290, 599–600 (although the date looks like '22 nov', the letter was

clearly written two days before his name day on 24 December.
15. BC 6290, 708, 714.
16. Cholewianka-Kruszyńska 2008, 178.
17. Ibid., 179.
18. Dwernicki, 43.
19. Cholewianka-Kruszyńska 2008, 180; Dębicki, IV/321; BC 6290, 607, 716; Niemcewicz 1909, 85.
20. BC 6290, 702, 605,612, 614.
21. BC 6290, 623–4, 622.
22. BC 6290, 742.
23. BC 6290, 668, 670.
24. Kicka, 403.
25. BC 6290, 680.
26. BC 6290, 726.
27. *Perepiska Imperatora Nikolaia Pavlovicha*, 4, 87; BC 6290, 759.
28. Prek, 181–2.
29. Duchińska, 38–9.

**Postscript**
1. Aleksandrowicz 2011, 101; BC 6111, 73ff., 103ff., 129ff.
2. Gontaut-Biron, 355–8; Maugras 1909, 527–8.

# Sources

## ARCHIVAL

Archives Nationales, Paris, 340 AP (Archives Poniatowski).
Archiwum Główne Akt Dawnych, Warsaw, Zespół 335, Archiwum Publiczne
Potockich, nr. 293. *Listy do Aleksandry z Lubomirskich Potockiej*; Zespół 355, Seria
I, Archiwum Radziwiłłów z Nieborowa; Archiwum Radziwiłłow IV, *Listy Anieli z
Radziwiłłów*; Zespół 358, *Listy Adama Kazimierza Czartoryskiego do Stanisława
Zamoyskiego*. Archiwum Radziwiłłów IV; Archiwum Radziwiłłów V, 2586: *Listy
Izabeli Czartoryskiej do Heleny i innych Radziwiłłów.*

Biblioteka Czartoryskich, Kraków
Izabela's reminiscences, notes, jottings, thoughts and writings in: 6066 II, 6067 IV t.
1 and 2, 6069, 6070 – 002 III, 6071 II and III, 6072 III, 6073 II; her catalogues
for the Gothic House: 21940, 21943, 21950; her correspondence: 6030 III, 6031-003
III t.3, 6103 III, 6107, 6034 IV, 6036, 6074 t. 1, 2 and 3, 6075, 6076, 6099, 6110,
6138, 6138, 6139 III, 6140 IV, 6141, 6155, 6158 t. 2; other family correspondence:
6029, 6032 III, 6033, 6057, 6091 IV, 6093 III, 6111, 6135 IV t. 2, 6136 II, 6146, 6147,
6148, 6149 III, 6150 t. 1 & 2, 6286, 006288 – 002 III, 6290, 6291, 6342 t. 2; other
family papers: 6008 IV, 6013 IV t. 1 and 2, 6108 t. 1 and 2; accounts, travel and
other expenses, personal expenses, staff, court and other, inventories, etc.: 6001 IV
t. 1 and 2, 6006 IV t. 106020, 6027 t. 1, 2, 3 and 4, 6028 IV, 6077 IV t. 1 and 2,
6078, 6079 t. 2 and 4, 6082; political papers: 1988 III, 1998 III, 199 IV, 2000 IV.

Biblioteka Kórnicka, Kórnik
01367 *Album księżnej Izabeli Czartoryskiej.*
07734 *Fragments du Journal de la ctesse Stanislas Zamoyska, née pcesse Czartoryska.*
07337 *Listy Cecylii Beydale do Celestyny Działyńskiej i różne do Cecylii Beydale.*
01324, 01327, 01577, 01637, *Gazetki pisane.*

Biblioteka im. H. Łopacińskiego, Lublin
521. *Listy Marii Wirtemberskiej i Izabeli Czartoryskiej.*

2110. *Kopie listów-gazetek pisanych przez Jana Magnuszewskigo, plenipotenta ks. Lubomirskiej do Józefa Konopki (1765–1807).*

Biblioteka Narodowa, Warsaw
*Osobliwsze zdarzenia przytrafione w Puławach w jesieni roku 1807 spisane po francusku w liście do księżnej Marii Wurtemberskiej.*
*Listy i autografy różnyvh osób ze zbiorów Bronisława Gubrynowicza.*

Geheimes Staatsarchiv, Berlin: Preussischer Kulturbesitz
BHP Rep. 47, Nr. 1078 Marianna von Württemberg to Frederick II.

Landesarchiv Baden-Württemberg, Hauptstaatsarchiv. Stuttgart
G 247 Bü 1, Friedrich Wilhelm von Württemberg to his bother Ludwig, Frederick II to Marianna von Württemberg, and documents relative to Ludwig's divorce.
G 246 Bü 3, Frederick II and Frederick William II to Ludwig von Württemberg.
G 252. Bü 3, Maria Feodorovna to Frederick of Württemberg.

Landesarchiv Berlin
Preussische Akademie der Künste, Band 1431: Nr. 4 (1695-1804) Part 1, Bl. 33.

Muzeum Narodowe, Warsaw, rkps. 520: *Conseils donnés par la princesse Czartoryska à Me Rautenstrauch.*

Oesterreichische Staatsarchiv, Vienna
Reports and interrogations concerning Izabela, Adam and Adam Jerzy: OeStA/AVA Inneres: PHSt331. 1797, PHSt333. 1797, PHSt691. 1798, PHS1000. 1798, PHSt1032. 1798, PHSt837. 1799, PHSt331. 1797, PHSt134. 1800, PHSt591. 1800, PHSt637. 11804, PHSt90a. 1808, PHSt438a. 1808, PHSt451a. 1808, PHSt649a. 1808, PHSt1284b. 1809, PHSt319. 1812.

Online: *Księgi Metrykalne Kościoła pw Świętego Krzyża w Warszawie*: https// metrykigenealodzy.pl/index.php?=pg&ar

Private Collection, London
Memoirs of Wirydianna Fiszerowa, French typescript.

# PRINTED

*Autographen aus allen Gebieten. Katalog 639*, ed. J. A. Stargardt, Marburg 1987
Bernardin de Saint-Pierre, Henri, *Oeuvres Posthumes*, Paris 1833
Berry, Mary, *Extracts from the Journals and Correspondence of Miss Berry from the year 1783 to 1752*, vol. III, London 1865
Beugnot, Claude comte, *Mémoires du Comte Beugnot, ancien ministre (1783–1815)*, vol. II, Paris 1866
Bignon, Edouard, baron, *Souvenirs d'un Diplomate. La Pologne (1811–1813)*, Paris 1864

# Sources

Błędowska z Działyńskich, H., *Pamiątka Przeszłości. Wspomnienia z lat 1794–1832*, Warsaw 1960

Boigne, Adèle d'Osmond, comtesse de, *Mémoires de la comtesse de Boigne, née d'Osmond*, vol. I, Paris 1908

Bourgoing, Baron P. de, *Souvenirs militaires*, Paris 1897

Broglie, Achille-Charles-Léonce duc de, *Souvenirs du feu duc de Broglie*, vol. I, Paris 1886

Bronikowski, Ksawery, ed., *Pamiętniki Polskie*, 2 vols, Przemyśl 1883

Buchholtz, Ludwig, *Powstanie Kościuszkowskie w świetle korespondencji posła pruskiego w Warszawie. Listy Ludwiga Buchholtza do Fryderyka Wilhelma II (styczeń-czerwiec 1794)*, Warsaw 1983

Bukar, S., *Pamiętniki z rękopisu po raz pierwszy ogłoszone*, Dresden 1871

*Bumagi Arsenia Andreevicha Zakrevskogo*, in *Sbornik Imperatorskogo Russkogo Istoricheskogo Obshchestva*, vol. 78, St Petersburg 1891

*Bumagi kniazia Nikolaia Vasilievicha Repnina*, in *Sbornik Imperatorskogo Russkogo Istoricheskogo Obshchestva*, vol. 5, St Petersburg 1870

*Bumagi kniazia N. V. Repnina za vremia upravlenia ego Litvoiu (gody s 1794 po 1796)*, in *Sbornik Imperatorskogo Russkogo Istoricheskogo Obshchestva*, vol. 16, St Petersburg 1875

Burnett, George, *View of the Present State of Poland*, London 1807

Catherine II, Empress of Russia, *Sochinienia*, ed. A. N. Pypin, vol. XII, St Petersburg 1911

Cieszkowski, L., *Pamiętnik anegdotyczny z czasów Stanisława Augusta*, Poznań 1867

Coke, Lady Mary, *The Letters and Journals of Lady Mary Coke*, vol. II, ed. James Home, Bath 1970

Coxe, William, *Travels into Poland, Russia, Sweden, and Denmark*, 2 vols, London 1785

Craven, Elizabeth, *The Beautiful Lady Craven. The Original Memoirs of Elizabeth Baroness Craven afterwards Margravine of Anspach and Bayreuth and Princess Berkeley of the Holy Roman Empire (1750–1828)*, ed. A. M. Broadley and Lewis Melville, vol. I, London 1914

Czacki, M., *Wspomnienia z roku 1788, po 1792*, Poznań 1862

Czajkowski, Michał, *Pamiętniki Sadyka Paszy*, Lwów 1898

Czartoryska, Izabela princess, *Myśli różne o sposobie zakładania ogrodów*, 2nd edn, Wrocław 1808

—, *Książka do pacierzy dla dzieci wiejskich podczas Mszy Św. Dla szkółki puławskiej napisana*, Wroclaw 1815

—, *Pielgrzym w Dobromilu, czyli nauki wiejskie*, Warsaw 1817, vol. 2 1821

—, *Poczet Pamiątek zachowanych w Domu Gotyckim w Puławach*, Warsaw 1828

—, *Pielgrzym w Dobromilu, czyli dalszy ciąg nauk wiejskich*, 1834

—, *Listy księżnej Izabeli z hr. Flemmingów Czartoryskiej do starszego syna księcia Adama*, ed. S. Duchińska, Kraków 1891

—, *Dyliżansem przez Śląsk. Dziennik podróży do Cieplic w roku 1816*, Wrocław 1968

Czartoryski, Adam Jerzy, *Mémoires du prince Adam Czartoryski et correspondance avec l'empereur Alexandre Ier*, 2 vols, Paris 1887

—, *Pamiętniki i memoriały polityczne 1776–1809*, ed. Jerzy Skowronek, Warsaw 1986

—, *Dziennik ks. Adama Jerzego Czartoryskiego 1813–1817*, ed. Małgorzata Karpińska, Warsaw 2016

Czartoryski, Adam Kazimierz, *Katechizm moralny dla uczniów Korpusu Kadetów*, Warsaw 1774

—, *Listy Jmci Pana Doświadczyńskiego*, Warsaw 1782

Czartoryski, Władysław, ed., *Alexandre Ier et le Prince Czartoryski. Correspondance particulière et conversations 1801–1823*, Paris 1865

Dębski, Jan Nepomucen, *Odgłos muzy na dźwięk weselnych okrzyków*, etc., Warsaw 1761

—, *Poloniae totius magnique ducatus Litvaniae*, etc., Warsaw 1761

Delaney, Mary Granville, Mrs, *The Autobiography and Correspondence of Mary Granville, Mrs Delaney*, ed. Lady Llanover, Second Series, vol. I, London 1862

Dembowski, Leon, *Moje wspomnienia*, 2 vols, St Petersburg 1898

Dino, Dorothée de Courlande, duchesse de, *Souvenirs de la duchesse de Dino*, Paris 1908

Dmochowski, Franciszek Salezy, *Wspomnienia od 1806 do 1830*, Warsaw 1959

Duchińska, Seweryna, *Wspomnienia z życia Marii z książąt Czartoryskich księżnej Wirtemberskiej*, Warsaw 1886

Dwernicki, Józef, *Pamiętniki*, Lwów 1878

Engelhardt, Lev Nikolaevich, *Pamiętniki Jenerała Lwa Mikołajowicza Englehardta*, trs. P. K. Stolnikowicz-Chełmski, Poznań 1873

Falkowski, Juliusz, *Obrazy kilku ostatnich pokoleń w Polsce*, 5 vols, Poznań 1882–7

Golovin, countess Varvara Nikolaevna, *Souvenirs de la comtesse Golovine, née princesse Galitzine 1766–1821*, Paris 1910

Grzegorzewska z Gostkowskich, Sabina, *Dziesięć dni w Puławach w roku 1828*, Kraków 1898

Johnson, Lieutenant-Colonel John, *A journey from India to England, through Persia, Georgia, Russia, Poland and Prussia in the year 1817*, London 1818

Karpiński, Franciszek, *Pamiętniki*, Poznań 1884

Kicka, Natalia, *Pamiętniki*, Warsaw 1972

Kitowicz, Jędrzej, *Pamiętniki do panowania Augusta III i Stanisława Augusta*, 4 vols, Lwów 1882

—, *Opis obyczajów za panowania Augusta III*, Wrocław 1970

Kniaźnin, *Dzieła*, 5 vols, Warsaw 1828

Kopeć, Józef, *Dziennik Józefa Kopcia brygadiera wojsk polskich*, Warsaw 1995

Koźmian, Andrzej Edward, *Wizerunki osób towarzystwa warszawskiego: Dwie siosty. Maria z książąt Czartoryskich Wirtemberska i Zofia Zamoyska*, in *Przeglad Pozański*, r. 24; 1857

—, *Wspomnienia*, in *Pamiętniki z XIXw.*, vol. I, Poznań 1867

Koźmian, Kajetan, *Pamiętniki*, 3 vols, Wrocław 1972

Kretowicz, Zygmunt August. *Puławy*, Lwów 1831

Lauzun, Armand de Gontaut-Biron, duc de, *Mémoires secrets du beau Lauzun, suivies de lettres adressées a l'auteur etc.*, ed. Edmond Pilon, Paris 1943

Lavater, Johann Caspar, *Thérèse Czartoriska*, Zurich 1780

Lehndorff, Ernst Anhasverus, *Tagebüchernach seiner Kammerherrenzeit*, ed. Karl Eduard Schmidt Lötzen, in *Mitteilungen der literarischen Gessellschaft Masovia*, vol. 24/25, 1920; vol. 30/30, 1925

Ligne, Charles Joseph, Prince de, *Coup d'oeil sur Beloeil et su une grande partie des jardins de l'Europe*, ed. Comte Ernest de Ganay, Paris 1922

*Liste des Seigneurs et Dames venus aux eaux minérales de Spa l'an 1768*, ditto 1772 and 1773, Liège 1768, 1772, 1773

# Sources

Lubomirski, Stanisław, *Pod władzą księcia Repnina. Ułamki pamiętników i dzienników historycznych (1764–1768)*, Warsaw 1971

Lucchesini, Girolamo, *Listy do Fryderyka Wilhelma II*, Warsaw 1988

Łętowski, L., *Wspomnienia pamiętnikarskie*, Wrocław 1956

Łojek, Jerzy, ed., *Rok nadziei i rok klęski 1791–1792. Z korespondencji Stanisława Augusta z posłem polskim w Petersburgu Augustynem Deboli*, Warsaw 1964

Mably, Gabriel Bonnot de, *De la Situation Politique de la Pologne en 1776*, Paris 1794

Malmesbury, James Harris Earl of, *Diaries and Correspondence*, vol. I, London 1845

Matuszewicz, Marcin, *Diariusz życia mego*, 2 vols, Warsaw 1986

Montesquiou, Comte Anatole de, *Souvenirs sur la Révolution, l'Empire, la Restauration et le Règne de Louis-Philippe*, Paris 1961

Moszczeński, A., *Pamiętnik do historii polskiej w ostatnich latach panowania Augusta III i pierwszych Stanisława Augusta*, in *Pamiętniki z ośmnastego wieku*, vol. IX, Poznań 1867

Nakwaska, A., *Wspomnienia z czasów pruskich i Księstwa Warszawskiego (1792–1830)*, in *Kronika Rodzinna*, 1891, nr. 4

Naruszewicz, Adam, *Sprawa między x. A. Czartoryskim [. . .] oskarżającym a Janem Komarzewskim [. . .] i Franciszkiem Ryxem [. . .] oskarżonymi roku 1785*, Warsaw n.d.

Niemcewicz, Julian Ursyn, *Zofia Zamojska*, Paris 1837

—, *Pamiętnik 1811–1820*, 2 vols, Poznań 1871

—, *Pamiętnik o czasach Księstwa Warszawskiego (1807–1809)*, Warsaw 1902

—, *Puławy w czterech pieśniach*, Brody 1907

—, *Pamiętnik 1830–1831*, Kraków 1909

—, *Pamiętniki czasów moich*, Warsaw 1957

Oberkirch, Henriette Louise, baronne d', *Mémoires*, vol. II, Paris 1869

Ochocki, Jan Duklan, *Pamiętniki*, 4 vols, Wilno 1857

Ostrowski, Teodor, *Poufne wieści z oświeconej Warszawy. Gazetki pisane z roku 1782*, Wrocław 1972

*Perepiska Imperatora Nikolaia Pavlovicha s Velikim Kniaziem Konstantinom Pavlovichom*, in *Sbornik Imperatorskogo Russkogo Istoricheskogo Obshchestva*, vol. 132, St Petersburg 1911

Poniatowski, Stanisław, *Pamiętniki synowca Stanisława Augusta*, Warsaw 1979

Potocka-Wąsowiczowa, Anna z Tyszkiewiczów, *Wspomnienia naocznego świadka*, Warsaw 2022

Potocki, Leon, *Urywek ze wspomnień pierwszej mojej młodości*, Poznań 1876

Pradt, Dominique Dufour de, *Histoire de l'ambassade dans le Grand Duché de Varsovie en 1812*, Paris 1816

Prek, Franciszek Ksawery, *Czasy i Ludzie*, Wrocław 1959

Radziwiłł, princesse Antoni, née princesse Louise de Prusse, *Quarante cinq années de ma vie*, Paris 1911

Recke, Elisa von der, *Mein Journal 1791–1793/95*, Leipzig 1927

*Recueil de Pièces relatives au procès entre S. A. Le Prince Adam Czartoryski, accusateur, & M. M. Komarzewski & Ryx, accusés du crime d'empoisonnement*, Warsaw 1785

Rulhière, Claude-Carloman de, *Histoire de l'Anarchie de Pologne, et du démembrement de cette république*, vol. II, Paris 1807

Rymszyna, Maria and Zahorski, Andrzej, eds, *Tajna Koresponencja z Warszawy 1792–1794 do Ignacego Potockiego*, Warsaw 1961

Rzewuska, Rosalie, *Mémoires de la comtesse Rosalie Rzewuska (1788–1865)*, Rome 1939

Sapieha, Leon xiąże, *Wspomnienia (z lat od 1803 do 1863 r.)*, Kraków 1912

Sekrecka, M., ed., *Correspondance inédite d'Isabelle Czartoryska avec Jean Gaspard Lavater*, in *Acta Universitatis Wratislaviensis*, nr. 117, *Romanica Wratislaviensia V*, Wrocław 1970

Senfft von Pilsach, Friedrich Christian, *Mémoires du comte de Senfft ancien ministre de Saxe*, Leipzig 1863

Skarbek, Fryderyk Count, *Pamiętniki Fryderyka hrabiego Skarbka*, Warsaw 2009

Soroka, Jerzy, *Paniętnik Jerzego Soroki, pazia i koniuszego księcia generała ziem podolskich 1772–1822*, ed. Dr Władysław Wisłocki, in *Tygodnik Illustrowany*, Seria III, t. 12, 1881

Staël-Holstein, Germaine de, *Dix années d'éxil*, Paris, n.d.

Stanisław II Augustus, King of Poland, *Mémoires*, Paris 2012

Szymanowski, J., *Listy do starościny Wyszogrodzkiej*, Warszawa 1973

Tarczewska, z Tańskich Aleksandra, *Historia mego życia*, Wrocław 1967

Tarnowska, z Ustrzyckich U., *Wspomnienia damy polskiej z XVIIIw.*, in *Archiwum Wróblewieckie*, Zeszyt 1, Poznań 1869

Vigel, Filip Filipovich, *Zapiski*, Moscow 2000

Voltaire, François Arouët, *Histoire de Charles XII*, vol. 23 in *Oeuvres Complètes*, Paris 1785

Walpole, Horace, *The Yale Edition of Horace Walpole's Correspondence*, Yale 1937–1983

Witt, J. (Stanisław Kostka Potocki), *Listy polskie pisane w roku 1785*

Wodzicka, z Potockich T., *Ze zwierzeń dziewcięcych. Pamiętnik Zofii z Matuszewiczów Kickiej (1796–1822)*, Kraków 1910

Wraxall, N. William, *Memoirs of the Courts of Berlin, Dresden, Warsaw and Vienna, in the years 1777, 1778 and 1779*, 2 vols, London 1806

Württemberg, Marianna Czartoryska princess (Maria Wirtemberska), *Niektóre zdarzenia, myśli i uczucia doznane za granicą*, Warsaw 1978

Wybicki, Józef, *Pamiętniki Józefa Wybickiego Senatora Wojewody królestwa polskiego*, 3 vols, Poznań 1840

Wyrwicz, Karol, *Mowa do J.O. Książąt Ichmościów Adama gen. Ziem podolskich i Izabeli z hr. Flemmingów Czartoryskich w dzień pożądanego ich ślubu[. . .] przez x. Karola Wyrwicza w Wołczynie dn. 19 listopada Roku 1761 Miana*

Zaleski, Michal, *Pamiętniki*, Poznań 1879

Zamoyska, Jadwiga, *Wspomnienia*, London 1961

Zamoyski, Andrzej hr, *Moje Przeprawy*, 2 vols, Kraków 1911

Zamoyski, Władysław, *Jenerał Zamoyski, 1803–1868*, vol. I, Poznań 1910

Zawadzki, Wacław, ed., *Polska Stanisławowska w Oczach Cudzoziemców*, 2 vols, Warsaw 1965

Żubr, Joanna, *Opis życia Joanny Żubr, byłej w Wojsku Polskim sierżantem, a teraz retretowanej w stopniu podporucznika własnoręcznie spisany d. 1 maja 1828*, in Ma. E. Kowalczyk, *Sierżant w spódnicy*, Łomianki 2016

# STUDIES

Aftanazy, Roman, *Materiały do dziejów rezydencji*, Andrzej J. Baranowski, ed., Warsaw 1986

Ajewski, Konrad, *Stanisława Kostki Zamoyskiego życie i działalność 1775–1856*, Warsaw 2010

Aleksandrowicz, Alina, ed., *Z kręgu Marii Wirtemberskiej. Antologia*, Warsaw 1978

—, *Izabela z Flemingów Czartoryska*, in Goliński, Zbigniew and Kostkiewiczowa Teresa, *Pisarze Polskiego Oświecenia*, vol. III, Warsaw 1996

—, *Izabela Czartoryska, Polskość i Europejskość*, Lublin 1998

—, *Różne drogi do wolności. Puławy Czartoryskich na przełomie XVIII i XIX wieku*, Pulawy 2011

—, *Twórczość Marii z ks. Czartoryskich ks. Wirtemberskiej. Literatura i Obyczaj*, Warsaw 2022

Aleksandrowska, Elżbieta, ed., *Monitor 1765–1785*, Warsaw 1976

—, *Sejm czteroletni i konstytucja 3 maja w kręgu Puław*,in *Rok Monarchii Konstytucyjnej. Piśmiennictwo polskie lat 1791-2 wobec konstytucji 3 maja*, ed. Teresa Kostkiewiczowa, Warsaw 1992

Askenazy, Szymon, *Wczasy historyczne*, Warsaw 1902

—, *Szkice i portrety*, Warsaw 1937

Bieliński, Józef, *Żywot ks. Adama Jerzego Czartoryskiego*, 2 vols, Warsaw 1905

Barnett, Gerald, *Richard and Maria Cosway*, Cambridge 1995

Cholewianka-Kruszyńska, Aldona, *Panny Czartoryskie*, Warsaw 1995

—, *Piękna i Dobra. Opowieść o Zofii z Czartoryskich Zamoyskiej*, Kozłówka 2008

Crane, Susan A., *Collecting and Historical consciousness in Early Nineteenth-Century Germany*, Cornell 2000

Dacka-Górzyńska, Iwona M., *O nieznanych dzieciach Magnaterii Polskiej w świetle Parafialnych metryk zmarłych kościoła Sw. Krzyża w Warszawie*, in Przegląd Historyczny, vol. 102, Warsaw 2011

Danilczyk, Adam, *W kręgu afery Dogrumowej. Sejm 1786 roku*, Warsaw 2010

Dębicki, Ludwik, *Puławy (1762–1830)*, 4 vols, Lwów 1887–8

Długoń, Iwona, *Znad Modrego Dunaju po leniwy San. Czartoryscy z Pełkiń*, unpublished doctoral thesis

Drozdowski, Marian Marek, ed., *Życie kultralne i religijne w czasach Stanisława Augusta Poniatowskiego*, Warsaw 1991

Frączyk, Tadeusz, *Adam Kazimierz Czartoryski. Biografia historyczno-literacka na tle przemian ideowych polskiego Oświecenia*, Kraków 2012

Garlick, Richard Cecil, *Philip Mazzei, Friend of Jefferson*, Baltimore, 1933

Głowacka,-Maksymiuk, *Aleksandra z książąt Czartoryskich Ogińska*, Siedlce 2003

Gołębiowska, Zofia, *Oświata i wychowanie w Puławach oraz kluczu końskowolskim w czasach Czartoryskich*, Lublin 2005

Gontaut-Biron, comte R. De, *Le duc de Lauzun 1747–1793*, Paris 1937

Grabski, Andrzej Feliks, *Myśl historyczna polskiego Oświecenia*, Warsaw 1976

Hertz, Paweł, *Rabbi Izrael z Kozienic i książę Adam Czartoryski*, in W Drodze, 1984, no. 9

Hyczko, Gustawa, *Instytut Panien polskich w Paryżu (1845–1899)*, in Zins, Henryk, ed., *Polska w Europie. Sudia Historyczne*, Lublin 1968

Inglot, Stefan, ed., *Historia Chłopów Polskich*, Wrocław 1992

Janion, Maria and Żmigrodzka, Maria, *Romantyzm i Historia*, Warsaw 1978
Kaleta, Roman, *Anegdoty i sensacje obyczajowe wieku oświecenia w Polsce*, Warsaw 1958
—, *Oświeceni i Sentymentalni*, Wrocław 1971
Kicińska, Urszula, *Zofia Maria z Sieniawskich Czartoryska – Życie w cieniu Matki i Męża?*, in Roćko Agata and Górska, Magdalena, eds, *Słynne Kobiety w Rzeczypospolitej XVIII wieku*, Wilanów 2017
Klimowicz, Mieczysław, *Oświecenie*, Warsaw 1975
Koneczny, Feliks, *Tadeusz Kościuszko na setną rocznicę zgonu Naczelnika*, Poznań 1917
Konopczyński, Władysław, *Kazimierz Pułaski. Życiorys*, Kraków 1931
Kraushar, Alexander, *Książe Repnin a Polska. W pierwszym czteroleciu panowania Stanisława Augusta (1764–1768)*, Kraków 1898
—, *Okruchy przeszłości*, Warsaw 1913
—, *'Pan Andrzej'. Żywot, zasługi, wygnanie i hołd narodowy pozgonny, oddany zwłokom ś. p. Andrzeja hr. Zamoyskiego*, Lwów 1925
Kseniak, Mieczysław, *Rezydencja Książąt Czartoryskich w Puławach*, Lublin 1998
Kukiel, Marian, *Banicja księcia Adama Czartoryskiego i katastrofa Puław*, Lwów 1930
—, *Książę Adam*, Paris 1950
Libiszowska, Zofia, *Życie polskie w Londynie w XVIIIw.*, Warsaw 1972
Lipowski, Z. J., *Benjamin Franklin as a Psychotherapist: A Forerunner of Brief Psychotherapy*, in *Perspectives in Biology and Medicine*, vol. 27, no. 3, Baltimore 1984
Maugras, Gaston, *Le duc de Lauzun et la cour intime de Louis XV*, Paris 1893
—, *Le duc de Lauzun et la cour de Marie-Angoinette*, Paris 1909
Michalski, Jerzy, *Duc de Lauzun i próba zbliżenia francusko-rosyjskiego*, in *Kwartalnik Historyczny*, Rocznik CIV, 1997, 1
Nieć, Juljan, *Młodość ostatniego elekta. St. A. Poniatowski 1732–1764*, Kraków 1935
Pauszer-Klonowska, Gabriela, *Pani na Puławach. Opowieść o Izabeli z Flemmingów Czartoryskiej*, Warsaw 1980
Perey, Lucien, *Histoire d'une Grande Dame au XVIIIe siècle. La Princesse Hélène de Ligne*, Paris 1888
Przeździecki, comte Renaud, *Diplomatie et Protocole à la cour de Pologne*, vol. II, Paris 1937
Putkowska, Jolanta, *Warszawska podmiejska rezydencja Izabeli Czartoryskiej w Powązkach*, in *Kwartalnik Architektury i Urbanistyki*, vol. 53, no. 3, Warsaw 2008
Radziwiłł, M. P., *Ostatnia wojewodzina wileńska*, Lwów 1892
Raz, Carmel and Finger, Stanley, *Musical Glasses, Metal Reeds and Broken Hearts. Two Cases of Melancholia Treated by New Musical Instruments*, in Gouk, P., Kennaway, J., Prins, J. and Thormählen, W. eds, *The Routledge Companion to Music, Mind and Wellbeing*, Abingdon 2018
Rolle, A. J., *Opowiadania historyczne*, vol. I, Warsaw 1882
Rosman, M. J., *The Lords' Jews. Magnate-Jewish Relations in the Polish-Lithuanian Commonwealth in the Eighteenth Century*, Harvard 1990
Rottermund, Andrzej, *Pałac Błękitny*, Warsaw 1970
Sidorowicz, Stanisław, *Czartoryscy. Trzydzieści sześć życiorysów*, Kraków 1938
Skałkowski, A. M., *Kościuszko w świetle najnowszych badań*, Poznań 1924
Skowronek, Jerzy, *Antynapoleońskie koncepcje Czartoryskiego*, Warsaw 1969
—, *Adam Jerzy Czartoryski 1770–1861*, Warsaw 1994
Strzałkowa, Maria, *Adam Klewański (1763–1843)*, Kraków 1960

# Sources

Waszczuk, Rafał, *Misja Piotra Maurycego Glayre'a w Paryżu, czerwiec-listopad 1772r.*
   *Wokół stosunków Stanisława Augusta z Francją po pierwszym rozbiorze*, in
   Ungiewski, Piotr, ed., *'Skłócony Naród, Król Niepewny, Szlachta Dzika'. Polska
   Stanisławowska w świetle najnowszych badań*, Warsaw 2020
Weston, Stephen, *Two Sketches of France, Belgium, & Spa, in two tours during the
   summers of 1771 and 1816*, London 1817
Whelan, Agnieszka, *Gesture and Performance. Princess Izabela Czartoryska and her
   Gardens, 1770–1831*, doctoral thesis, UCL.
—, *Izabela Czartoryska – Fety, Jarmarki i amour propre*, in Roćko Agata and Górska,
   Magdalena, eds, *Słynne Kobiety w Rzeczypospolitej XVIII wieku*, Wilanów 2017
Wroczyński, Ryszard, *Dzieje oświaty polskiej do roku 1795*, Warsaw 1987
Zahorski, Andrzej, *Warszawa za sasów i Stanisława Augusta*, Warsaw 1970
Zaleski, Bronisław, *Żywot Księcia Adama Jerzego Czartoryskiego*, vol. I, Poznań 1881
Zamoyski, Adam, *The Last King of Poland*, London 1992
Zawadzki, W. H., *A Man of Honour. Adam Czartoryski as a Statesman of Russia and
   Poland 1795–1831*, Oxford 1993
Zdrada, Jerzy, *Zmierzch Czartoryskich*, Warsaw 1969
Żychliński, Teodor, *Złota Księga Szlachty Polskiej*, Rocznik VIII, Poznań 1886
Żygulski, Zdzisław, *Dzieje zbiorów puławskich*, Kraków 1962
Żywirska, Maria, *Ostatnie lata życia króla Stanisława Augusta*, Warsaw 1978

## ONLINE:

Pasaż Wiedzy. Muzeum Pałacu Króla Jana III w Wilanowie:
Dumanowski, Jarosław, *Polskie Prawo Ziemskie. Zawarcie Małżeństwa*
—, *Polskie Prawo Ziemskie. Stosunki Majątkowe Między Małżonkami*
Kleśta-Nawrocka, Aleksandra, *Kryzys Staropolskiego Małżeństwa*

# Index

Aigner, Piotr, 157, 158–9
Alexander I, emperor of Russia, 136, 137, 143, 144–5, 155–6, 164–9, 170, 171–2, 206; alliance with Prussia, 168, 169; armies move west to Germany (1813), 191; at Congress of Vienna (1814–15), 196, 197–8, 199; death of (November 1825), 220; defeated at Austerlitz (1805), 168–9, 170; defeated at Friedland (1807), 170; desire to recreate Polish state, 195–6, 197; forces Périgord-Dorothée marriage, 175–6; in Germany (1814), 195; Grand Duchy of Warsaw in hands of (1813), 188–9; as increasingly reactionary, 207, 208, 211–12, 215; masses large army on Grand Duchy border (1809), 179; meets Napoleon at Tilsit (1807), 170; opens Sejm in Warsaw, 206–7, 208; stays at Puławy (1814), 196–7; in Warsaw on return from Paris (1815), 200–1
Amiens, Peace of, 158
Angoulême, duchesse d', 152
Anhalt-Zerbst, Duchess of, 17
Argyll, Archibald Earl of, 9
Armfeldt, Baron Gustav von, 172
Artois, comte d' (future Charles X), 58
Augustus II ('the Strong'), king of Poland, 12–13, 14
Augustus III, king of Poland, 14, 17, 18, 19, 23
Austerlitz, Battle of (1805), 168
Austria, 12, 23, 107, 123–4; Adam Czartoryski commands imperial troops,

72–3, 177, 178, 214; defeat at Wagram (1809), 178; defeated at Austerlitz (1805), 168–9, 170; and final dismemberment of Poland (1795), 141–2; and French Revolutionary/Napoleonic Wars, 126, 167, 168–9, 170, 177–9, 187, 188; and partition of Poland (1772), 46, 57–8, 63, 67; and Polish insurrection (1830–1), 225–6; and Russian invasion of Poland (1792), 126, 127; and third partition of Poland (1795), 131–2, 139; troops in Grand Duchy of Warsaw (1809), 177–9
Auvigny, Louis-Aimé d', 78
Bardejov (Slovakian spa), 146
Barclay de Tolly, Field-Marshall, 196, 197, 198
Barrington, Lady, 45
Barry, Madame du, 45
Bartolini, Lorenzo, 229
Bassano, duc de, 185
Bastiani, Abbé, 90
Bath, 116
Batowski, Count Aleksander, 172, 176
Bavaria, 177
Benedict XIV, Pope, 8
Bentham, Jeremy, 25–6
Berlin, 88–93, 105–6
Berlin Academy of Arts, 66
Berlioz, Hector, 231
Berry, Mary, 95
Beydale, Cecylia, 153–4, 179, 180, 196, 224, 226–7, 228, 229, 231

257